JAVABEANS BY EXAMPLE

Henri Jubin
and the
Jalapeño Team

To join a Prentice Hall PTR Internet
mailing list, point to:
http://www.prenhall.com/mail_lists/

Prentice Hall PTR
Upper Saddle River, NJ 07458

ISBN 0-13-790338-3

90000

9 780137 903382

Library of Congress Cataloging-in-Publication Data

Jubin, Henri.
      JavaBeans by example / Henri Jubin and the Jalapeño Team.
        p. cm.
      Includes bibliographical references and index.
      ISBN 0-13-790338-3 (paper)
      1. Java (Computer program language)   I. Jalapeño Team.
      II. Title.
      QA76.73.J38J83   1997
      005.2'762--dc21   97-36744
                                                  CIP

Editorial/production supervision: *Patti Guerrieri*
Cover design director: *Jerry Votta*
Cover designer: *Bruce Kenselaar*
Cover illustration: *Karen Strelecki*
Manufacturing manager: *Alexis R. Heydt*
Marketing manager: *Stephen Solomon*
Acquisitions editor: *Mike Meehan*
Editorial assistant: *Barbara Alfieri*

 Published by Prentice Hall PTR
Prentice-Hall, Inc.
A Simon & Schuster Company
Upper Saddle River, NJ 07458

Prentice Hall books are widely used by corporations and government agencies
for training, marketing, and resale.

The publisher offers discounts on this book when ordered in bulk quantities.
For more information, contact: Corporate Sales Department, Phone: 800-382-3419;
Fax: 201-236-7141; E-mail: corpsales@prenhall.com; or write: Prentice Hall PTR,
Corp. Sales Dept., One Lake Street, Upper Saddle River, NJ 07458.

IBM, VisualAge, OS/2, SQL, DB2 and DB2/6000 are trademarks of International Business
Machines Corporation. C-bus is a trademark of Corollary, Inc. PC Direct is a trademark of Ziff
Communications Company and is used by IBM Corporation under license. UNIX is a registered
trademark in the United States and other countries licensed exclusively through X/Open Company
Limited. Microsoft, Windows, Windows NT and the Windows 95 logo are trademarks or registered
trademarks of Microsoft Corporation. Java, JavaBeans and HotJava are trademarks of Sun
Microsystems, Inc. All other products or services mentioned in this book are the trademarks or
service marks of their respective companies or organizations.

Printed in the United States of America
10 9 8 7 6 5 4 3 2

ISBN 0-13-790338-3

Prentice-Hall International (UK) Limited, *London*
Prentice-Hall of Australia Pty. Limited, *Sydney*
Prentice-Hall Canada Inc., *Toronto*
Prentice-Hall Hispanoamericana, S.A., *Mexico*
Prentice-Hall of India Private Limited, *New Delhi*
Prentice-Hall of Japan, Inc., *Tokyo*
Simon & Schuster Asia Pte. Ltd., *Singapore*
Editora Prentice-Hall do Brasil, Ltda., *Rio de Janeiro*

Contents

Chapter 3
Building Blocks—The JavaBeans API, 23

Chapter 7
Examples Used in the Book, 195

Preface

Java, in a relatively short period of time, has emerged as the de facto standard for creating applications for the Internet, and, consequently, for enterprise intranets. "Write once, run anywhere" has become a reality with Java. Java Virtual Machines (JVMs) are available for nearly every computing platform, including all IBM operating systems (from OS/2 Warp to OS/390), Microsoft Windows, Apple Macintosh, UNIX, and even new devices such as the IBM Network Station and telephony devices. Java is ideally suited to the Internet (and intranets), with compact code size, robust security features, windowing toolkits, database access capabilities, multimedia features, and more. For the enterprise, in-house Java applications can be more easily and quickly distributed, even to customers outside the enterprise who might need selective access to information. Furthermore, because Java is platform neutral, both in-house and public versions of Java applications reach the widest possible audience, now and in the future.

While Java itself is a highly object-oriented language, until recently there was no standard technology to help programmers build Java components which interact with one another in common ways. Consequently, "beans" were born. JavaBeans can be created, reused, modified and assembled into feature-rich applications. This book focuses on the benefits of JavaBeans and how to take advantage of them, particularly in the enterprise.

Introduction

Understand what JavaBeans are, how they are built and how they can be used and reused. Although the focus is on JavaBeans, special attention is paid to the enterprise environment. For anyone trying to build applications for the enterprise environment, topics such as distributed objects and accessing legacy databases become important.

JavaBeans provide an interesting solution to many of the issues which arise in the enterprise environment. They provide a means of packaging functionality into reusable units which can then be spread throughout the enterprise. In addition, beans are designed to be able to be manipulated visually using a visual builder tool.

The Authors

This book was written by the Jalapeño Team, an international group of IBM software engineers.

The organizer and guiding spirit for the Jalapeño Team is Henri Jubin. Henri currently works for the International Technical Support Organization (ITSO) in Austin, where he covers the area of Object Oriented Technology. Henri has previously worked in various support and consulting positions within IBM France. He has dealt with topics such as Object-Oriented Technology and OS/2. Henri has lived in France and Spain.

Following, in alphabetical order, is a list of the authors and developers of the Jalapeño Team.

Jacques Dubuquoy is a member of the Object Technology University group of IBM's International Education Center in Belgium. He teaches courses in C++ and Object-Oriented Analysis and Design. Jacques previously worked as an assistant professor for the engineering faculty of the Catholic University of Louvain in Belgium. Jacques is a native of Belgium.

Robert Insley is a consultant with IBM's Information Technology Practice in Switzerland. His specialization is in Object-Oriented Technology, particularly Smalltalk and Java. Robert previously worked for Credit Suisse, an international Swiss bank, developing Smalltalk applications. Robert has lived in the United States and Switzerland.

Takashi Itoh works for the IBM Advanced Software Systems Laboratory in Makuhari Chiba in Japan. Takashi has worked with diverse technologies such as AIX, RS6000, virtual reality and CASE tools. Takashi is a native of Japan.

Mario Kosmiskas is a member of IBM's Network Computing and Open Systems Center in São Paolo, Brazil. He has experience in developing Java, C++ and Smalltalk applications. In addition he is responsible for the design and testing of AIX and HACMP solutions. Mario is a native of Brazil.

Abhay Parasnis works for TISL, a joint IBM and Tata company in India. Lately, Abhay has been working on Java and C++ solutions. He has also worked on Networking solutions. Abhay is a native of India.

Mats Pettersson is a consultant with IBM Global Services in Stockholm, Sweden. Recently, Mats has been involved with developing Java and C++ applications. Previously, he worked on MQSeries solutions. Mats is an absolute chili pepper fanatic. He is a native of Sweden.

Contributors

The Jalapeño Team would like to thank the following people for their help and contributions:

Bob Matta, IBM ITSO Rochester

Joaquin Picon, IBM France

Noel Javier Sales, IBM The Netherlands

Acknowledgment

The Jalapeño Team would like to thank all our friends, spouses, girlfriends, children and colleagues for all their support and patience over the last several months. In addition, special thanks to the team at the ITSO in Austin, Texas, for making us feel so at home during our stay in Austin.

The following people provided invaluable advice, answers, text and support: Helene Armitage, Ron Martin, John Cook, Tod Wiese, and Sheila Richardson.

We would like to thank Marcus Brewer, the editor at ITSO-Austin Center, for his many contributions to this book, as well as Steve Gardner for his logistic coverage.

Henri Jubin would like to thank the whole team and in particular their families for their silent and patient support.

Chapter 1

How to Use This Book

▼ INTRODUCTION

▼ THE CHILI PEPPER STORY

▼ THE STRUCTURE OF THE BOOK

This chapter is divided into three sections: an introduction to the contents of the book, an introduction to a story used throughout the book to illustrate ideas and concepts, and a guide on how the book is to be used.

Introduction

The purpose of this book is to give the reader an overview of what JavaBeans are, how they are built, and how they can be used and reused. Although the focus is on beans, special attention is paid to the enterprise environment. For anyone trying to build applications for the enterprise environment, topics such as distributed objects and accessing legacy databases become particularly important. Beans provide an interesting solution to many of the common problems that arise in enterprise application development. They provide a means of packaging functionality into reusable units that can then be shared throughout the enterprise. However, beans cannot by themselves ensure reusability. Several conditions must be met in order to exploit the potential that beans offer. In particular, an object reuse policy and philosophy must be implemented and enforced throughout the enterprise.

Beans are designed to be manipulated visually by using a visual builder tool. Consequently, enterprises that have already begun to use visual programming techniques will find it relatively easy to use beans. Visual programming allows for the separation and concentration of skills among developers. Highly skilled developers build and make available beans for other developers with more business knowledge (and perhaps less technical expertise) to assemble into custom applications.

In reading this book the discerning reader will find many references to chili peppers, brokers and growers as well as recipes for using chili peppers. Lest the reader worry that Java has spawned a new generation of edible and delectable components, rest assured this is not the case. The authors have simply made use of their common love for "hot, hot" foods to spice up the book. Many of the examples used to explain beans, as well as the sample application developed using beans, relate back to a story about a chili pepper broker.

The Chili Pepper Story

One of the great features of the American Southwest is the abundance of hot, spicy foods. A key ingredient in these foods is the chili pepper, usually small, little devils in various shades of red, yellow and green. In order to ensure a constant supply of peppers, brokers provide the crucial link between the growers and the distributors or consumers. A broker knows which peppers are available from which grower. When a broker is contacted by a customer for peppers, the broker knows which grower to contact to fill the order. The grower puts together a shipment and notifies the broker that the order has been filled. The broker then contacts a food and health inspector in order to have the shipment inspected. The inspector notifies the broker of the results. If the shipment has passed inspection, it must be insured before being shipped to the customer. After all, who wants to risk having an uninsured cargo of highly volatile peppers being lost? The insurer provides a policy for the shipment and notifies the broker that the shipment has been insured. At this point, the shipment can finally be sent to the customer. The customer, in turn, cooks a great meal at his restaurant, thus providing the sorely needed fuel for the authors of this book.

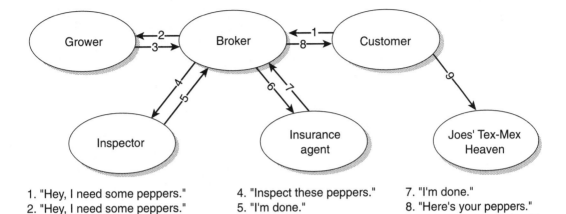

1. "Hey, I need some peppers."	4. "Inspect these peppers."	7. "I'm done."
2. "Hey, I need some peppers."	5. "I'm done."	8. "Here's your peppers."
3. "Here's them peppers."	6. "Insure this shipment."	9. "Now this is good food!"

The Structure of the Book

This book is designed with more than the just the technical reader in mind. The reader is not expected to read the book from cover to cover. Depending on your background and interests, certain chapters will be more useful or interesting than others.

Most chapters are self-contained, and can be read in almost any order. This first chapter provides a guideline for using the book. In addition, it introduces a common metaphor, the chili pepper story mentioned above. This chapter should be read by all. The remainder of the book is divided into three major sections: one on beans, one on building and using beans, and a final section that addresses additional topics such as reusing beans, tools that support beans, and more.

The first section is split into two chapters. The first chapter provides a high-level introduction to beans: what they are, the concepts behind them, and how they can be used. The following chapter provides a detailed explanation of the terms introduced in the previous chapter. The less technically versed reader may choose to look only at the summaries provided for each unit.

The second section describes the building of a chili pepper application using beans. It is also split into two chapters. The first chapter describes the actual building of the application. Again, summaries are provided for those who wish to skip the details. The second chapter describes additional features which are very important in the enterprise environment, such as printing, distributed objects, access to an existing database and support for international users. Although the chili pepper application itself will not be extended, detailed examples are provided for each feature.

The last section of the book discusses additional topics relating to beans. The packaging of beans using JAR files is discussed, as well as certain security issues related to the use of beans in applets. The use of signed applets can help beans in applets enjoy many of the same rights and privileges as beans in applications. A discussion of visual developments which support the development and reuse of beans is provided as well. To conclude this section, a detailed list of all the examples used in the book is provided as a quick reference for the reader who is looking for specific application ideas.

The appendix contains the programming guidelines used in writing the code found in this book as well as a complete documentation for the sample chili application (source code, analysis, design artifacts and the JavaDoc listing for the application).

Throughout the book, references to program code (including class names, methods, parameters and properties) are indicated by a fixed-width font. As an example: `ClassName`.

It is important to note that this is not a book about Java per se. There are a number of excellent books available that provide a detailed introduction to Java. References to some of these sources can be found throughout this book. This book discusses the features of the Java language that need to be understood in order to work with JavaBeans. A working knowledge of Java is not mandatory for readers of the book. However, for those readers who plan to use the book as a guide for actually working with beans, a working knowledge of Java is recommended.

Finally, exercise caution when trying out the examples and the recipes. You need to be careful not to burn yourself after handling the fresh chili peppers. Do not rub your eyes or other sensitive areas, and always wash your hands thoroughly after handling fresh chilis. In other words, the programs are examples, not ready-to-go applications. We designed them to illustrate how beans work, not necessarily how businesses work. Use the concepts, not the code, to create reliable, functional enterprise applications.

5

Spiced Escabèche Anguilles

Origin: South of Belgium with a hint of something else

The ingredients are: 2 lbs. of medium sized eels, one pint of fish stock (court-bouillon), 2 sliced onions, 3 cloves, the rind of a lemon, 1/4 pint of white vinegar, flour, 2 red or green bell peppers.

Wash and skin the eels, cut them into pieces about 3 inches long; salt them and lay them into a stew-pan. Pour over the fish stock, the vinegar, the sliced onions and the lemon peel. Stew gently for half an hour (or more) and lift them to a dish. Drain the court-bouillon, stir in sufficient flour to thicken, add the peppers, and boil for 2 minutes. Pour over the eels and refrigerate before serving.

Chapter **2**

Introducing Beans

▼ DEFINITION - WHAT IS A BEAN?

▼ CHARACTERISTICS

▼ WHERE AND HOW BEANS CAN BE USED

▼ BUILDING A SIMPLE BEAN

The purpose of this chapter is to provide a high level introduction to beans. After reading this chapter, the reader should understand what beans are, how beans are defined, what they promise, and how they can be used. The principle ideas that need to be understood when talking about beans are introduced. The next chapter provides an in-depth explanation of the individual concepts. A broad range of possible uses for beans is discussed, ranging from applets that animate a Web page to sophisticated distributed solutions. The reader is provided with enough background to be able to understand the various possibilities. In addition, at the end of the chapter, an example is given that shows how to build a simple bean. The example reinforces the introduction to the concepts behind beans.

Definition—What Is a Bean?

According to its creators, the engineers at JavaSoft, "A JavaBean is a *reusable software component* that can be *manipulated visually* in a *builder tool."*

Let's start from the beginning. A *reusable software component* is a piece of program code that provides a well defined functional unit. The functionality is encapsulated in such a way that it can be reused in other larger components or pieces of code. The scope of the functionality can be something very simple and small like the label for a button on a window or it can be something as large as an entire application.

Let's use an example. Habanero Software is a medium-size software company with various products on the market. The company wants to have its logo and copyright notice displayed every time one of its software products starts running. Joe Developer writes a little piece of code that displays the logo, an animated Habanero pepper spelling out the name of the company, and a copyright notice. Joe provides his piece of code to each of the development teams at Habanero Software and explains to them how to embed it in their applications and how to trigger the on-screen message. This piece of code Joe has created fits the definition of a *reusable software component*.

So what is a *builder tool,* and what does it mean to be *manipulated visually*? A builder tool is a program that allows a developer to quickly and easily assemble code into larger units of code. A developer using such a tool does not typically have to physically merge units of code. Rather, the developer sees an on-screen representation of a unit of code (an icon perhaps) which can in some way be connected or combined with a representation of another unit of code. Builder tools differ in the type of "glue" they provide to combine code. Some tools may simply provide hooks for code which implement the link, and some tools provide a simple scripting language to implement the links between units of code. Other tools provide the ability to specify the type of link and actually generate the required "glue" code. Many builder tools allow components to be *manipulated visually,* allowing the developer to establish connections between components by pointing and clicking (or dragging and dropping).

The JavaSoft definition allows for a broad range of components which can be thought of as beans. Beans can be visual components, such as buttons or entry fields, or even an entire spreadsheet application. Beans can also be non-visual components, encapsulating business tasks or entities such as processing employee paychecks, a bank account, or even an entire credit rating component. Non-visual beans still have a visual representation, such as an icon and/or name, to allow visual manipulation. While this visual representation may not appear to the user of an application, non-visual beans are depicted on-screen so developers can work with them.

Beans can only be manipulated and reused if they are built in a standardized way. In other words, there must be an architecture or blueprint for building JavaBeans. JavaSoft provides such an architecture with its JavaBeans API. According to Java-soft, the goal of the Beans API is to "define a software component model for Java." In providing an API for JavaBeans, JavaSoft delivers four key benefits:

1. **Support for a range of component granularity**. Beans can come in different shapes and sizes. JavaSoft expects that most beans will be relatively small components. Consequently, simple components are easy to implement. However, while the JavaBeans API provides a reasonable amount of default behavior, larger and more customized components can be created for more complex purposes.

2. **Portability**. The API is platform neutral. A bean which is developed under Windows, for example, should behave the same whether it is run under OS/2 Warp, UNIX, Macintosh OS, or any other platform. However, the port-ability is not absolute. Certain components which are closely tied to specific operating system resources, such as buttons and entry fields, may look or even act differently on different operating systems. The great majority of components, especially non-visual components, are portable across all plat-forms that support Java.

3. **Uniform, high-quality API**. Ideally, every platform that supports Java will support the entire JavaBeans API. In fact, there are exceptions, as discussed above. However, each platform that is unable to support a feature from the API is expected to provide a reasonable default behavior. The color red might be mapped to a certain shade of gray, for example. On the other hand, not every platform that ultimately supports Java will need to support the entire JavaBeans API. Depending on the platform and the application or applications being run, some features may not be necessary.

4. **Simplicity**. The easiest way to reduce the risk of having a large number of unsupported features in the API is to keep the API simple, universal and compact. The JavaBeans API makes the simple cases easy while at the same time making the difficult cases possible. By keeping the API simple, it is eas-ier to learn and begin to use.

The Beans API defines the distinguishing characteristics of a bean—how they look and feel. The next unit introduces these characteristics.

Characteristics

Although the JavaBeans API does not say anything about the functionality an individual bean can support, it does define the distinguishing characteristics of a bean. These characteristics are:

- A **public interface**. The public interface defines the way a bean interacts with other beans. The public interface is made up of three groups:

  Properties are named attributes of beans. They can be read and/or set by other beans. Beans can provide "customizers" (see below) that allow a developer to set properties that govern a bean's appearance or behavior. For example, a bean that creates a button called "Push Me" might have a property that sets the color of the button (red, blue, yellow, and so forth.)

  Methods are Java methods that can be triggered by other beans. Methods are the gateways to the functionality a bean provides. When a bean triggers a method provided by a second bean, it is in effect asking the second bean to initiate the action associated with the method. For example, the "Push Me" bean might have a method which draws and positions the button in a certain screen location.

  Events are the messages used by beans. They are the means by which beans communicate with one another. Beans trigger events to notify all who are interested that something has taken place. An event might indicate that a particular method has been activated or that a state change has taken place. For example, an event might be generated if the "Push Me" button is pushed. Beans can react to events that have been initiated by other beans (by invoking a method or by triggering events of their own).

- **Introspection**. Introspection allows a builder tool to find out how a bean works. A builder analyzes a bean by looking at an instance of a class and making a list of all the public members (properties, methods and events) that it finds.

- **Customization**. Customization allows a developer to set properties that govern a bean's behavior or appearance. Examples include the width and height of a button or the background color of an entry field.

- **Persistence**. Persistence provides a mechanism for filing away the customized state of a bean so that it can be saved and reloaded at a later time. One of the key features for enabling persistence is serialization, the ability to generate a byte stream representation of the actual state of a bean.

In addition to those defined by the JavaBeans API, there are additional characteristics associated with beans:

- **Visual and non-visual beans.** Beans are either visual or non-visual. Visual beans usually provide behavior for a graphical user interface (GUI), including buttons, entry fields, menus, and so on. Non-visual beans most often provide application logic. For example, a non-visual bean can total all customer accounts in a banking application. Non-visual beans can be either visible or invisible. An invisible bean is a bean without its own user interface representation at development time. In certain cases, such a bean may be able to use a default GUI representation provided by another class in the hierarchy. In other cases, a tool may provide an invisible bean with a default appearance in order to make the bean visible to the developer. Aside from not having their own GUI representation, invisible beans are the same as "normal," visible beans.

- **Design time behavior and appearance.** The appearance and behavior of a bean at runtime can differ from its appearance and behavior at development time. The visibility of a bean in a visual development tool, or the ability to customize properties of the bean, are not relevant at runtime. Such behavior should be factored out using interfaces and helper classes in order to avoid delivering code that is not relevant to the runtime application.

- **Mapping class libraries to beans.** It is not always advantageous to build an entire application using beans. Beans are useful in situations where the characteristics defined above can be exploited. Code that does not benefit from visual manipulation can be left as standard Java classes in the class libraries. In other words, in using visual development to build applications, it is not necessary to map the entire class library, or libraries that contain the application code, to beans.

- **Multi-threading.** The Java environment supports multi-threading. However, having a bean running in several threads at the same time can cause problems. The same method running simultaneously in several threads can lead to conflicting results for a bean. The methods defined on a bean must be defined in such a way that parallel execution will lead to predictable results. A simple remedy is to set all the methods for a particular bean to `synchronized`. More complicated methods or functionality will require more complex synchronization.

- **Remote and distributed beans.** Java currently supports three mechanisms that enable the development of distributed applications.

  Remote Method Invocation (RMI). RMI allows local Java objects to refer to and use remote (over-the-network) Java objects as if they were local. This capability is possible because both the client and server are written in Java.

Java Interface Definition Language (IDL). The IDL implements the industry standard OMG CORBA distributed object model. The interfaces are defined using the IDL. The CORBA IDL represents a multi-language and multi-vendor environment. Through the Java IDL interfaces, Java clients can access or be accessed by IDL servers. The servers can be Java or non-Java servers. Compared to RMI, the Java IDL allows the design of more robust, heterogeneous distributed systems.

Java Database Connection (JDBC). The Java database API allows access to industry standard SQL databases, such as IBM's database server (DB2). JDBC, unlike RMI or CORBA, is not a true facility for distributed applications. Nevertheless, it does offer access to remote data and functions from Java.

- **Internationalization.** Internationalization allows the development of components that adapt to different languages and cultures. Components can be extended with functionality to support a number of different languages and cultures instead of being tied to a single language and culture (usually that of the developer).

- **Address space.** Typically, JavaBeans run in the same address space as their container. If the container is an application, the virtual machine running the application will also run the bean. If the container is a non-Java application (a Web browser, for instance), the virtual machine associated with the application will run the bean. Typically, the virtual machine associated with the non-Java application will run in the same address space as the application.

- **Security.** Beans are governed by the standard Java security model. There are no special modifications for beans in the security model. As such, Sun advises beans developers to design and develop beans for use in an untrusted applet. In other words, "Build beans with the worst case in mind, and they will run in all conditions." Designing beans to run in untrusted applets has certain ramifications:

  Introspection. The standard Java security model allows untrusted applets to access only public fields and methods. As a result, a bean should only use the high-level Introspection API.

  Persistence. Access to random files for untrusted applets is clearly restricted. As a result, beans should not attempt to control where the streams containing their serialized data should be written to or read from (see Chapter 3 for more information concerning serialization).

  Beans that are clearly meant to be used as part of full-fledged, trusted Java applications can ignore these security recommendations.

The next unit discusses what beans can do and how they can be used once they are defined.

Where and How Beans Can Be Used

The previous section discussed what beans are and what defines a typical bean. This unit outlines the basic uses for beans. Because Java first became popular as an extension to Web-page design, JavaBeans work well inside Web pages. This unit introduces the most common architectures for Web-based applications with JavaBeans. Later in this unit, more traditional, non-Web approaches to application design are discussed to see how beans extend well beyond Web technologies.

"The Web is changing the way the world does business" is one of the many phrases used to describe the Internet. With the advent of Java, the Web has matured from a simple one-way presentation medium to a complete, two-way (or even multi-way) vehicle for sophisticated applications. There are several new ways of presenting information and communicating which take advantage of the Web. This unit summarizes the most important ones and shows how beans can be used to implement such solutions.

Using Beans to "Liven Up" a Web Page

Beans can be used to move beyond static Web pages, which simply display information, to interactive pages that are more interesting, appealing and useful. The functionality is typically added in the form of one or more Java applets that are embedded in the page. The applet is downloaded to the Web browser along with the page. Once the applet has been downloaded, it begins to run automatically, provided the Web browser's Java capability is turned on. The applet continues to run as long as the page is active. Web pages that contain a rotating globe, moving ticker tape, or other animated feature most often contain Java applets. Beans can be used to develop such applets. Indeed, the entire applet can be packaged as a bean, making reuse in different situations much simpler. While such applets provide more interesting content, the Web pages are still somewhat static.

Using Beans to Provide a Web Page with the Ability to Communicate

Designing a dynamic Web page with the ability to communicate is somewhat more involved than simply embedding a rotating globe applet. Yet the principle is the same: One or more embedded applets provide the desired functionality. The applet(s) may present the user with the ability to communicate with another system on the network and/or to look up or send information. For example, an on-line reservations system can use Java applets to allow a customer to search for a preferred flight and pay for an airline ticket. The Java applets may communicate with an existing in-house reservations system, thus providing limited access to information on flights and seating. The customer may only be allowed to view flights between two cities, or more elaborate capabilities, such as car rental reservations, may also be provided, depending on the complexity of the Java applets. The same Java applets could be adapted so that airline employees have more complete access to the reservations system.

Applets that provide this kind of two-way communication do not typically start by themselves. Often, they must be triggered by clicking on a button or by choosing a menu option. Applets providing two-way communication can also be constructed with beans. As beans, the applets can be reused for other users in other situations.

Using Beans to Implement an Application

At first glance, Web pages and applets could be used to implement comprehensive applications with beans. However, applications and applets ("little applications") are somewhat different in how they are created. Applets are "little" in the sense that they cannot be run as standalone programs. Rather, they are meant to be embedded in Web pages, to be run when the page is displayed. In addition, applets generally run in a more restricted and more secure environment, with limited or no access to a Web browser's own disk drive, for example. Applets are not "little," however, in the sense that they must be small applications with limited functionality. In fact, there is no restriction on the size of applets.

Applications (as opposed to applets) can be constructed with other programming languages such as C, Smalltalk, Pascal, COBOL, and so on. And until recently, JavaSoft and Sun did not suggest that Java should be used for "heavyweight" applications. However, Java's advantages in "lightweight" programming, combined with new, rich function introduced in the latest Java Development Kits, has propelled the language into one preferred for large-scale application development. In fact, entire office application suites, such as Lotus Kona and Corel Office for Java, have already been written entirely in Java.

Consequently, there are no apparent limitations to developing "large" applications with beans. A Java application can be constructed entirely of beans, completely without beans, or as a hybrid, with some use of beans. Beans can be used to build the GUIs for an application, a typical use of visual programming. Beans can also be used to build other interfaces, such as communications and database interfaces. In addition, beans can be used for the core of the application, the actual business logic, such as the calculation of monthly loan payments in a banking application. Beans become most useful when taking advantage of visual programming techniques. Also, code that can (and should) be encapsulated for later reuse (in the same or other applications, by the same or different programmers) is a perfect candidate for incorporation into bean(s).

Using Beans to Implement a Distributed Web-Based Application

Beans hold the most promise in the designing, testing, and implementing of complex, distributed, Web-based applications. Such applications are becoming increasingly common (and necessary) to a wide range of businesses. Java is attractive for developers of network computing solutions because of its ability to address many of the drawbacks associated with current client/server approaches. For example, client/server architectures demand enormous maintenance efforts. New software versions in a client/server environment often must be individually installed, supported and upgraded on the client systems. However, client software written in Java can be "pushed" onto client machines from one (or a few) central server(s).

Client/server designers face significant obstacles in supporting multiple platforms. Writing to just one or several operating systems results in applications that don't serve all enterprise users, much less the public at large. Most businesses try to reach the widest possible audience to market their products, and client/server solutions tend to leave out significant numbers of users. In contrast, Java's "write once, run anywhere" philosophy addresses this problem. A Java application is written for one machine, the Java virtual machine, which in turn runs on just about every computing device which supports the virtual machine. The virtual machine translates Java bytecode into native machine code for each platform. Not all Java Virtual Machines (JVMs) function precisely the same; however, the degree of standardization is impressive, and JavaSoft continues to enhance the compatibility test suite so that products labeled "100% Pure Java" conform to the standard. This compatibility testing relieves most of the burden of cross-platform support from application developers.

Distributed applications are often categorized into two-tier and three-tier (or "n-tier") models, depending on how the workload is distributed. Java and JavaBeans work well with both models. In the two-tier (also known as "fat client") approach, the client contains both presentation logic (the GUI) and application logic. That is, the client is responsible not only for displaying results (and handling input into forms or other documents) but also for some processing of information (such as sorting a list of names). The server shares responsibility for application logic. In the three-tier ("thin client") solution, the client only handles presentation logic. The actual application logic resides on the server. With the advent of network computers and other non-traditional computing devices with JVMs, most with limited disk space, three-tier solutions become especially attractive. Networks and "thin clients" help promote sensible distribution of application workload, with decisions based less on the limits of technology and more on support, upgrade and other costs. For example, software version control becomes simpler and less costly because most (if not all) changes can be made on one or a few central servers. Protecting data against loss, theft, or corruption becomes less costly if most information can be shared from a central location. Employees work better together if they can share higher quality information more often, more quickly.

Network computing, particularly over the public Internet, is not without its risks and challenges. For example, in an intranet environment, network traffic demands can be reasonably anticipated. In-house corporate networks can be designed to allow employees speedy access to needed information. However, it is much more difficult to ensure consistent, reliable, high performance links to company information on the public Internet. Most businesses are not responsible for building the Internet, and most must depend on communications companies for access to their public applications and information.

Quite simply, Java and JavaBeans were uniquely designed with network computing in mind. The same advantages stressed before (small code size, object-oriented technology, "write once, run anywhere," and so forth) become most evident with distributed, three-tier applications, although these advantages exist for every application.

The next section discusses the creation of a simple bean. This will allow us to become better familiarized with the ideas presented in the previous sections before launching into a detailed explanation of the Beans API in the next chapter.

Building a Simple Bean

In this unit we will build a simple "Hello Pepper" bean. The idea is to illustrate the concepts introduced earlier in this chapter in a lighthearted way before launching into the detailed technical explanations of the Beans API in the next chapter. The "Hello Pepper" bean will draw a bitmap of its flaming fiery self on the screen along with the text "Hello Pepper."

We begin by defining the class `HelloPepper` for our bean. Since we just want to build a simple bean, and we don't plan to build a standalone application or an applet, we define our class to be a subclass of `Canvas`. This allows our bean to inherit a great deal of its behavior from its superclasses since we want to build a bean that can draw a bitmap of itself. Making `HelloPepper` a subclass of `Canvas` allows us to inherit all the drawing behavior that we need. A `Canvas` object is one that can be used to display drawings and images. We simply have to add code for finding and loading the correct bitmap. Once the bitmap is loaded, we make use of the drawing behavior we have inherited to draw the bitmap and the "Hello Pepper" text in the correct place on the screen. Using our favorite editor, we write the following:

```
package HelloPepper;

import java.awt.Color;
import java.awt.Font;
import java.awt.FontMetrics;
import java.awt.Graphics;
import java.awt.Image;
import java.awt.Toolkit;
import java.awt.image.ImageProducer;
import java.io.IOException;
import java.io.Serializable;
import java.net.URL;

/*
 * The HelloPepper bean is a simple bean which displays an icon
 * of itself in addition to the text "Hello Pepper."
 */

public class HelloPepper extends java.awt.Canvas implements
Serializable {
private String greeting = "Hello Pepper";
private Image pepperImage;
```

In addition to making our class a subclass of Canvas we have done some additional work. Our bean implements the Serializable interface in order to be able to take advantage of one of the characteristics of beans mentioned in the previous unit, the ability to generate a stream containing the current state of the bean. We have defined two instance variables. The instance variable greeting of type String holds the current greeting. It is initialized to the default greeting "Hello Pepper." The instance variable pepperImage points to the image being displayed, the bitmap of the fiery pepper. We have also defined a package for our bean. We will need this package later when we define a second class that contains information about our bean. We have also imported a number of classes. These are the classes which we will reference in the code for the HelloPepper bean.

The next step is to define some methods to provide our bean with some functionality. We begin by defining the constructor method for the bean. The constructor, which returns a new instance of the bean, sets a default size for the bean of 100 by 100 pixels.

```
public HelloPepper() {
   setSize(100, 100);
}
```

We continue by defining get and set methods for our two instance variables. These methods will allow us to read and set the contents of our instance variables. (The comments for the methods contain keywords necessary for generating Java-Doc documentation for the code. For a detailed explanation of JavaDoc, refer to the section on generating JavaDoc in the Appendix.)

```
public synchronized String getGreeting() {
  return greeting;
}

public Image getPepperImage() {
  if (pepperImage == null) {
    this.setPepperImage(this.loadPepperImage());
  }
  return pepperImage;
}

public void setGreeting(String aString) {
  greeting = aString;
}

public void setPepperImage(Image aImage) {
  pepperImage = aImage;
}
```

The method getPepperImage() uses lazy initialization to set the value of the image. If the variable does not point to an image, the pepper image is loaded, and the value of the instance variable pepperImage is set to it. The next step is to define the method that actually loads the image when necessary.

```
public Image loadPepperImage() {
  try {
    URL url = this.getClass().getResource("iconpepp.gif");
    Toolkit tk = Toolkit.getDefaultToolkit();
    return tk.createImage((ImageProducer) url.getContent());
  }
  catch (Exception ex) {
    return null;
  }
}
```

The loadPepperImage() method uses the class loader to locate the desired GIF file. Using the class loader has the advantage of being able to locate files, such as GIF files, that have been placed in a JAR file. Using the class loader also means we can work with relative references. In other words, the class loader tries to find the

desired file in the same place it found the class files. If the desired file is found, a
URL for the file is returned. The default toolkit is then instantiated to create an
image using the contents of the URL, which was returned by the class loader, as
the image source. The image is then returned. The load procedure is protected
with an exception handler. If the GIF file cannot be located, or if the image cannot
be created, an exception is raised. The exception is caught by the exception handler, and the exception handler returns null in this case. (Even if you do not plan
to explicitly handle an exception, you should still catch it.)

We now have defined all the methods for loading and accessing what we wish to
display. Now all that remains is to define the code to display the image and text.

```
public synchronized void paint(Graphics g) {
   int width = this.getSize().width;
   int height = this.getSize().height;

   // Prepare and draw the greeting string.

   this.resetFont(g);
   FontMetrics fm = g.getFontMetrics();
   String theGreeting = this.getGreeting();
   g.drawString(theGreeting,
     (width - fm.stringWidth(theGreeting)) / 2,
     (height - fm.getHeight() + fm.getMaxAscent())));

   // Prepare and draw the pepper image.

   int iheight = height - fm.getHeight();
   g.drawImage(this.getPepperImage(), 0, 0, width, iheight,
     Color.yellow, this);
   }

public void resetFont(Graphics g) {
   Font oldFont = g.getFont();
   Font newFont = new Font(oldFont.getName(), oldFont.BOLD, 12);
   g.setFont(newFont);
   }
```

The first method, the paint() method, is the method that does the actual drawing. It is called every time the bean needs to display itself. It is passed an instance
of Graphics by the method that calls it. A Graphics object is a device-indepen-
dent interface to graphics services. It encapsulates the state information needed
for the various rendering operations that Java supports. This state information
includes:

- The component (an instance of a subclass of `Component`) to draw on
- A translation origin for rendering and clipping coordinates
- The current clip
- The current color
- The current font
- The current logical pixel operation function (XOR or Paint)
- The current XOR alternation color

`Graphics` is the abstract base class for all graphics contexts that allow an application to draw onto components realized on various devices, such as a print device, or onto the screen. Subclasses of `Graphics` exist for different platforms and graphics output devices. An instance of one of the subclasses of `Graphics` is capable of drawing lines, painting images, copying areas, clipping images, and more. A `Graphics` object can be used to draw our bean since we have made our bean a subclass of `Canvas`. A `Canvas` object is one that can be used to display drawings and images. When the paint method is called, the `Graphics` object that is passed as a parameter is used to draw the image and text our bean displays.

The first thing we do is find the current size of the bean and store the current width and height in temporary variables. The first time the bean is drawn, the size will correspond to the default size of 100 x 100. The next thing we do is reset the font to one that is more to our liking before we draw our greeting. The second method, `resetFont()`, resets the font for us. We pass along the `Graphics` object as the parameter. The `Graphics` objects holds on to the current font as one of the parameters it uses to draw text. Since each `Font` object cannot be changed, we create a new `Font` object with the same name as the current font, but with the bold style and a larger face size. The `Graphics` object is given the new `Font` object to use.

Once we have reset the font, we can go ahead and draw the greeting. The greeting is centered and written along the bottom edge of the bean in an area that is as high as the font and as wide as the bean. The image is then drawn in the remaining space with a background color of yellow.

Aside from one small detail, we are now finished. When the bean is loaded into a visual tool, we would like to give it a visual representation (an icon). We will use the same GIF file as above. However, in order to specify the icon for the bean, we must define a new class. The new class is called `HelloPepperBeanInfo` and inherits from `SimpleBeanInfo`. Instances of `HelloPepperBeanInfo` are not meant to be used as beans. Rather, they can be thought of as helper objects that return information about the bean. Here we are just interested in giving the

HelloPepper bean its own icon. As a result, we only have to override the getIcon() method from SimpleBeanInfo in order to have our GIF file used as the icon. The HelloPepperBeanInfo class is placed in the same class as the HelloPepper bean.

```
package HelloPepper;

import java.beans.SimpleBeanInfo;
import java.awt.Image;

/*
 * This bean info provides the icon in the form of a gif file
 * which is displayed in the toolbox.
 */

public class HelloPepperBeanInfo extends SimpleBeanInfo {
  public Image getIcon(int iconKind) {
    Image img = loadImage("iconpepp.gif");
    return img;
  }
}
```

When loaded into a visual builder tool and placed on a composition surface, the HelloPepper bean looks like this:

The bean in icon form appears as follows:

Since the `HelloPepper` class is defined as a bean, we automatically inherit default editors for changing the properties of the bean. The default properties editor allows us to change the greeting from "Hello Pepper" to something else, adjust the background color of the bean, and more.

The `HelloPepper` bean is intended to be a fun introduction to the ideas and concepts introduced earlier in this chapter. In this example, we have shown how to define a class so that instances of it can be serialized. We have shown how defining a bean involves defining one or more Java classes. We have made use of the simple framework for beans in defining the `HelloPepperBeanInfo` class. We have demonstrated how classes that are not themselves beans can be used to provide a bean with specific features (such as an icon). In the next chapter, we discuss the ideas and concepts introduced throughout this chapter in much more detail.

Green Chilaquiles

The market basket:

A dozen of each tortillas and green tomatos. 2 fresh garlic cloves. 1 sprig of epazote. Olive oil, salt. Serrano chilis (as much as you can or you like). 1/2 cup of sour cream. 1/2 cup of queso fresco (fresh cheese). 1 onion, sliced.

How to:

Cut the tortillas in small pieces and fry them in the olive oil until brown. Drain off the oil.

Liquefy the tomatos together with the chili and garlic. Fry them until they season. Add salt and a sprig of epazote. Add three cups of water. If you want to peel the tomatos just pour boiling water over the tomatos and let them sit for a minute. Then, you can easily peel them.

When the salsa boils, add the tortillas. Leave them only a minute so they do not soften too much. Remove from heat.

Serve with queso fresco crumbled on top and sour cream as desired.

Chapter 3

Building Blocks—
The JavaBeans API

▼ EVENTS

▼ PROPERTIES

▼ INTROSPECTION

▼ BEANINFO CLASS

▼ CUSTOMIZATION

▼ PROPERTY EDITORS AND THE PROPERTY SHEET

▼ SERIALIZATION

This chapter provides an in-depth explanation of the concepts necessary in order to start building and using beans. The concepts were introduced in the previous chapter. Each concept is discussed in its own unit. Each unit begins with a summary for those who would like to skip the technical details. Many of the examples used in this chapter refer to parts of our little chili pepper story. Writing, as we all know, is hard work, and the prospect of good food is one way of rewarding oneself. The sample application that will be developed in the next chapter will provide the glue to pull together and provide a living example of some of these rather technical concepts.

We begin by focusing on the public interface of a bean. In the first unit, we will look at the events mechanism, the mechanism which enables beans to communicate with one another. In the next unit, we look at the properties of beans, the things which govern their existence, behavior and appearance. We will not discuss the third part of the public interface, methods, in detail. Methods for classes which have been defined as beans do not differ from other methods in Java. We continue by looking at introspection, the mechanism which allows a builder tool to find out how a bean works by examining its public interface. In the next unit, we discuss customization, a feature which allows a developer to set properties which govern a bean's behavior and appearance. Finally we discuss serialization, the ability to make a bean, including customized beans, persistent by generating a stream representation of the bean's current state.

Events

Events are the notification mechanism used by Java Beans, but any Java class can send and receive events. The event notification in Java works using method invocation. The object that is the source of an event calls a method on the destination object for one event when the event is triggered. The destination of the message, called the event listener, must implement the method (or methods) to be notified when the event occurs. The method name and signature are defined by the event source. They are grouped in an interface event listener interface, which must be implemented by all the objects that want to be notified of the event.

The event source is able to notify as many event listeners as desired. The event source maintains a list of the listeners for each event that it can trigger. It is the responsibility of the event source to create and maintain the list of listeners and to provide public methods to add and remove listeners from the list.

When notifying the listeners that an event has occurred, the event source may need to describe the event or send additional information to the listeners. The event object encapsulates all the information about an event. It is sent to each registered listener every time the event is triggered.

There are four elements involved in Java events:

- event object
- event listener
- event listener interface
- event source

All four elements are necessary to implement events in Java.

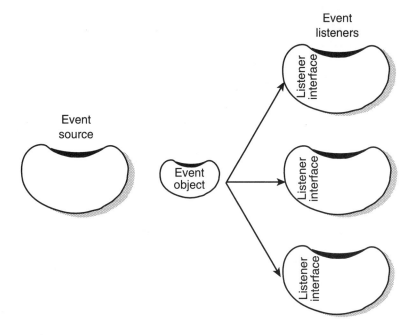

Event Object

Event objects encapsulate the information that the event source passes to registered listeners of the event. Event objects are instantiated by the event source. They are sent by the source to each registered listener for the event listener when the event is triggered.

All the event objects defined by a bean must be subclasses of `java.util.EventObject`. The coding guidelines for event objects state that the name of a custom event object must end in Event. So for example, a custom button could use the event object `ButtonPressedEvent`. `EventObject` implements two methods; `toString()` and `getSource()`. `toString()` returns a string representation of the event object. `getSource()` returns a reference to the event source. The `getSource()` method can be used by listeners that receive messages of the same type from various event sources to differentiate each source and take the correct action.

If a window has two buttons labeled YES and NO and these buttons are instances of the same class, then they use the same event object classes. When either of the buttons is pressed, the same methods on the event listener (the window in this example) are called. In order to know which button was pressed, the event listener looks at the source of the event object received. It can then perform the appropriate action corresponding to the button which was pressed. All four elements are necessary to implement events in Java.

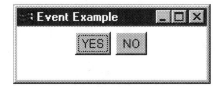

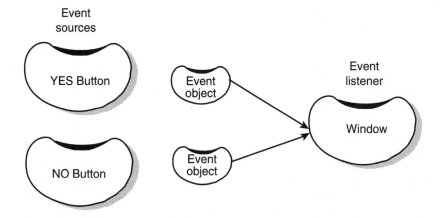

Let's look at another example. A graphics system could use the `PaintEvent` defined below to know which area of the screen must be painted. The event source creates a `PaintEvent` object when an area of the screen needs to be repainted. It sends the event to all the graphics objects that have registered themselves as listeners on the event. The graphics objects receive the event object and see if they are located inside the area that is going to be repainted. If so, they perform the appropriate action.

```
public class PaintEvent extends java.util.EventObject {

    /**
     * Defines the area to be repainted
     */
    Rectangle iArea;
```

```
/**
 * Constructor
 */
public PaintEvent(Component aSource, Rectangle anArea) {
    super(aSource);
    iArea = anArea;
}


/**
 * Returns the rectangle representing the area that needs to be
 * repainted.
 */
public Rectangle getUpdateArea() {
    return iArea;
}
}
```

Note the absence of set methods on the event object. Event objects usually describe a new state of the event source and only the source object should set the attributes. The attributes are set using the constructor at instantiation. Instead of changing variables in an old event object, a new event object should be instantiated with new values. Some event listeners may implement methods which avoid processing duplicate events. Resending the same event object instance may cause problems with such listeners.

Event sources should not use instances of EventObject. Instead, they should use subclasses of EventObject. EventObject must always be subclassed, even if no additional information is added to the event object. For example, a button that wants to notify other objects when it has been pressed may not send instances of EventObject. Instead, it could send instances of Button-PressedEvent defined below. No information is needed to be sent to the listeners, just the notification of the event.

```
public class ButtonPressedEvent extends java.util.EventObject {

    public ButtonPressedEvent(Object aSource) {
        super (aSource);
    }

}
```

Event Listeners

Event listeners are objects that can receive and handle events sent from other objects. To be able to receive events, a listener object must:

- implement one or more event listener interfaces;
- register itself with the event sources.

Event Listener Interfaces

The Java event notification works through method invocation. When a source fires an event it calls certain defined methods on each registered listener. Before starting to send events, the source needs to know if the listeners have implemented the methods to be called. This is done by checking the implementation of an event listener interface. The event listener interface defines all the event handling methods for a specific event. An event listener interface may define as many event handling methods as necessary. As stated above, the event listener must implement the event listener interface corresponding to the events it is interested in.

All event listener interfaces must inherit from `java.util.EventListener`. The coding guidelines for event listener interfaces state that the interface name must end in Listener.

```
interface <interfaceName>Listener extends java.util.EventListener
```

The coding guideline for the naming of all the methods in the event listener interface is:

```
void <methodName>(<EventObjectType> anEvent);
```

There is no convention for the actual name of the event handling method, so <methodName> can be anything. The parameter has to be an event object, so <EventObjectType> specifies the type of an existing subclass of `java.util.EventObject`.

For certain special situations where the use of events is not appropriate, such as interfacing with other languages, it is possible to deviate from the guidelines presented above. It is possible to define event handling methods which accept other arguments in addition to event objects. However, the use of event handling methods which accept an arbitrary list of arguments has potential drawbacks and is therefore discouraged. For those cases where it is necessary, the alternative coding guideline is presented here.

```
void <methodName>(<ArbitraryParameterList>);
```

The following is an example of the definition of a standard event handling interface.

```
public interface PaintListener extends java.util.EventListener {

    public void paintArea(PaintEvent anEvent);
    public void eraseAllAndPaint(PaintEvent anEvent);

}
```

Each event listener interface is associated with one type of event. To receive events from different sources, an event listener class must implement different event listener interfaces. However, it is possible for different event source objects to use the same type of event object and event listener interface. This happens, for example, with some AWT components that respond to user actions, such as `Button`, `List`, `TextField` and `MenuItem`. They all use the `ActionEvent` event object and the `ActionListener` event listener interface. In cases like this, only one listener interface needs to be implemented, but the event handling method needs to look at the source of the event to properly handle the event.

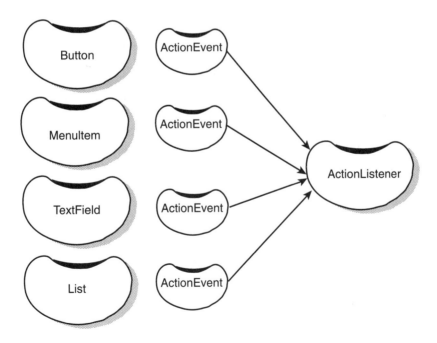

Listener Registration

Event source objects are responsible for maintaining a list of listeners to be notified when an event is fired. In order to be able to receive events from a source, a listener must be registered (or added to the list of listeners) at the source. Only objects that have implemented the correct event listener interface are allowed to register.

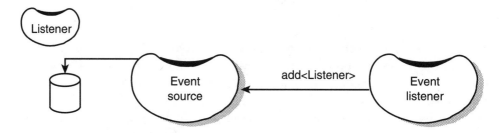

The event source provides a method to allow the registration of listeners. The coding guideline for this method is:

```
add<ListenerType>(<ListenerType> aListener);
```

where <ListenerType> is the type of listener interface used by this event. The registration can be done by the listener itself or by a controller object. A method to remove event listeners is provided as well. It is presented in the Event Source section below. The coding guidelines do not include the keyword synchronized for the event handling methods. The use of synchronous event handling methods is strongly recommended although not required. Synchronized event handling methods avoid problems when listening for events from many event sources.

Event Listener Example

This example of event listener uses the PaintEvent and the PaintListener classes presented previously. It shows a possible skeleton for implementing an event listener. It is not a running example.

```
public class ListenerExample implements PaintListener {

    public ListenerExample(anSource) {
        ...
        // Register itself as a listener
        anSource.addPaintListener(this);
        ...
    }
```

```
// Event handling methods
public void paintArea(PaintEvent anEvent) {
    ...
}

public void eraseAllAndPaint(PaintEvent anEvent) {
    ...
}
}
```

Event Sources

Event sources are any objects capable of sending events. It is the responsibility of the event source to maintain a list of registered listeners for each event that it can fire. These lists are used by the source to locate the listeners when sending an event. As shown above in the coding guidelines for methods that manage the list of listeners, the methods are not required to be synchronized, although the use of synchronous methods for modifications to the listener list are strongly recommended. The use of a `synchronized` method to fire an event is not recommended because a listener could lock the thread if something goes wrong during the event processing. During event generation, an event source should use a synchronized block to identify all the listeners and then do the notification from unsynchronized code. This practice avoids deadlocks and makes the event delivery thread-safe. Event delivery uses normal method invocation: The event source calls the listener's event handling method. Just as in any standard method invocation, the caller's thread is used to run the event handling method. If other behavior is desired, separate threads must be created for each event delivered.

While an event is being sent, the list of listeners may be updated, either by another thread or by one of the listeners. It is an implementation decision how to operate in these circumstances. One possible solution is to make a copy of the list of listeners before starting to send the event. The drawback of this solution is that when an object is removed from the list during the event delivery, it will still receive the last notification. This solution is implemented in the events example below.

Multicast Delivery

This is the most common behavior of an event source object. Multicast delivery means that event sources are capable of notifying as many listeners as necessary. Whenever possible, object sources should support multicast event delivery. There is no predefined order for multicast event delivery. It is an implementation decision to create an order for the delivery. The same delivery order should not be expected from different event sources.

The coding guidelines for multicast delivery are:

```
public void add<ListenerType>(<ListenerType> aListener);

public void remove<ListenerType>(<ListenerType> aListener);
```

where <ListenerType> is the listener interface defined for the event.

Upon receiving the event notification, one of the listeners may throw an exception. The event source may either continue or stop delivering the event notifications.

Unicast Delivery

For design or implementation reasons, a source object may need to notify only one listener. In such cases, the event source must keep track of a single listener and notify it when the event is fired.

The coding guidelines for unicast delivery are:

```
public void add<ListenerType>(<ListenerType> aListener) throws
java.util.TooManyListenersException;

public void remove<ListenerType>(<ListenerType> aListener);
```

Note that the coding guidelines are the same for multicast event delivery, except that unicast event delivery throws an exception when more than one listener tries to register.

Complete Events Example—Pizza Delivery

This is a complete example that shows the use of event objects, interfaces, sources and listeners.

An event source, a `Bakery` object, simulates a pizza oven. It is capable of preparing one pizza in regular time intervals. Every time a new pizza is ready, it multicasts an event to any customers who are out there listening. The customers are registered as event listeners to be notified when a new pizza is available. When customers receive the event notification that a new pizza is available, they automatically receive one slice. After finishing eating the pizza slice, the customers wait for new pizza slices (a new event notification). The customers ignore any notification that occurs while they are eating.

To provide an output that illustrates the event delivery and handling, the bakery prints out a message when a new pizza is ready. The customers print out a message each time they take a bite of pizza. The customers also count the number of slices they receive.

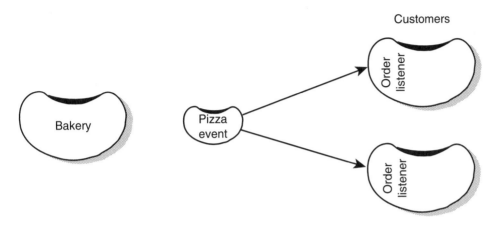

The `PizzaEvent` is the `Event` object. It does not contain any special information about the event. All that is needed for this example is the occurrence of the event. Even so, we have to create a subclass *EventObject*.

```
public class PizzaEvent extends java.util.EventObject {

  public PizzaEvent(Object aSource) {
    super(aSource);
  }
}
```

`OrderListener` is the listener interface that must be implemented by the listeners.

```
public interface OrderListener extends java.util.EventListener {
  public void pizzaStatus(PizzaEvent anEvent);
}
```

`Bakery` is the event source. It simulates a pizza oven that is capable of preparing a new pizza in regular time intervals. It generates an event when a new pizza is ready. The time interval is four seconds. To make it possible to know when a new pizza is ready, a message is sent to the console just after the delivery of the events.

```
import java.lang.Thread;
import java.util.*;

public class Bakery implements Runnable {
  private Vector iCustomers = new Vector();
  private Thread iThread;
```

```
   public Bakery() {
     iThread = new Thread(this);
     iThread.start();
   }

   public void run() {
     while(true) {
       try {
         iThread.sleep(4000);
         PizzaEvent event = new PizzaEvent(this);
         sendMessage(event);
       } catch (InterruptedException e) {}
     }
   }

   public synchronized void addOrderListener(OrderListener
aListener) {
       iCustomers.addElement(aListener);
   }

   public synchronized void removeOrderListener(OrderListener
aListener ) {
       iCustomers.removeElement(aListener);
   }

   private void sendMessage(PizzaEvent anEvent) {
     Vector v;
     synchronized(this) {
       v = (Vector)icustomers.clone();
     }
     for (int i=0; i<v.size(); i++) {
       OrderListener ol = (OrderListener)v.elementAt(i);
       ol.pizzaStatus(anEvent);
     }
     System.out.println("Pizza ready...");
   }
 }
```

The Customer is the event listener. He eats a slice of pizza when he has one.
When he has no slices, his thread is suspended because no work is done by the
customer during this interval. A new pizza slice is received when the source, the
bakery, sends an event and the thread is resumed.

```
import java.lang.Thread;
import java.util.Random;

public class Customer implements OrderListener, Runnable {
  private int iNumber;
  private boolean iHaveSlice;
  private Thread iThread;
  private Random iRandom;
  private int iSliceNumber;

  public customer(int aNumber) {
    iNumber = aNumber;
    iRandom = new Random(aNumber);
    iThread = new Thread(this);
    iThread.start();
  }

  public void run() {
    while(true) {
      if (iHaveSlice) {
        for (int bites=0; bites<4; bites++) {
          System.out.println("customer:" + iNumber + " bite " +
          bites + " slice:" + iSliceNumber);
          try {
            iThread.sleep((int)(iRandom.nextFloat()*3000));
          } catch (InterruptedException e) {}
        }
        synchronized(this) {
          iHaveSlice = false;
        }
        iThread.suspend();
      }
    }
  }

  public synchronized void pizzaStatus(PizzaEvent anEvent) {
    if (!iHaveSlice) {
      iHaveSlice = true;
      iSliceNumber++;
      iThread.resume();
    }
  }
}
```

TestApp is the application that instantiates the Bakery and Customer classes. As many customers as desired may be added.

```
public class TestApp {

  public static void main(String args[]) {
    TestApp t = new TestApp();
  }

  public TestApp() {
    Bakery b = new Bakery();
    Customer c1 = new Customer(1);
    Customer c2 = new Customer(2);
    b.addOrderListener(c1);
    b.addOrderListener(c2);
  }
}
```

Testing the Application

This is an output example. The actual order of the messages depends on the platform and JDK implementation of threads. Note that the customers start eating just after a new pizza is ready (when the source sends an event).

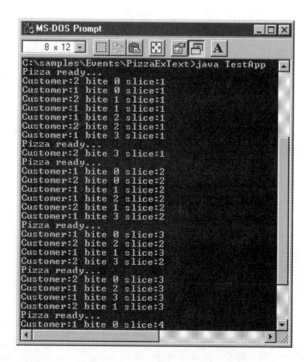

Extending the Example with Graphical Output

The previous example works fine, but it is difficult to visualize the message flow. With graphical output from the source and the listeners, it is easier to visualize the output, even with many more listeners. This example uses three customers, but others can easily be added just by instantiating more customers and registering them as listeners.

The following files must be replaced to make the graphical version work. They work the same way as their text counterparts; the only modifications done are to support the graphical output.

The Bakery.

```
import java.lang.Thread;
import java.util.*;
import java.awt.*;

public class Bakery extends Label implements Runnable {
  private Vector iCustomers = new Vector();
  private Thread iThread;

  public Bakery() {
    super();
    setAlignment(Label.CENTER);
    iThread = new Thread(this);
    iThread.start();
  }

  public void run() {
    Color oldBackground = getBackground();
    PizzaEvent event = new PizzaEvent(this);
    while(true) {
      try {
        iThread.sleep(6000);
      } catch (InterruptedException e) {}
      setBackground(Color.yellow);
      setText("Pizza");
      sendMessage(event);
      try {
        iThread.sleep(1500);
      } catch (InterruptedException e) {}
      setText("");
      setBackground(oldBackground);
    }
  }
```

```
 public synchronized void addOrderListener(OrderListener
    aListener) {
   iCustomers.addElement(aListener);
 }

 public synchronized void removeOrderListener(OrderListener
    aListener ) {
   iCustomers.removeElement(aListener);
 }

 private void sendMessage(PizzaEvent anEvent) {
   Vector v;
   synchronized(this) {
     v = (Vector)iCustomers.clone();
   }
   for (int i=0; i<v.size(); i++) {
     OrderListener ol = (OrderListener)v.elementAt(i);
     ol.pizzaStatus(anEvent);
   }
 }
}
```

The Customer.

```
import java.lang.Thread;
import java.util.Random;
import java.awt.*;

public class Customer extends Panel implements OrderListener,
Runnable {
  private boolean iHaveSlice;
  private Thread iThread;
  private Random iRandom;
  private Label iBites = new Label("0");
  private Label iMoreSlices = new Label();
  private int bug;

  public customer(int aNumber) {
    iRandom = new Random(aNumber);
    iHaveSlice = true;
    setBackground(Color.cyan);
    setLayout(new BorderLayout());
    add(iMoreSlices, "North");
    iMoreSlices.setAlignment(Label.CENTER);
    Panel southPanel = new Panel();
    southPanel.setLayout(new FlowLayout());
    add(southPanel, "South");
```

```
    southPanel.add(new Label("Bite:"));
    southPanel.add(iBites);
    bug = aNumber;
    iThread = new Thread(this);
    iThread.start();
  }

  public void run() {
    while(true) {
      if (iHaveSlice) {
        iMoreSlices.setText("");
        for (int bites=1; bites<5; bites++) {
          iBites.setText(Integer.toString(bites));
          try {
            iThread.sleep((int)(iRandom.nextFloat()*3000));
          } catch (InterruptedException e) {}
        }
        synchronized(this) {
          iHaveSlice = false;
          iMoreSlices.setText("MORE Pizza!");
          iBytes.setText("");
        }
        iThread.suspend();
      }
    }
  }

  public synchronized void pizzaStatus(PizzaEvent anEvent) {
    if (!iHaveSlice) {
      iHaveSlice = true;
      iThread.resume();
    }
  }
}
```

The `TestApp`.

```
public class TestApp extends java.awt.Frame {

  public static void main(String args[]) {
    TestApp t = new TestApp("Events Example");
  }

  public TestApp(String title) {
    super(title);
    setSize(540,160);
    setLayout(null);
```

```
    setVisible(true);

    Bakery b = new Bakery();
    b.setBounds(240,135,50,20);
    add(b);

    Customer c1 = new Customer(1);
    Customer c2 = new Customer(2);
    Customer c3 = new Customer(3);
    c1.setBounds(55,40,100,75);
    c2.setBounds(220,40,100,75);
    c3.setBounds(385,40,100,75);
    add(c1);
    add(c2);
    add(c3);

    b.addOrderListener(c1);
    b.addOrderListener(c2);
    b.addOrderListener(c3);

    paintAll(getGraphics());
  }
}
```

To run the graphical version of the example, type `java TestApp` on a command line. You should see a window like this.

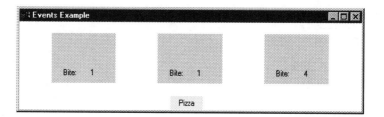

The bakery displays "Pizza" on the window while it is delivering the events. Customers are presented as blue boxes. When a customer is waiting for a new slice of pizza, the "MORE Pizza!" text is displayed. Only in this state do they accept a new slice of pizza from the bakery. This version does not count the number of slices eaten.

The `java.awt.Frame` class does not handle the window close event. This is the reason why you will not be able to close the window using the close button or the system menu. Switch to the command window used to start the program and cancel the execution from there (usually done by hitting CONTROL+C).

Conclusion

This concludes the events example and the events unit. The next unit continues with properties, the attributes of bean's Properties control things like a beans' state, appearance and behavior. We will see how events can be used to notify other objects that a bean's state has changed. Events can also be used to give other objects veto power over the setting of properties of a bean.

Properties

Properties are named attributes of beans. They can be read or set by other beans. If we look at beans as simply being Java classes with additional behavior, then properties are the attributes of those classes. When using properties with beans, it is necessary to provide get and set methods for accessing the properties. For example, in the `Pepper` class shown below, a get and set method provides access to the name of the chili pepper.

```
public String getPepperName() {
  return iPepperName;
}

public void setPepperName(String aName) {
  iPepperName = aName;
}
```

Accessibility to the properties of a bean is governed by the presence of the get and set methods. In other words, the properties will only be recognized as such if the appropriate get and set methods are defined. Introspection, the ability of a development environment to discover the public interface of a bean, requires the presence of the get and set methods. If the methods are missing, the properties are not recognized as being part of the public interface of the bean.

There are various possibilities for reacting to changes in the value of a property. A simple solution is to program the code directly into the get and set methods. However, this is poor style. The method performs more than one task and unnecessary dependencies are created. A more elegant solution is to define the get and set methods to generate events when the property is accessed. Interested objects "listen" for such events in order to be able to react. It is also possible to constrain the value of a property to certain limits. Again, a simple solution would be to place the constraints directly in the set method. Caution should be exercised when doing this in order to avoid the problems described for the simple solution above. The following example shows a set method which can generate an exception for the case of an unacceptable value.

```
public void setKind(String aKind)
            throws java.lang.Exception {
    if(aKind == "Strawberry") {
        Exception ex = new Exception("Not a chili pepper");
        throw ex;
    }
    else
        iKind = aKind;
}
```

The code which calls the above method must be able to catch the exception.

```
Pepper pepper = new Pepper();
try {
    pepper.setKind("Strawberry");
}
catch (Exception ex) {
    System.out.println("Exception - Message is: " +
                        ex.getMessage() );
}
```

An additional solution is to define the property to be a constrained property. Constraining a property gives other objects a veto power over the values of the property. Other objects which are listening for property changes can accept or reject the proposed value. It is possible to make a property read-only or to remove a property from the public interface of a bean.

In this unit, we will discuss the various ways of defining properties as they were introduced above.

Indexed Properties

Indexed properties are like normal properties, except that an index is used to reference the value. The index is always a Java `int`. The conventions for coding the access to the indexed property kind where the values are strings are as follows:

- Get and set all the values.

```
String[] getKind();
void setKind(String kinds[]);
```

- Get and set a specific value.

```
String getKind(int anIndex);
void setKind(int anIndex, String aKind);
```

For example, imagine that there are different kinds of chili peppers. The get method for accessing a kind of pepper would be called as follows:

```
String pepper = getKind(1);
```

The getter method may throw an `ArrayIndexOutOfBoundsException` if the `int` passed in is not within the bounds of the array.

Bound Properties

A bound property is a property which generate events when its value is changed. It is used to notify other beans that the value of a property has changed. A bean which generates such events must implement the `java.beans.Property-ChangeListener` interface. Events are broadcast or signaled by behavior defined using the interface. Objects which are interested in being notified of such events must register themselves with the bean as listeners for those events. This ensures that those objects receive the events when they are generated. Once they have received the events, they may react as desired. A detailed explanation of events can be found in the previous unit.

Let's look at an example. Let's assume a shipment of chili peppers can have the following states:

- Initialized
- Loaded
- Inspected
- Insured
- Sent
- Not Loaded

The shipment is modeled using the class `Shipment`. `Shipment` defines the property `shipmentState` of type `ShipmentState` to store the value of its state.

```
public class Shipment extends Object
            implements PropertyChangeListener {
private  ShipmentState shipmentState;
```

In order for other objects to be able to react when the state of the shipment changes, `shipmentState` must be a bound property. Interested objects may register themselves by calling the method `addShipmentStateListener()` and passing themselves along as a parameter. `addPropertyChangeListener()` adds the object to the collection of listeners returned by `getStateListeners()`. A corresponding `removePropertyChangeListener()` removes listeners from the collection of listeners.

```
public void addShipmentStateListener(
            PropertyChangeListener pcl) {
   getStateListeners().addPropertyChangeListener(pcl);
}


 public PropertyChangeSupport getStateListeners() {
    return iStateListeners;
 }
```

The collection of listeners is implemented using the class `java.beans.PropertyChangeSupport`.

```
private transient PropertyChangeSupport iStateListeners;
```

The listeners are notified by firing the property change event to the collection of state listeners. In this example, the event has the name state and it points to the old and the new state.

```
this.getStateListeners().firePropertyChange(
                      "state", oldState, newState);
```

In order to respond, a listener must first have registered itself using

```
shipment.addShipmentStateListener(this);
```

When the state of the shipment changes, the `propertyChange()` method of the listener is invoked. In this example, the broker would like to be informed of changes in the state of a shipment. The broker analyzes the property change event to see how the property has changed in order to decide how to respond. The source of the event tells the broker which shipment is affected.

```
public void propertyChange(PropertyChangeEvent anEvent) {
   if (anEvent.getPropertyName().equals("state")) {
      String newValue = (String)anEvent.getNewValue();
```

```
        if (newValue.equals("Initialized")) {
            System.out.println(
            "... EVENT \"Initialized\" ignored by Broker");
        }
        if (newValue.equals("NotLoaded")) {
            System.out.println(
            "... EVENT \"NotLoaded\" received by Broker");
            this.cancelShipment((Shipment)anEvent.getSource());
        }
        if (newValue.equals("Loaded")) {
            System.out.println(
            "... EVENT \"Loaded\" received by Broker");
            this.inspectShipment((Shipment) anEvent.getSource());
        }
        if (newValue.equals("Inspected")) {
            System.out.println(
            "... EVENT \"Inspected\" received by Broker");
            this.insureShipment((Shipment) anEvent.getSource());
        }
        if (newValue.equals("Insured")) {
            System.out.println(
            "... EVENT \"Insured\" received by Broker");
            this.deliverShipment((Shipment) anEvent.getSource());
        }
    }
}
```

Constrained Properties

A constrained property is defined as a property of a bean whose potential changes generate events. Recipients of the event may raise an Exception, vetoing the potential change. Constrained properties are used to allow other beans which are listening for a property change to accept or reject the new value for the property. In this case, the bean is not listening to the propertyChange event, but to the vetoableChange event. In response to this event, the listening beans can throw the java.beans.PropertyVetoException event to hinder the change.

The setter method for a constrained property must support PropertyVetoException. For example:

```
protected void setKind(String aKind)
        throws PropertyVetoException {
iKind = aKind;
}
```

The collection of listeners is implemented using the class `java.beans.VetoableChangeSupport`.

```
private transient VetoableChangeSupport iStateListeners;
```

The `java.beans.VetoableChangeListener` interface is used instead of the `PropertyChangeListener` interface. In order to provide support for adding listeners, we use the following method. It will add the listener using the `VetoableChangeSupport` class.

```
public void addShipmentStateListener(
            VetoableChangeListener vcl) {
    getStateListeners().addVetoableChangeListener(vcl);
}
```

The listener registers itself in the same way as for a bound property

```
shipment.addShipmentStateListener(this);
```

When the property in the `Shipment` changes, the `vetoableProperty-Change()` method is invoked.

```
public vetoablePropertyChange(VetoableChangeEvent anEvent)
        throws PropertyVetoException {
    if (anEvent.getPropertyName().equals("state")) {
        String newValue = (String)anEvent.getNewValue();
        if (newValue.equals("NotLoaded")) {
            System.out.println(
            "... EVENT \"NotLoaded\" received by Broker");
            throw new java.beans.PropertyVetoException(
                    "Not accepted!", anEvent);
        }
    }
}
```

Read Only and Private Properties

There are various ways of making a property read-only or private. If the set method is not implemented or if it is private, the property will be read-only. Not implementing the methods or making both the get and set methods private will remove the property from the public interface of the bean. In addition, a `Bean-Info` class associated with the class can be used to set properties to read-only or to remove them from the public interface.

Conclusion

In this unit we have discussed the properties of beans. We have discussed the various possibilities that exist when defining properties. We have shown how events can be used to inform other interested objects when the properties of a bean change. We have also shown how events can be used to give other objects a veto power when the properties of a bean are set. We have shown how properties can be added, removed or constrained in their accessibility in the public interface of a bean. This unit concludes the discussion of the public interface of a bean. The next unit introduces introspection, a mechanism which is typically used by development tools to examine the public interface of a bean.

Introspection

Introspection is the process that Java uses to analyze the components of the public interface of a bean: properties, methods and events. Introspection only works on objects; it does not analyze source code. The biggest benefit of introspection is the increased reusability of beans. A development tool can look directly into the component object to discover its behavior. A development tool will not look at the source code of a bean; rather, an instance of the bean is created and introspection is applied to analyze the bean. This reduces the need for the component developer to send extra information or source code along with the component. All the necessary information about a bean can be discovered by the tool using introspection.

BeanInfo Class

All the information about a components' properties, methods and events are provided by a `BeanInfo` object. `BeanInfo` is an object that specifies which properties, methods and events of a bean are to be exposed. It does not necessarily present all the information about a bean. A `BeanInfo` could explicitly identify which properties one component has by answering the `getPropertyDescriptors()`, and it could answer `null` to the `getMethodDescriptors()` meaning the methods should be discovered by analysis. This makes it simple to create `BeanInfo` classes, because the developer of a component does not have to describe everything about a class, only what he/she thinks is important. There is a one-to-one relation between beans and `BeanInfo`'s. One `BeanInfo` can describe only one bean.

It is not necessary for a bean to have a corresponding `BeanInfo` class that explicitly describes its contents. It is possible to create a default `BeanInfo` object for a bean dynamically when none is provided (see Introspector section) using the low level reflection API. This method creates a `BeanInfo` object for the target bean containing all the public properties, methods and events of the bean. The result is called implicit information and no private information about a bean can be exposed in implicit information.

The name of a `BeanInfo` class is formed by appending the word "BeanInfo" to the class name of the component that it describes. For example, the `BeanInfo` for a class called `Pepper` should be `PepperBeanInfo`.

Pepper.class

PepperBeanInfo.class

A BeanInfo Class for a Bean

The class `java.beans.SimpleBeanInfo` is provided with the JDK to facilitate the implementation of `BeanInfo` classes. To make a new `BeanInfo`, subclass `SimpleBeanInfo` and overwrite the necessary methods. All the methods in this class return null or -1, meaning no explicit information is available. When null or –1 is returned, the inquirer should look for implicit information. This behavior is implemented by the `Introspector` class presented further down.

These are the methods implemented by the `SimpleBeanInfo` class:

```
public PropertyDescriptor[] getPropertyDescriptors();
public MethodDescriptor[] getMethodDescriptors();
public EventSetDescriptor[] getEventSetDescriptors();
public BeanDescriptor getBeanDescriptor();
public int getDefaultEventIndex();
public int getDefaultPropertyIndex();
public BeanInfo[] getAdditionalBeanInfo();
public java.awt.Image getIcon(int iconKind);
public java.awt.Image loadImage(String resourceName);
```

The main methods are `getPropertyDescriptors()`, `getMethodDescriptors()` and `getEventSetDescriptors()` which return an array of descriptors for properties, methods and events. These methods return all the properties, methods and events that are to be exposed by a bean. The caller of these methods expects null or an array of descriptors. When a null is returned, the caller will look for implicit information. Otherwise, the caller assumes that the information received is all that is to be exposed and does not try to discover any other information about what the bean exposes in its public interface. It is not possible to implement the getPropertyDescriptors() to describe just one property and expect the other properties to be discovered. If the method is implemented as described, all the other properties will be hidden.

The loadImage() method is provided for ease in loading an image. It will look for the file specified by the resourceName parameter and will create an Image object from it. The image file must be in GIF format but future implementations of the JDK should support other formats.

The getIcon() method is responsible for returning the icon that represents the bean. It is optional for a bean to have an icon. This icon is not the actual visual representation of the bean; it can be used by tools to represent it in a tool bar or to identify a bean with no visual interface (non-visible bean) on the assembly surface. Icons are GIF images with predefined sizes and number of colors (actually, only color and black and white are defined). The getIcon() method receives the kind of icon required as a parameter. There are constants defined in java.beans.BeanInfo which specify the different types of icons. The following table shows the possible values for the iconKind parameter:

Size	Color type	Monochrome Type
16x16	ICON_COLOR_16x16	ICON_MONO_16x16
32x32	ICON_COLOR_32x32	ICON_MONO_32x32

It is not necessary for a bean to have all the different types of icons. The example below shows how a bean with just one icon can implement the getIcon() method. It uses the loadImage() method to load and create an Image object.

```
public java.awt.Image getIcon(int iconkind) {
   java.awt.Image img = loadImage("iconpepp.gif");
   return img;
}
```

Refer to the JavaSoft documentation for further information about the other methods of SimpleBeanInfo.

BeanInfo Example

We will use a simple bean to create a BeanInfo for the Pepper bean, the same bean which was used previously in the Properties unit. It is a bean with just two properties, kind and heatLevel, and no events. It is not intended to have any special behavior and it is just used to illustrate the creation of BeanInfo classes. The BeanInfo for the Pepper class, the PepperBeanInfo class, describes only one of the Pepper properties while hiding the other. Note that is possible to hide properties, methods and events using the BeanInfo, but it is not possible to define "fake" or additional ones. A run time error is generated if a property, method or event is described that does not exist.

```java
public class Pepper implements java.io.Serializable {
  private String iKind;
  private int iHeatLevel;

  public Pepper() {}

  public String getKind() {
    return iKind;
  }

  public void setKind(String aKind) {
    iKind = aKind;
  }

  public int getHeatLevel() {
    return iHeatLevel;
  }

  public void setHeatLevel(int aHeatLevel) {
    iHeatLevel = aHeatLevel;
  }
}


import java.beans.*;
public class PepperBeanInfo extends SimpleBeanInfo {

  public PropertyDescriptor[] getPropertyDescriptors() {
    PropertyDescriptor[] pdArray = new PropertyDescriptor[1];
    try {
      pdArray[0] = new PropertyDescriptor("heatLevel",
        Pepper.class);
    } catch (IntrospectionException e) {
      System.out.println("Error creating a PropertyDescriptor");
    }
    return pdArray;
  }
}
```

Introspector

The class java.beans.Introspector is provided as a way for applications (or applets) to discover information about a bean's behavior. An instance of Intros-pector examines a bean, seeking a corresponding BeanInfo. If no BeanInfo can be found, the introspector uses the low level reflection API and coding guide-lines to generate implicit information about the bean. A BeanInfo is created by the introspector using the implicit information generated. If a BeanInfo is found, it is examined to see what information it contains. A developer defined Bean-Info provides explicit information in the form of descriptors (see A BeanInfo Class for a Bean section earlier in this chapter). If any of the descriptors return null, the introspector examines the instance of the bean using the reflection API to generate implicit information for the category. Categories for which the descrip-tors return something other than null are not looked at using reflection. The resulting BeanInfo is then returned to the application or development tool which initiated the introspection. The application always receive a BeanInfo object from the introspector, unless an exception occurs during the introspection. The application or development tool does not have to worry about how to create and populate a BeanInfo for a bean.

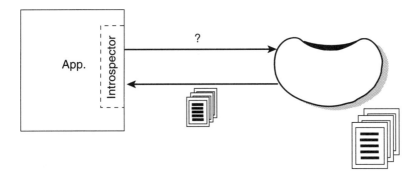

When a bean has superclasses, the introspector gathers information from the superclasses as well as from the class to create a new BeanInfo object for the bean. For each class in the tree, the approach described above is used. The infor-mation from the class and its superclasses is merged in the BeanInfo returned by the introspector. This approach makes the development of extensions to existing beans easy because subclasses need only specify the new properties, methods and events. All the information defined by the superclasses will continue to be used.

Coding Guidelines

Coding guidelines are a set of stated rules for defining and naming methods and signatures. Introspection uses an automatic identification algorithm based on coding guidelines to identify properties, methods and events. It is not mandatory to follow the guidelines. In fact, a bean may work even if the guidelines were not followed. However, it is strongly recommended to follow the guidelines. Following the guidelines makes code consistent. It also makes introspection possible. It is possible for a beans developer to define `BeanInfo` classes for beans that do not follow the coding guidelines. However, there is a risk that the beans will not interact correctly with other beans or work correctly in development tools.

When analyzing an object, an introspector must parse the signature of methods which refer to properties and events in order to discover the true names of the properties and events. The coding guidelines for such methods specify how the names of properties and events are used. Typically, the first letter of the name is capitalized and a verb is placed before it. For example, the signature for a method which returns the value of the property `heatLevel` is `getHeatLevel()`. When parsing, the introspector finds the coding guidelines for the category of method being parsed. Using the coding guidelines, the name is picked out and the first letter is converted to lower case. However if the first three letters of the name in the method are capitalized, the first letter does not revert to lower case. For example:

N≈ame in method	True name
`...ShipmentState...`	`shipmentState`
`...TCP...`	`TCP`

The coding guidelines used in introspection to determine the behavior of beans are listed here by category.

Properties

A property may be read/write, read-only or write-only. By default, properties are neither bound nor constrained. The `is<PropertyName>()` method must be defined for `Boolean` properties. The `get` method is optional in this case.

```
public <PropertyType> get<PropertyName>();
public void set<PropertyName>(<PropertyType> value);
public boolean is<PropertyName>();
```

When the property is an `Array`, the following methods are necessary:

```
public <PropertyElement> get<PropertyName>(int position);
```

```
public void set<PropertyName>(int position, <PropertyElement>
  value);
```

Events

Introspection looks for the add/removeListener pair of methods to define an event. Methods for unicast and multicast events have the same signature, but the unicast event may throw a TooManyListenersException exception.

```
public void add<ListenerType>(<ListenerType> listener)
  throws java.util.TooManyListenersException;
public void remove<ListenerType>(<ListenerType> listener);
```

Methods

All the public methods are included in the bean description. There are no coding guidelines for writing general purpose public methods in order for them to be recognized through introspection.

Introspection example—Descriptor

The following example illustrates how introspection can be used. The Descriptor application uses introspection to analyze an object and print out information about its methods, properties and events. It can be used on any local class that has a void constructor (a constructor that receives no parameters). It is started from the command line. Descriptor uses introspection to return a BeanInfo for the target class. The target class is named on the command line when the application is started. Two parameters can be set: -m and -a. -m changes the way method names are presented, making the output simpler to read. -a controls the depth of introspection in the target bean. By default, the descriptor only introspects the target class and does not present any information about its superclasses. When -a is set, introspection covers the entire tree of the target class. The complete source code is explained below.

```
import java.beans.*;

public class Descriptor {
  private BeanInfo iBeanInfo;
  private boolean iAllClasses;
  private boolean iOnlyMethodsNames;
```

import java.beans.*; makes the beans classes available for the Descriptor class. This is needed because all the Introspection classes are part of this package. iBeanInfo stores the introspection result. iAllClasses and iOnlyMethod-

`Names` are boolean variables. If `iAllClasses` returns true, the entire tree of the target is introspected. If `iOnlyMethodNames` returns true, only the method names are displayed.

```java
public static void main(String[] args) {
    if ((args.length == 0) || (args.length > 2)) {
        System.out.println("Usage: Descriptor -[am] <bean>");
        System.out.println("        -a   Introspect into the class
          hierarchy");
        System.out.println("        -m   Print only the methods names");
        System.exit(1);
    }
    Descriptor bd = new Descriptor(args);
}
```

The `main()` method is the method which starts a Java application. In this case, the number of command line parameters is checked to see if they match the requirements. If the requirements are met, a descriptor is instantiated.

```java
public Descriptor(String[] args) {
    String beanName;
    if ((args[0].charAt(0) == '-') || (args[0].charAt(0) == '/')) {
        if (args[0].indexOf('a') != -1)
            iAllClasses = true;
        if (args[0].indexOf('m') != -1)
            iOnlyMethodsNames = true;
        beanName = args[1];
    } else
        beanName = args[0];
    try {
        ClassLoader cl = Class.forName(beanName).getClassLoader();
        Object bean = Beans.instantiate(cl, beanName);
        Class beanClass = bean.getClass();
        if (iAllClasses)
            iBeanInfo = Introspector.getBeanInfo(beanClass);
        else
            iBeanInfo = Introspector.getBeanInfo(beanClass,
beanClass.getSuperclass());
    } catch (ClassNotFoundException e) {
        System.out.println("Bean " + beanName + " not found.");
        System.exit(1);
    } catch (IntrospectionException e) {
        System.out.println("Introspection failed on bean: " +
beanName);
        System.exit(1);
    } catch (Exception e) {
```

```
      System.out.println("Descriptor error.");
      e.printStackTrace();
      System.exit(1);
    }
    System.out.println("Introspection Results on bean " + beanName);
    describeMethods();
    describeProperties();
    describeEvents();
  }
```

The constructor creates a descriptor for the target. The description process is then started. The name of the class to introspect, the target, is received from the command line. The `ClassLoader` locates the class file for the target and loads the class. `Beans.instantiate()` is used to create an instance of the target. Java uses the class `Class` to internally represent classes at runtime. All objects have access to the `getClass()` method defined in `Object`. The method returns an instance of `Class` corresponding to the object's type. The `Introspector` class uses this instance of `Class` to extract the information necessary to build a Bean-Info object for the target. The `getBeanInfo()` method is overloaded. The first form takes the target class as a parameter and run through the entire tree of the target to generate the `BeanInfo`. The second form has two parameters: the target class and one of its superclasses. Only the portion of the tree between the target and up to but not including the specified superclass is introspected. In this case, we just pass the superclass of the target class. As a result, only the target class is analyzed. The instance of `BeanInfo` resulting from the introspection is assigned to the `iBeanInfo` instance variable.

```
  /**
   * Display the targets' methods.
   */
  private void describeMethods() {
    MethodDescriptor[] md = iBeanInfo.getMethodDescriptors();
    if (md.length > 0)
      System.out.println("\nMethods\n");
    for (int i=0; i<md.length; i++) {
      if (iOnlyMethodsNames)
        System.out.println(md[i].getName());
      else
        System.out.println(md[i].getMethod());
    }
  }

  /**
   * Display the beans' properties.
```

```
*/
private void describeProperties() {
  PropertyDescriptor[] pd = iBeanInfo.getPropertyDescriptors();
  if (pd.length > 0)
    System.out.println("\nProperties\n");
  for (int i=0; i<pd.length; i++) {
    // Property name
    System.out.print(pd[i].getName() + " - ");
    // Property Type
    System.out.print((pd[i].getPropertyType()).getName());
    // Property Attributes
    String PropertyAttributes = pd[i].isBound()?",Bound":"";
   PropertyAttributes += pd[i].isConstrained()?",Constrained":"";
    System.out.println(PropertyAttributes);
  }
}

/**
 * Display the beans' events.
 */
private void describeEvents() {
  EventSetDescriptor[] ed = iBeanInfo.getEventSetDescriptors();
  if (ed.length > 0)
    System.out.println("\nEvents\n");
  for (int i=0; i<ed.length; i++) {
    System.out.print(ed[i].getName());
    System.out.println(" - " +
(ed[i].isUnicast()?"Unicast":"Multicast"));
    System.out.println("\tListener type:     " +
ed[i].getListenerType());
    System.out.println("\tRegister method:    " +
ed[i].getAddListenerMethod());
    System.out.println("\tUnregister method: " +
ed[i].getRemoveListenerMethod());
  }
}
}
```

Each of these three private methods describes a specific category of a bean's elements. Each asks the `BeanInfo` for an array of descriptors for the category being described. Each descriptor describes a specific element. There are a number of different descriptors; `BeanDescriptor`, `EventSetDescriptor`, `IndexedPropertyDescriptor`, `ParameterDescriptor` and `PropertyDescriptor`. All are subclasses of `FeatureDescriptor`. Not all of the subclasses are used in this example. The application can easily be extended to include the remaining classes. Each descriptor can provide more information than is used in this example. Refer to the JavaSoft documentation for further information on descriptors.

Running the Descriptor Application

The result of running the descriptor on the `Pepper` class without a `BeanInfo` is shown.

```
C:\>java Descriptor Pepper
Introspection Results on bean Pepper

Methods

public java.lang.String Pepper.getKind()
public int Pepper.getHeatlevel()
public void Pepper.setHeatlevel(int)
public void Pepper.setKind(java.lang.String)

Properties

heatLevel - int
kind - java.lang.String
```

When a `PepperBeanInfo` class is defined, the result of running the application on `Pepper` changes. `PepperBeanInfo` only describes the `heatLevel` property, kind no longer appears.

```
C:\>java Descriptor Pepper
Introspection Results on bean Pepper

Methods

public java.lang.String Pepper.getKind()
public void Pepper.setHeatLevel(int)
public int Pepper.getHeatLevel()
public void Pepper.setKind(java.lang.String)

Properties

heatLevel - int
```

Conclusion

As we have seen throughout this unit, introspection is a very powerful and useful tool for developers and development tools alike. The next unit discusses another important aid for development—customization. Using customization, it is possible to change the appearance and behavior of a bean by setting the appropriate properties.

Customization

The behavior and appearance of a bean can be modified by setting the values of its properties at development time. This process is known as customization. The properties can be edited using a properties editor. There are two kinds of properties editors:

- A property sheet, the system default. The property editor allows the values of individual properties to be edited one at a time. A property editor is provided for each property which can be edited. Default editors, usually entry fields, are provided for some Java types. User defined property editors are also possible. User defined editors can be very simple, allowing a string representation of the type to be edited. More advanced property editors may use a separate window which is launched from the property sheet.

- The customizer allows higher level editing of a bean. The customizer is a separate editor. It can be used to set several properties simultaneously, making dependencies among properties transparent. The customizer is not intended to replace the property sheet; it works together with the property sheet to provide additional editing capabilities. Changes made using a customizer are reflected in the property sheet.

For simple beans, the property sheet, with or without customized property editors, may be sufficient. However, more complex beans, particularly those where dependencies exist between properties, will most likely require customizers as well. It is important to note that the customizer does not replace the property sheet. In those cases where a customizer is defined, it is used to provide a higher level of editing capabilities. Development tools vary in the way they deal with customizers. If a customizer exists for a bean, it may be shown automatically. In other environments, the customizer must be displayed explicitly. This is the case in the BDK from Sun.

We will begin by discussing the property sheet and the three kinds of property editors that may appear in it. We will provide examples for each kind of property editor. We will show how the development environment recognizes the presence of additional property editors. We will show how the property sheet is assembled if additional property editors are specified. We will conclude by discussing customizers. We will include an example of a customizer for the `Pepper` bean. Introspection and the `BeanInfo`, introduced in the previous unit, play a crucial role in providing the development tool with information on how to locate and assemble all the parts of the properties editors for a bean.

Property Editors and the Property Sheet

Every bean has a property sheet associated with it. It contains property editors which edit the values of individual properties at development time. Each property which can be edited has its own property editor. Unless otherwise specified, property editors are assigned on the basis of type. The development tool goes through the following process when assembling the property sheet for a bean. It first uses introspection to generate the `BeanInfo` for the bean. If a specific `Bean-Info` is defined for the bean, it is examined to see which property editors are defined for the properties of the bean. If no specific property editor is defined for a property, the tool attempts to find a property editor which corresponds to the type of the property. If no `BeanInfo` was defined for the bean, introspection returns a `BeanInfo` containing implicit information about the bean. Please see the previous unit for a discussion of introspection. The tool attempts to find property editors which correspond to the type of the properties contained in the `BeanInfo`. Java provides default editors for certain basic types (see Default editors below). Developers must provide property editors for the remaining types. It is up to the development tool to decide what happens if no property editor is found. For example, the BDK from Sun simply does not show the property on the property sheet. The tool uses a class called `PropertyEditorManager` to handle the mechanics of finding property editors for the editable types.

Custom property editors may be a graphical component that is launched from the property sheet or a very simple class that can be integrated in the property sheet. In order to become a property editor, a class must implement the `java.beans.PropertyEditor` interface. A support class called `java.beans.PropertyEditorSupport` implements the `PropertyEditor` interface. It adds functionality for handling `PropertyChange` listeners. The simple property editor uses `PropertyEditorSupport`, and the graphical property editor implements the `PropertyEditor` interface. The examples and sample code provided show the use of both `PropertyEditor` and `PropertyEditor-Support`.

A property can be hidden, read-only, write-only or read/write. If both the getter and setter methods for the property are not public, the property is hidden and will not appear on the property sheet. Read-only properties are displayed, but cannot be edited. Furthermore, the BeanInfo may also be used to qualify the access rights of properties of a bean.

Default Property Editors

Default property editors are provided for the following Java types:

- `boolean`

- `byte`

- `short`

- `int`

- `long`

- `float`

- `double`

- `String`

- `Color`

- `Font`

The property sheet of the `Pepper` class in the BeanBox from Sun, the BDK is shown below. Note that the property sheet shows the names of the properties in lower case regardless of the spelling of the property in the code.

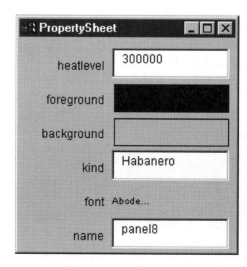

The properties specific to `Pepper` are `kind` and `heatlevel`. The other properties are related to the class `java.awt.Panel`. They are displayed because the
`Pepper` bean is a graphical component. The `kind` is of type `String`, and the
`heatlevel` is an `int`. In the example above, the default editors for `String` and
`int` are used to provide access to the `kind` and `heatlevel` properties.

The following diagram describes how the visual development environment puts
together the property sheet in this case.

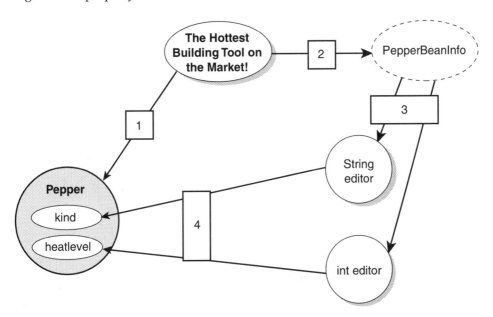

1. The `Pepper` bean is selected from the palette of beans.

2. Since no `PepperBeanInfo` class is available, the tool uses introspection
   (see the section on introspection for more detail) on the bean. It creates an
   instance of a default `PepperBeanInfo` for itself in memory containing
   properties and methods for the bean.

3. Since no property editors are specified, Java provides default property editors for all the types it supports.

4. The `String` editor is used for the `kind` property, and the `int` editor for
   `heatlevel` property. These editors are default editors, so no extra code is
   needed to be able to edit the properties.

Simple Property Editors

A simple property editor can be integrated directly into the property sheet. It may
appear as an entry field or as a drop down list for example. A simple property editor may only implement the `getAsText()` and/or `setAsText()` methods. The
`getAsText()` method simply returns a string representation of the property.
`setAsText()` provides the functionality to set the property based on a string. In
order to be able to use simple property editors for properties where a default
property editor for the type already exists, a `BeanInfo` class corresponding to the
bean must be defined to specify which editors to use. If no default editor exists for
the type, it is not absolutely necessary to specify the simple editor in the `Bean-`
`Info`. The development tool will find the correct editors on the basis of type
matching. However, it is considered good style to specify the editors explicitly in
the `BeanInfo`.

The following example shows how to define a `BeanInfo` class for the `Pepper`
bean. For further information on the `BeanInfo` class, please refer to the section
on Introspection.

```
public class PepperBeanInfo extends SimpleBeanInfo {

  public java.beans.PropertyDescriptor[] getPropertyDescriptors()
{
    PropertyDescriptor pd[];
    try {
      pd = new java.beans.PropertyDescriptor[2];
      // Specify the editor for kind.
      pd[0] = new java.beans.PropertyDescriptor("kind",
Pepper.class);
      pd[0].setDisplayName("Kind of Pepper");

pd[0].setPropertyEditorClass(Property.Simple.KindEditor.class);
      // Specify the editor for heatlevel.
      pd[1] = new java.beans.PropertyDescriptor("heatlevel",
Pepper.class);
      pd[1].setDisplayName("Heatlevel of Pepper");

pd[1].setPropertyEditorClass(Property.Simple.HeatEditor.class);
      return pd;
    }
  }
}
```

An array is created with two `PropertyDescriptors`, one for each of the properties. A property descriptor describes one property of a bean, accessible via a `get` and a `set` method. A property descriptor also specifies if the property is bound or constrained. Note that the property name is lower case. The `getPropertyDescriptors()` method returns the array of property descriptors for a bean. The `setDisplayName()` method specifies the name that will be shown for the property in the property sheet.

The property sheet for the `Pepper` class now looks like this:

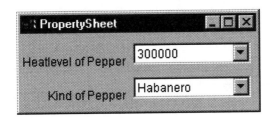

The drop down lists are provided because we have implemented the `getTags()` method in each of the property editors. `getTags()` returns an array of strings containing the possible values for the property being edited.

```
public String[] getTags() {
   String tags[] = {
      "Habanero",
      "Serrano",
      "Jalapeno",
      "Bell Pepper"};
   return tags;
}
```

When the user selects one of the items in the drop down list, the `setAsText()` method is invoked. `setAsText()` sets the value of the target property.

```
public void setAsText(String text) throws
IllegalArgumentException {
   setValue(text);
}
```

The diagram illustrates how the development tool assembles the property sheet using the new editors.

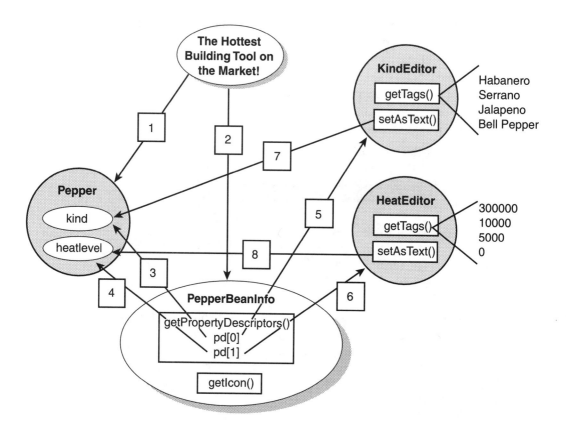

1. The Pepper bean is selected from the palette of beans.

2. The building tool checks to see if a BeanInfo class for Pepper exists and finds PepperBeanInfo. This BeanInfo class points to two specific editors that are to be used when editing the properties in the Pepper bean. This is done in the getPropertyDescriptors() method. It returns an array of property descriptors.

3. The first property descriptor is associated with the kind property.

4. The second property descriptor is associated with the heatlevel property.

5. The kind property descriptor specifies the editor to be used for kind. In this case, it is the KindEditor. The KindEditor provides a drop down list with four different chili peppers: habanero, serrano, jalapeño and bell pepper. The getTags() method is invoked by the property sheet in the building tool to obtain the list.

6. The heatlevel property descriptor specifies the HeatEditor. The get-Tags() method returns four heat levels.

7. Let's assume habanero is selected as the kind of pepper. This selection calls the setAsText() method. The parameter for the setAsText() method is a String. The string is used to update the kind property in the Pepper class. The setValue() method is called with the String value received in setAsText().

8. Logically, you should not really be able to select the heatlevel for the pepper. A habanero is usually 300000 heat units; it is not likely to find a habanero that is only 1000 heat units. Perhaps you like the taste and smell of the habanero, but want it to be milder? (Very unlikely!) Let's assume 300000 is selected. The setAsText() method is invoked. Since the target property is an int, the string 300000 must be converted to an int. This is done by calling:

```
setValue(java.lang.Integer.valueOf(text));
```

9. The editor is completed! Time to eat the habanero! We suggest that you use it in a nice salsa with carrots, onion and garlic. Saute the carrots and the onion, and then boil in water and a little vinegar. Add garlic and the habanero and make a nice salsa in your mixer. This one is a real eye opener at your parties.

Graphical Property Editors

More elegant graphical property editors can also be used in the property sheet. Such editors are typically launched by the property sheet when the value of the property is selected. They can be used in addition to or in place of the simple editors and default editors introduced above. Adding a graphical property editor to the property sheet is similar to the way in which simple editors were added above. However, instead of adding the entire editor, only a widget displaying the value of the property is added. When the widget, typically an entry field, is selected, the property editor for the property is displayed. Both the widget which displays the value of the property and the actual editor may be defined in the class of the property editor. The following methods may be implemented in the class of the editor:

- getMinimumSize()
- isPaintable()
- paintValue()
- supportsCustomEditor()
- getCustomEditor()

It is not necessary to draw the entire graphical editor. Defining `supportsCus-tomEditor()` to return true indicates to the development tool that a separate editor is supported. A frame with a button is provided by the tool. The developer must define a panel containing the editor. The panel is placed within the frame provided by the tool. The panel may be defined in the same class. In this case, `getCustomEditor()` returns itself. The panel may also be defined in another class. In this case, `getCustomEditor()` must return an instance of the appropriate class. `getMinimumSize()` is used to define the minimum size in pixels required by the panel. `isPaintable()` is a flag which indicates if the class defines how the value is presented in the property sheet. If this is the case, the method returns true and the method `paintValue()` must be implemented. `paintValue()` is used to specify how the value of the property is presented in the property sheet.

Let's look at an example which will allow us to edit the kind of the `Pepper` bean using a separate editor. We will define the panel which contains the editor and the presentation of the value in the property editor in the same class. The class `KindEditor` is a subclass of `Panel`. It implements the `PropertyEditor` and `ItemListener` interfaces.

```
package Property.GUI;

import java.beans.*;
import java.awt.*;

public class KindEditor extends Panel implements PropertyEditor,
ItemListener {

    private Checkbox iCbHabanero, iCbSerrano, iCbJalapeno, iCbBell;
    private CheckboxGroup iCbGroup;
    private Label iTextSelect;
    private PropertyChangeSupport iPropertyChangeSupport;
    private String iKind;
```

We have defined a number of instance variables. The checkboxes, the checkbox group and the label are all components of the panel. The string is used to represent the actual value of the property in the property sheet. The property change support is used by the development tool to synchronize the value of the property between the editor and the instance of the bean which the development tool is referencing.

```
public KindEditor() {
  setLayout(null);

  iPropertyChangeSupport = new PropertyChangeSupport(this);
  iCbGroup      = new CheckboxGroup();
  iCbHabanero = new Checkbox("Habanero", iCbGroup, true);
  iCbSerrano  = new Checkbox("Serrano",  iCbGroup, false);
  iCbJalapeno = new Checkbox("Jalapeno", iCbGroup, false);
  iCbBell     = new Checkbox("Bell Pepper", iCbGroup, false);
 iTextSelect = new Label("Choose your favorite chili pepper!",
Label.CENTER);

  iCbHabanero.addItemListener(this);
  iCbSerrano.addItemListener(this);
  iCbJalapeno.addItemListener(this);
  iCbBell.addItemListener(this);

  add(iTextSelect);
  iTextSelect.setBounds(5,   5, 200, 15);
  add(iCbHabanero);
  iCbHabanero.setBounds(20, 30, 100, 15);
  add(iCbSerrano);
  iCbSerrano.setBounds( 20, 50, 100, 15);
  add(iCbJalapeno);
  iCbJalapeno.setBounds(20, 70, 100, 15);
  add(iCbBell);
  iCbBell.setBounds(    20, 90, 100, 15);
}
```

We first set up the check box group and the text which appears in the panel. We define a check box for each kind of pepper and add it to the check box group. We then define the editor to be a listener for changes for each of the check boxes. This allows the editor to know when one of the check boxes has been selected. We then define the placement and sizing of the components in the panel.

```
public void itemStateChanged(ItemEvent anEvent) {
  Object obj = anEvent.getItemSelectable();
  if(obj == iCbHabanero)
    setValue((String)"Habanero");
  if(obj == iCbSerrano)
    setValue((String)"Serrano");
  if(obj == iCbJalapeno)
    setValue((String)"Jalapeno");
  if(obj == iCbBell)
    setValue((String)"Bell Pepper");
}
```

The `itemStateChanged()` method allows the panel to react when an item in the check box group is selected. It sets the value of the property to correspond to the check box which was selected.

```
public void addPropertyChangeListener(PropertyChangeListener
aPropertyChangeListener) {

iPropertyChangeSupport.addPropertyChangeListener(aPropertyChange
Listener);
}

public void removePropertyChangeListener(PropertyChangeListener
aPropertyChangeListener) {

iPropertyChangeSupport.removePropertyChangeListener(aPropertyCha
ngeListener);
}
```

These two methods handle the addition and removal of listeners of changes in the value property. These methods are used to allow the development tool to know when the value of the property has changed within the editor. When the value changes, the tool must update the property sheet. The tool calls the `paint-Value()` method if one is defined; otherwise a default representation is used.

```
public Object getValue() {
  return iKind;
}

public void setValue(Object anObject) {
  iKind = (String)anObject;
  iPropertyChangeSupport.firePropertyChange("", null, null);
}
```

The `getValue()` and `setValue()` methods handle access to the instance variable which stores the value of the property within the editor. When the value of the kind property is set, the *iPropertyChangeSupport.firePropertyChange()* method generates an event, and listeners will be able to reflect the new value.

```
public Dimension getMinimumSize() {
  return new Dimension(200, 150);
}
```

The `getMinimumSize()` returns the minimum rectangular space the panel needs within the frame provided by the tool.

```
public String getJavaInitializationString() {
   return "new Property.GUI.KindEditor(" + getAsText() + ")";
}
```

The `getJavaInitializationString()` method sets a label for the frame which contains the panel.

```
public boolean supportsCustomEditor() {
   return true;
}
```

```
public java.awt.Component getCustomEditor() {
   return this;
}
```

The `supportsCustomEditor()` returns true, meaning that a custom editor is supported. We have defined the panel in the same class as the painting of the value in the property sheet. As a result, `getCustomEditor()` returns itself.

```
public String getAsText() {
   return iKind;
}
```

```
public void setAsText(String aString) throws
java.lang.IllegalArgumentException {
   setValue(aString);
}
```

The `getAsText()` and `setAsText()` methods allow the tool to get the value of the property from the property sheet and to set the initial value of the property in the property sheet.

```
public boolean isPaintable() {
   return true;
}
```

The `isPaintable()` method indicates whether the painting of the property value in the property sheet is defined in the class. We return true, since we are planning to specify how the value is to appear.

```
public void paintValue(Graphics aGraphics, Rectangle aRect) {
   FontMetrics fm = aGraphics.getFontMetrics();
   int fontheight = fm.getHeight();
   int align = (aRect.height - fontheight) / 2;
```

```
aGraphics.setColor(Color.yellow);
aGraphics.fill3DRect(aRect.x + 1, aRect.y + 1, aRect.width - 4,
aRect.height - 4, false);
aGraphics.setColor(Color.black);
aGraphics.drawString(iKind, aRect.x + 4, aRect.y + aRect.height
- 4 - align);
}
```

The `paintValue()` method specifies how the property value is displayed in the property sheet. We are provided with a graphics context for drawing and a rectangle to draw in. We size the rectangle relative to the font used to display the value and we set the background color of the rectangle to yellow. Finally, we draw the string representing the value of the property.

The resulting property sheet is shown below. It uses a simple editor to set the `heatLevel` and displays the value of the `kind` as we have specified.

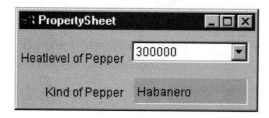

Selecting the value "Habanero" will bring up the editor. It looks like this:

Property Editor Managers

A `PropertyEditorManager` is responsible for locating the properties editor for a class. It manages tables containing types and property editors registered for the type. It contains additional behavior for locating editors for types which are not in the tables. A `PropertyEditorManager` can only handle property editors which implement the `PropertyEditor` interface. It is the class used by the development tool to locate the appropriate editor for the editable properties. `PropertyEditorManager` provides the following methods:

- `registerEditor(Class, Class)` is used to register a property editor class that is specified as the first parameter. This editor will be used to edit the values of the class specified as the second parameter.

- `findEditor(Class)` returns a subclass of `PropertyEditor` that is to be used for editing the values of the class specified as the parameter.

- `getEditorSearchPath()` returns an array of strings. The array contains the names of packages that will be searched to locate property editors if no editor for a type has been registered. The method initially returns {"sun.beans.editors"} as the default path.

- `setEditorSearchPath(String[])` can be used to set the list of packages to be searched when searching for property editors.

There are three ways for a `PropertyEditorManager` to find the right property editor for a type.

1. First the `PropertyEditorManager` checks if there is an editor registered for the type using the `registerEditor()` method.

2. If no editor is registered, it will try to locate a class by adding the string "Editor" to the class name with the fully qualified package name of the given type. For example, to locate an editor for `myBeans.Pepper`, the `PropertyEditorManager` searches for a class corresponding to `myBeans.PepperEditor`.

3. If no property editor is found in the package containing the type, the `PropertyEditorManager` searches for a class named `PepperEditor` in all the packages defined in the current editor search path.

Specifying a property editor for a property in the `BeanInfo` for a bean calls the `registerEditor()` method in `PropertyEditorManager`.

Customizers

Defining a customizer for a bean allows a developer to deal with situations where a higher level of editing logic is necessary. For example, they can be used in situations where dependencies exist between individual properties such that the properties must be edited simultaneously. The changes made will be reflected in the property sheet, however the properties must be defined in such a way that it is not possible to edit the same properties from the customizer and the property sheet. Unlike the property editors described above, the customizer receives the instance of the bean from the tool. As a result, the customizer can access properties which have public access methods defined for them even if the property has been defined to be read-only in the `BeanInfo` for the bean. Setting a property to read-only prevents the property sheet from displaying a property editor for the property. The property sheet simply displays the value of the property. Customizers are defined using the `java.beans.Customizer` interface. The customizer for a bean is specified using the `BeanInfo`.

Customizers must implement the `Customizer` interface. Typically, three methods are defined:

- `setObject()`. This method is called by the development tool when the customizer is displayed. It is used to pass in the instance of the bean, the target, to the customizer.

- `addPropertyChangeListener()`. When the value of a property is changed by the customizer, a property change event is generated by the customizer. Property change events are also generated directly by the bean when the values from the customizer are sent to the target bean. The event generated directly by the customizer seems redundant at first glance. However, it is used to allow objects which are not listeners on the target bean to know when the customizer has changed a value. The property sheet in the BDK from Sun uses the events generated by the customizer to synchronize the values it displays with those set by the customizer. This method allows listeners on the change events generated by the customizer to register themselves.

- `removePropertyChangeListener()`. This allows listeners to unregister for the property change event generated by the customizer.

A customizer is specified using the `BeanInfo` for a bean. The method `getCustomizerClass()` must be defined to return the class of the customizer in the `BeanDescriptor` for the bean. The `BeanInfo` provides access to the `BeanDescriptor`. The diagram below illustrates how the development tool finds the customizer if one has been specified.

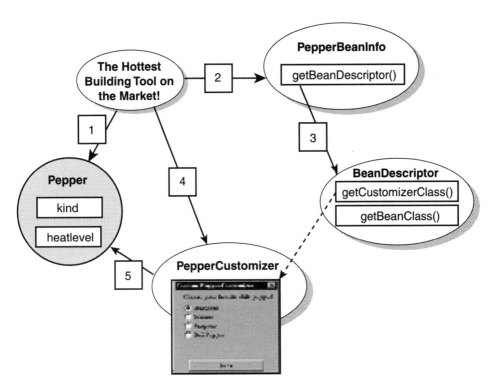

1. A `Pepper` bean is selected from the palette in a development tool.

2. The tool searches for a corresponding `PepperBeanInfo` class. The PepperBeanInfo implements a `getBeanDescriptor()` method. The getBeanDescriptor() returns the `BeanDescriptor` for the `Pepper` bean.

3. The `BeanDescriptor` contains information about the bean's class. It also contains information about the customizer to be used to customize the bean. In this case, the specified customizer is the `PepperCustomizer`.

4. The tool instantiates a `PepperCustomizer`.

5. When the `PepperCustomizer` is created, it is given a reference to the target bean using the `setObject()` method implemented in the customizer.

```
public void setObject(Object aPepper)
```

To illustrate, we will define a customizer for the `Pepper` bean which will allow us to set the `heatLevel` and `kind` properties simultaneously. We will use the same visual component we used for the GUI property editor described previously. However, we will set both the `kind` and the `heatLevel`, not just the `kind`. When a checkbox corresponding to a type of pepper is selected, the customizer invokes the appropriate get and set methods on the target bean. For example: Selecting the habanero will invoke the `setKind("Habanero")` method and the `setHeatLevel(300000)` method on the target pepper bean. Selecting a serrano will cause the `heatlevel` to be set to 50000 and so on. We will use of the `PropertyChange` event to inform listeners when a change has occurred in the customizer. When using the BeanBox for example, the property sheet is a listener on these events. They are used to synchronize the values of the properties displayed in the property sheet.

In the customizer example provided, the property editors for `kind` and `heatLevel` in the property sheet have not been disabled. There are various options for disabling the property editors in the property sheet. One possibility was mentioned in the introduction to customizers above, Another possibility is to remove the `PropertyDescriptors` for the properties from the `getPropertyDescriptors()` method in the `BeanInfo`.

The code is very similar to the code used to define the GUI property editor example explained above. We begin by defining the class `PepperCustomizer` as a subclass of Panel. The class implements the Customizer and `ItemListener` interfaces.

```
package Property.Custom;

import java.beans.*;
import java.awt.*;

public class PepperCustomizer extends Panel implements Customizer,
ItemListener {

  private Pepper iPepper;
  private Label iTextSelect;
  private CheckboxGroup iCbGroup;
  private Checkbox iCbHabanero, iCbSerrano, iCbJalapeno, iCbBell;
  private PropertyChangeSupport iPropertyChangeSupport;
  private static final String HABANERO = new String("habanero");
  private static final String SERRANO  = new String("serrano");
  private static final String JALAPENO = new String("jalapeno");
  private static final String BELL     = new String("bell pepper");
```

Instance variables are defined for the components of the panel and for the target bean. The customizer is similar to the GUI property editor. It is not necessary to define a frame for the customizer. The frame is provided by the customizer framework.

```
public PepperCustomizer() {
  setLayout(null);
  setFont(new Font("Serif", Font.PLAIN, 12) );

  iPropertyChangeSupport = new PropertyChangeSupport(this);
  iCbGroup     = new CheckboxGroup();
  iCbHabanero = new Checkbox("Habanero", iCbGroup, true);
  iCbSerrano  = new Checkbox("Serrano",  iCbGroup, false);
  iCbJalapeno = new Checkbox("Jalapeno", iCbGroup, false);
  iCbBell     = new Checkbox("Bell Pepper", iCbGroup, false);
  iTextSelect = new Label("Choose your favorite chili pepper!",
Label.CENTER);

  iPepper = (Pepper)aPepper;
  iCbHabanero.addItemListener(this);
  iCbSerrano.addItemListener(this);
  iCbJalapeno.addItemListener(this);
  iCbBell.addItemListener(this);

  add(iTextSelect);
  iTextSelect.setBounds(5,   5, 200, 15);
  add(iCbHabanero);
  iCbHabanero.setBounds(20, 30, 100, 15);
  add(iCbSerrano);
  iCbSerrano.setBounds( 20, 50, 100, 15);
  add(iCbJalapeno);
  iCbJalapeno.setBounds(20, 70, 100, 15);
  add(iCbBell);
  iCbBell.setBounds(    20, 90, 100, 15);
}
```

The constructor creates the components of the panel, adds the panel as a listener for changes in the checkboxes and places the components on the panel.

```
public void setObject(Object aPepper) {
  String kind = iPepper.getKind();
  if(kind.toLowerCase().compareTo(HABANERO) == 0)
    iCbHabanero.setState(true);
  if(kind.toLowerCase().compareTo(SERRANO) == 0)
    iCbSerrano.setState(true);
  if(kind.toLowerCase().compareTo(JALAPENO) == 0)
    iCbJalapeno.setState(true);
  if(kind.toLowerCase().compareTo(BELL) == 0)
    iCbBell.setState(true);
}
```

The setObject() method is called by the development tool when the constructor is displayed. It is used by the tool to pass along the target bean. In this case, the target is an instance of Pepper. The kind of the target is used to set the initial state of the customizer when it is displayed.

```
public void itemStateChanged(ItemEvent anEvent) {
  Object obj = anEvent.getItemSelectable();
  if(obj == iCbHabanero) {
    iPepper.setKind("Habanero");
    iPepper.setHeatlevel(300000);
  }
  if(obj == iCbSerrano) {
    iPepper.setKind("Serrano");
    iPepper.setHeatlevel(10000);
  }
  if(obj == iCbJalapeno) {
    iPepper.setKind("Jalapeno");
    iPepper.setHeatlevel(5000);
  }
  if(obj == iCbBell) {
    iPepper.setKind("Bell Pepper");
    iPepper.setHeatlevel(0);
  }
  // Notify the listeners that the property has changed.
  iPropertyChangeSupport.firePropertyChange("", null, null);
}
```

The itemStateChanged() method allows the panel to react when an item in the check box group is selected. It sets the values of kind and heatLevel in the target bean to correspond to the check box which was selected. Since the customizer is a registered Checkbox ItemListener, the itemStateChanged() method is invoked when a user selects a checkbox.

```
public void addPropertyChangeListener(PropertyChangeListener
aPropertyChangeListener) {

iPropertyChangeSupport.addPropertyChangeListener(aPropertyChange
Listener);
}

public void removePropertyChangeListener(PropertyChangeListener
aPropertyChangeListener) {
  iPropertyChangeSupport.removePropertyChangeListener
(aPropertyChangeListener);
}
```

These two methods handle the addition and removal of listeners of changes in the property by the customizer. When the values changes, the property sheet must be updated. The `PropertyChangeSupport` object that was created in the constructor is used to keep track of all the listeners.

```
public Dimension getMinimumSize() {
   return new Dimension(200, 150);
}
```

The `getMinimumSize()` returns the minimum rectangular space the panel needs within the frame provided by the customizer framework.

The finished customizer is shown below:

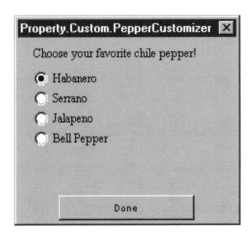

Conclusion

Customization provides an effective way of changing the behavior and appearance of a bean at development time. Properties can be edited individually using the property sheet and property editors. Java provides a number of default property editors, as well as a framework for defining custom property editors. Customizers provide an additional level of functionality. They can be used when dependencies exist between properties which require that properties be edited simultaneously. Once again, a framework is provided for defining customizers for a bean.

The next unit introduces serialization, a technique which allows the customized state of a bean to be transformed into a byte stream. The byte stream can be written to a file. The customized state can be retrieved from the file using the reverse process. Serialization allows development tools to keep track of modifications made to beans using customization.

Serialization

Serialization is the process which transforms an object into a stream of bytes representing the current state of the object. The byte stream contains the necessary information to recreate the instance on any system which supports Java. This process is known as deserialization.

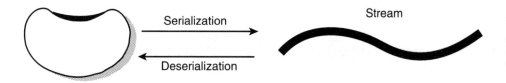

Serialization is typically used for simple persistency. For example, a development tool can keep track of the customized state of a bean using serialization. When a component or a bean is serialized, the byte stream can be saved in a file, in a binary database field or in a system registry database like other binary information. Remote Method Invocation (RMI) also uses object serialization to send beans across the network. RMI is explained later in the book.

The `Serializable` and the `Externalizable` interfaces define the serialization protocol. An object must implement one of these interfaces in order to be serialized. Serializable classes have their fields automatically saved by the object serialization process. Externalizable classes must specify the stream format and data to be contained in the stream. Serialization always writes an object identification to the beginning of the stream. The identification prevents different classes from reading the same streamed object. It also provides support for class evolution (as described in Version Control below).

When an object is serialized the resulting byte stream is out of the scope of the Java security control. Thus, objects containing sensitive data should not implement in either of the interfaces mentioned above in order to prevent them from being serialized.

Object Streams

The JDK provides classes for reading from and writing to a byte stream as well as classes for representing a byte stream. Instances of such classes are able to read field values from a serializable bean, convert the values into a platform-independent format and write them to a byte stream. Conversely, they can read data from the stream, convert it into the platform-dependent format required by the bean and write the data to the bean's fields. They also provide a way to minimize the data necessary to represent objects in the stream. They assign handles to each serialized object so that the same object is not written twice. If an object appears twice, only the handle of already serialized object is written in the stream.

The classes used to represent the object streams are `java.io.ObjectOutput-Stream` and `java.io.ObjectInputStream`. They implement respectively the `java.io.ObjectOutput` and `java.io.ObjectInput` interfaces which provide the interfaces for object serialization. The object stream classes are subclasses of the abstract classes `java.io.OutputStream` and `java.io.InputStream`. The `ObjectOutput` and `ObjectInput` interfaces define a set of methods for reading and writing to and from a stream. The methods can handle objects as well as primitive data types. They define `readObject()` and `writeObject()` to work with objects. Examples of methods for serializing primitive data types are: `readBoolean()`, `readChar()`, `readInt()`, `readDouble()` and their write counterparts. Please refer to the JDK documentation for further information on these two interfaces.

ObjectOutputStream

`ObjectOutputStream` (OOS) implements object serialization using the `ObjectOutput` interface. The class provides a complete set of methods for writing objects and primitive data types to a stream.

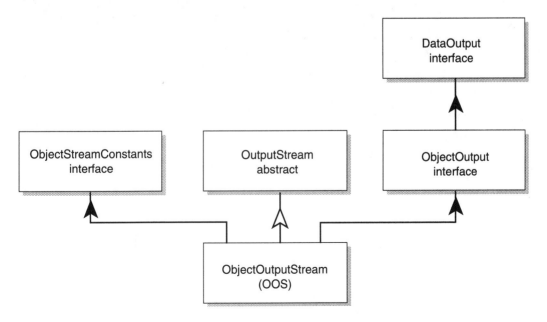

The name and a special representation (UID) of the class are saved at the beginning of the stream for each object being serialized. The special representation of the class is a 64-bit hash value of the class name, implemented interface names, methods and fields. Therefore, it is possible to identify different classes with the same name and allow only the correct class to read the serialized information. The information is encapsulated by the ObjectStreamClass class.

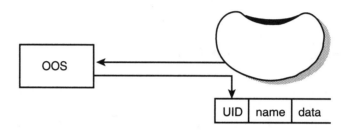

The data written after the name of the class depends on which serialization interface, Serializable or Externalizable, is implemented by the class being serialized.

The writeObject() method is responsible for writing an object to a stream. If the object passed as the parameter is serializable, it is written to the stream using the defaultWriteObject() method. If the object passed is externalizable, the writeExternal() method is used. If the object is neither serializable nor externalizable, a NotSerializableException is thrown. The defaultWriteObject() method implements the default serialization behavior. It first writes all the non-transient and non-static fields of the class and its superclasses to the stream. What is meant by writing a field is that information about the field, such as the name and type, is written. The values of the fields are written after the field information for all the fields is written.

Please refer to JavaDoc for more information on ObjectOutputStream.

ObjectInputStream

ObjectInputStream (OIS) implements object deserialization by using the ObjectInput interface. The class provides a complete set of methods to read objects and primitive data types from a byte stream. It inherits from InputStream as shown.

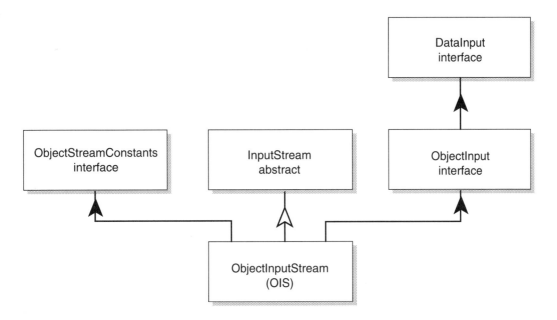

When reading objects from a stream, the object serial identification or serial unique identifier (serial UID) written during the serialization mechanism is compared with the one for the object to be instantiated. The data will be loaded only if the serial UIDs match.

The readObject() method reads an object from a byte stream. If the object is an instance of a class that is externalizable, the default constructor, the constructor which takes no parameters, is called to create a new instance. The readExternal() method is then used to recreate the object. In the Externalization section you will find further details on externalization. If the object is an instance of a class that is serializable, defaultReadObject() is used. The defaultReadObject() method implements the default deserialization behavior for classes which implement the Serializable interface. It first reads the fields' types and names from the stream. Any field of the object which does not appear in the stream is set to the default value. Values of fields that appear in the stream but not in the object are discarded. Classes with different fields have different serial UID numbers to prevent them from reading the same serialized version. However, the serialization mechanism supports the evolution of classes. Information serialized using an older version of a class can be written to an object instantiated using a newer version of the class and vice-versa. The Version Control section will give you more information.

Serialization Using the Serializable Interface

All that is needed for a class to support serialization is for it to implement the `Serializable` interface. This interface does not specify any methods. It only serves as a flag to identify classes that can/may be serialized. Within a serializable class, the `transient` keyword is used to mark variables that do not need to be saved when the object is serialized. Variables marked `static` are not serialized either.

When a serializable object is stored, all the other objects referenced by it are stored also. This is important to maintain the relationships between objects. However, this behavior is sometimes undesirable. References to other objects that are not supposed to be saved must be marked with the `transient` keyword. If a referenced object does not support serialization, it is not saved, and serialization continues normally with the next referenced object. When restoring the object, the field that references the object that didn't support serialization will be set to null. This may affect the components' normal operations. Fields that can be recalculated or do not determine the state of an object should also be marked as `transient`.

All the necessary information to recreate a "target" bean with an identical state as the "source" is saved when the component is serialized. This is only possible when the object hierarchy is respected and each level in the inheritance tree of a component is serialized. The `ObjectStreamOutput` saves all the fields of the serializable class (and its superclasses) before sending the data to the output stream.

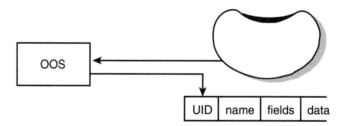

To illustrate the ideas, we present an example using the class `SimplePepper`. `SimplePepper` implements the `Serializable` interface. A second class named `SerPepper` (Serialization of `Pepper`) is an application that is capable of saving and restoring `SimplePepper` objects from files. It has a convenient, simple GUI that allows the user to set the `kind` property of the pepper (a property of type `String` that can be set to any value) and to choose the name of the file used for serialization/deserialization.

We begin by defining the class SimplePepper. It implements the Serializable interface. It has an instance variable of type String for storing the kind of the pepper. We define get and set methods to provide access to the variable.

```
import java.io.*;

public class SimplePepper implements Serializable {
  private String iKind;

  public String getKind() {
    return iKind;
  }

  public void setKind(String aKind) {
    iKind = aKind;
  }
}
```

The next step is to define the application that controls the serialization of a SimplePepper. We define the class SerPepper as a subclass of Frame in order to inherit the functionality we need to define the GUI. We implement the ActionListener interface in order to have the behavior we need to be able to react when the PushButton's on the GUI are pressed.

```
import java.awt.*;
import java.awt.event.*;
import java.io.*;

public class SerPepper extends Frame implements ActionListener {
  private  TextField iFileNameTextField = new TextField(0);
  private  TextField iKindTextField = new TextField(0);
  private  Button iBrowsePushButton = new Button("Browse");
  private  Button iWritePushButton = new Button("Write");
  private  Button iReadPushButton = new Button("Read");
```

We define instance variables to hold the components of the GUI. We instantiate the components and provide them with default values. The next step is to define the main() method, the method called to start the application.

```
public static void main(String[] args) {
  SerPepper aSerPepper = new SerPepper();
  aSerPepper.setVisible(true);
}
```

The application begins by creating a new instance of the class and displaying it. The next step is to define the constructor to create an instance of SerPepper.

```
public SerPepper() {
  super("Pepper (De)Serializer");
  setLayout(null);
  setBounds(20, 20, 360, 224);
  setBackground(Color.lightGray);

  Label lbl1 = new Label("File");
  Label lbl2 = new Label("Kind");
  lbl1.setBounds(12, 25, 47, 27);
  lbl2.setBounds(14, 94, 27, 29);

  iFileNameTextField.setBounds(67, 24, 271, 28);
  iKindTextField.setBounds(67, 94, 271, 28);

  iWritePushButton.setBounds(204, 181, 104, 30);
  iBrowsePushButton.setBounds(268, 55, 70, 27);
  iReadPushButton.setBounds(50, 180, 104, 30);

  this.add("LabelFilename", lbl1);
  this.add("iFileNameTextField", iFileNameTextField);
  this.add("iBrowsePushButton", iBrowsePushButton);
  this.add("LabelKind", lbl2);
  this.add("iKindTextField", iKindTextField);
  this.add("iWritePushButton", iWritePushButton);
  this.add("iReadPushButton", iReadPushButton);

  iBrowsePushButton.addActionListener(this);
  iWritePushButton.addActionListener(this);
  iReadPushButton.addActionListener(this);
  this.enableEvents(AWTEvent.WINDOW_EVENT_MASK);
}
```

This rather lengthy method defines the sizing and layout for the components of the GUI on the frame. After placing the components on the frame, we define the frame to be a listener on events generated by the pushbuttons when they are clicked. We want to be able to react when one of the buttons is pressed. The last step defines the frame to be a listener on all the window events it generates. This allows the frame to catch the close window event and close the window when it is generated. We now need to define a method that specifies how to react when a button is pressed.

```
public void actionPerformed(ActionEvent anEvent) {
  toggleButtonState();
  if (anEvent.getSource() == iBrowsePushButton)
    selectFile();
```

```
    if (anEvent.getSource() == iWritePushButton)
      serializePepper();
    if (anEvent.getSource() == iReadPushButton)
      deserializePepper();
    toggleButtonState();
  }
```

We first disable all the pushbuttons to prevent having to deal with more than one pushbutton event at a time. We analyze the source of the event to find out which button was pressed. Once we know which button was pressed, we can define what to do next. When we are finished, we re-enable all the pushbuttons. The next step is to define the methods that are called for each of the buttons. We begin with the behavior for the "Browse" pushbutton. This button brings up the platform file browser. It allows the user to select a file to read from or write to.

```
    private void selectFile() {
      String fileName;
      FileDialog iFileDialog = new FileDialog(this);
      iFileDialog.setVisible(true);
      if (iFileDialog.getFile() == null)
        fileName = "";
      else
        fileName = iFileDialog.getDirectory() +
  iFileDialog.getFile();
      iFileNameTextField.setText(fileName);
      iKindTextField.setText("");
      }
```

If no file is selected, an empty string is written to the "File" entry field. If a file is selected, the name of the file is written to the entry field. The "Kind" entry field is set to an empty string. The next method we need is the `serializePepper()` method. This method is called when the "Write" pushbutton is pressed.

```
    private void serializePepper() {
      SimplePepper pepper = new SimplePepper();
      pepper.setKind(iKindTextField.getText());
      try {
        FileOutputStream fos = new
  FileOutputStream(iFileNameTextField.getText());
        ObjectOutputStream oo = new ObjectOutputStream(fos);
        oo.writeObject(pepper);
        oo.flush();
        fos.close();
      } catch (Exception e) {}
      iKindTextField.setText("");
    }
```

The `serializePepper()` method is responsible for serializing and storing an object in a file. A `FileOutputStream` is defined to reference a file with the name specified in the file name entry field. The `FileOutputStream` is associated with the `ObjectOutputStream` that is responsible for serializing the object. Once the object has been serialized, both streams are closed and the "Kind" entry field is reset. We now need a method for deserializing peppers from a file.

```
private void deserializePepper() {
  try {
    FileInputStream fis = new
        FileInputStream(iFileNameTextField.getText());
    ObjectInputStream oo = new ObjectInputStream(fis);
    SimplePepper pepper = (SimplePepper)oo.readObject();
    fis.close();
    iKindTextField.setText(pepper.getKind());
  } catch (Exception e) {}
}
```

The `deserializePepper()` method restores the serialized object into a new instance of `SimplePepper`. It is called when the "Read" button of the GUI is pressed. It uses an `ObjectInputStream` associated with a `FileInputStream` to read the object from the file. When the object has been restored, the stream is closed, and the "Kind" entry field is updated with the `kind` value of the restored `Pepper` instance. The last two methods we need to define are private methods to handle the enabling and disabling of the pushbuttons and the handling of window events generated by the frame.

```
private void toggleButtonState() {
  boolean newState = !iBrowsePushButton.isEnabled();
  iBrowsePushButton.setEnabled(newState);
  iWritePushButton.setEnabled(newState);
  iReadPushButton.setEnabled(newState);
}

protected void processWindowEvent(WindowEvent anEvent) {
  if (anEvent.getID() == WindowEvent.WINDOW_CLOSING) {
    dispose();
    System.exit(0);
  }
}
```

The `processWindowEvent()` method is called when the frame generates a window event. When the close event is generated, the frame disposes of all its resources and closes the application. All other window events are ignored. We are now ready to run the application.

In order to run this example, you need to create a subdirectory (for instance, Serial). Type or load the previous two class files and compile them. Run the SerPepper class using the java command.

The application user window should look like this:

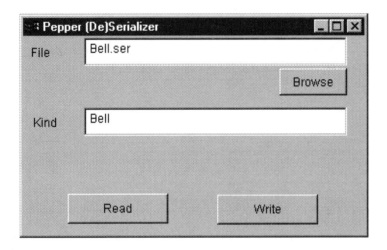

Using the application, the kind property of an instance of SimplePepper can be set to a value (e.g., Bell) and saved to a file (e.g., Bell.ser) by pressing the Write pushbutton. Pressing the Read push button causes the serialized bean to be read from the file specified. A new instance of SimplePepper is created with the same state as the original instance. After recreating the bean, the value of the kind property is displayed in the Kind entry field. It is the same value as the original value that was entered, in this case "Bell".

The serialization process from the example, including the contents of the byte stream, is shown below for a better understanding of how the process works.

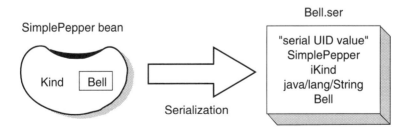

Controlling Serialization

Java provides a way to control the information sent to the byte stream by serializable objects. ObjectOutputStream implements the default serialization behavior for serializable objects in the defaultWriteObject() method. When writeObject() is called with a serializable object as its parameter, the defaultWriteObject() method is used to serialize the object. However, before using the default method to serialize an object, the writeObject() method checks for the presence of two methods in the target object, the object to be serialized.

```
private void writeObject(java.io.ObjectOutputStream out)
    throws IOException;

private void readObject(java.io.ObjectInputStream in)
    throws IOException, ClassNotFoundException;
```

If present, these methods are used instead of the behavior to read and write the contents of the serializable object to the byte stream. In other words, writeObject() from the target is used in place of defaultWriteObject() as defined in ObjectOutputStream. Likewise, readObject() in the target replaces defaultReadObject() from ObjectInputStream.

The writeObject() and readObject() methods act only on the data of the object to be serialized. The field information for all the classes in the inheritance tree of the object is always written. This rule holds only if all the objects in the tree are serializable. The results become unpredictable if some of the objects in the tree are externalizable. Data for fields defined by the object's superclasses is stored/retrieved using its own serialization behavior. The fact that an object writes its data to the stream using writeObject() has no effect on the way remaining objects in the tree write their data. The field information for a class that implements writeObject() is written regardless of what writeObject() specifies. A writeObject() can be defined that writes no data to the stream. However, the field information for the fields is still written to the stream. If the data for a field is not present in the stream at the time of deserialization, the value is set to null. Additional information written to the stream by a writeObject() method that is not used by the object is ignored during deserialization.

If additional information is needed in the stream, the defaultWriteObject() can be called in the writeObject() method to write the object's contents before the extra data is written. It is important to call defaultWriteObject() before writing any information to keep the stream compatible with the serializable pro-

tocol. If data is written to the stream before the actual object, the readObject()
method must read the additional data in the correct order before calling
defaultReadObject().

The following version of SimplePepper defines the writeObject() and
readObject() methods to control the information on the data stream. It writes a
time stamp after the objects' data on the stream. When retrieving an object, the
readObject() method reads the time stamp and checks when the object was
saved. If it was saved more than one minute ago, an error message is written on
the Kind field.

The entire source code for the new version of SimplePepper is provided for
completeness. For details on the implementation of the SerPepper class, refer to
the section on Serialization above.

```
import java.io.*;
import java.util.*;

public class SimplePepper implements Serializable {
  private String iKind;

  public String getKind() {
    return iKind;
  }

  public void setKind(String aKind) {
    iKind = aKind;
  }

  private void writeObject(ObjectOutputStream anOutput) throws
IOException {
    anOutput.defaultWriteObject();
    anOutput.writeObject(new Date());
    anOutput.flush();
  }
```

The writeObject() method first calls defaultWriteObject() to write the
standard data to the byte stream. Following that, the date is written, and the
stream buffer is flushed.

```
  private void readObject(ObjectInputStream anInput) throws
IOException,
    ClassNotFoundException {
    anInput.defaultReadObject();
    try {
      Date serialDate = (Date)anInput.readObject();
```

```
      if (((new Date()).getTime() - serialDate.getTime()) > 60000)
        setKind("Protection error");
      } catch (Exception e) {
        setKind("Date note Initialized.");
      }
  }
```

The `readObject()` method first calls `defaultReadObject()` to read the standard information from the byte stream. After that, it reads the date and checks to make sure that the serialized information is less than a minute old. If the information is older, an error is raised. If no date is found in the serialized information, an exception is raised.

To run this version of the application, create another directory and place this version of `SimplePepper` in it. Copy `SerPepper.class` from the previous example above to this directory and run the application using `java SimplePepper`.

Using the `SerPepper` application, create a file named `Jalapeno.ser` with jalapeño as the kind of pepper. If you try to deserialize the bean right after serializing it, the process will work correctly. If you wait more than one minute and then try to deserialize, an error message will be displayed on the Kind text field because the information is too old. If you try to read the `Bell.ser` file saved with the version from the previous example, you will receive another error message because the `readObject()` method tries to read the date from an empty stream. The previous version did not save a date object after the standard data, so the stream is already empty after `defaultReadObject()` completes. The following picture illustrates what is written to and read from the byte stream.

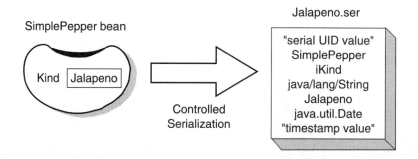

Serialization Using the Externalizable Interface

Instead of implementing the `Serializable` interface to make its current state persistent, a bean can use the `Externalizable` interface. Using this interface, a class is entirely responsible for saving its contents and that of its superclasses. The data of the superclasses is not stored automatically when the `Externalizable` interface is used. To implement the `Externalizable` interface, a class must support the following two methods:

```
public void writeExternal(ObjectOutput anOutput) throws
IOException;

public void readExternal(ObjectInput anInput) throws IOException,
   ClassNotFoundException;
```

When reconstructing an externalized object, an instance is created using the default constructor of the target class. The `readExternal()` method is then called to recreate the original state. Therefore, an externalizable class must provide a default constructor in order to be deserialized.

During externalization, the `ObjectStreamClass` writes the serial UID and class name to the byte stream as shown below. Any additional data is written by the `writeExternal()` method. The field information is not written automatically as is the case in serialization.

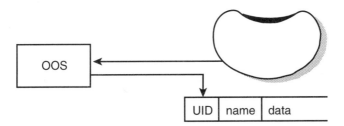

The `writeExternal()` and `readExternal()` methods are always public methods. They can be called by any other object. Any object can read and modify the resulting stream. In most cases, the stream is smaller than the stream produced using the `Serialization` interface since the field information is not written automatically.

A version of `SimplePepper` that implements the `Externalizable` interface is shown below. Note that no constructors are defined for this version of the class. When no constructors are provided, the constructor of the parent class is used. In this case, the parent class is `Object`. By default, all classes extend `Object` when a specific superclass is not defined. `Object` provides a default constructor. If a constructor is provided by `SimplePepper` (for instance, `public SimplePepper(String aKind)`), it would cause an error unless a void constructor is also defined.

```java
import java.io.*;
import java.util.*;

public class SimplePepper implements Externalizable {
  private String iKind;

  public String getKind() {
    return iKind;
  }

  public void setKind(String aKind) {
    iKind = aKind;
  }

  public void writeExternal(ObjectOutput anOutput) throws
IOException {
    anOutput.writeObject(getKind());
    anOutput.flush();
  }
```

The writeExternal() method calls writeObject() and passes along the
string returned by its getKind() method. The resulting byte stream contains the
UID, the name SimplePepper and the serialized information generated by performing writeObject() on an object of type String. The byte stream contains
no field information for the iKind variable. However, the stream contains field
information for the variables used by the instance of String that iKind points
to, to store its data.

```java
  public void readExternal(ObjectInput anInput) throws
IOException,
    ClassNotFoundException {
    setKind((String)anInput.readObject());
  }
```

The readExternal() method reads the information from the byte stream, casts it
to an object of type String and assigns it to the new instance of SimplePepper.

To try the new version of SimplePepper, create a new directory (for example,
External), place the above code in a file SimplePepper.java, compile and
place the class file in the directory together with the SerPepper.class file. You can
use the same SerPepper class used in the previous examples to save/restore
objects from files. Try this version and create a file called Serrano.ser with the
kind set to "Serrano." The resulting byte stream is noticeably different from previous versions as can be seen in the diagram below.

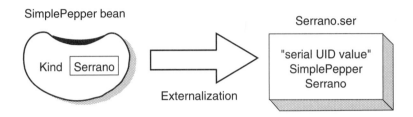

The format of the serialized object (.ser file) is different from that resulting from using either default serialization or customized serialization. It is not possible to read the files saved by the other versions of SimplePepper with this version.

Version Control

The ObjectOutputStream object writes the serial UID and the class name at the beginning of the serialized byte stream. The serial UID is a 64-bit hash value of the class name, implemented interface names, methods, and fields. This is done the same way for both serializable and externalizable objects. The reason for putting this information at the beginning of the stream is to avoid having classes try to read information saved by another class, even if the two share the same name. However, a class may evolve in different releases of an application. Adding or removing fields, methods and interfaces will result in different serial UID, making the serial representations incompatible.

What happens if two different versions of the same application must exchange data? Or what if two different versions of an object want to exchange information through RMI?

For externalizable classes, those that are responsible for the data format and content of the byte stream, the only thing that needs to be changed in the stream is the serial UID. When all versions use the same UID, different versions of an externalizable class will be able to read the same streamed object. However, the developer must keep track of the different versions of the class and keep them compatible.

For serializable classes, Java provides a way to allow newer versions of a class read to the stream generated by an older version and write data to a stream in a format compatible to that of the older version. The newer class is responsible for maintaining compatibility with the older class. The only changes that can be made are those that do not affect the information the older class is expecting in the stream. Changes that can be made to a class while keeping the stream compatible are:

Compatible Change	Description
Appending additional data to the stream	All the data in the stream after the data that a class is expecting is ignored.
Adding fields	Extra fields in the stream are ignored and missing fields are initialized to the default value.
Changing the access modifiers of a field (public, private, protected, package)	Access modifiers have no influence on the ability to serialize a class.
Changing a static field to non-static	Same as adding a field.
Changing a transient field to non-transient	Same as adding a field.

Examples of incompatible changes are:

Incompatible change	Description
Removing fields	Missing fields will be initialized to the default value, which may cause the deserialized version to fail.
Changing the position of the class in the class hierarchy	The class name in the beginning of the stream contains the full identifier of the class. The class id changes, making it incompatible for the previous class.
Changing a non-static field to static	Same as removing a field.
Changing a non-transient field to transient	Same as removing a field.
Changing the type of a field	The loading class will not be able to read the data for the field and will initialize it to the default value.
Removing data from the stream	Missing fields will be initialized to the default value, and missing data on readObject() will raise an exception.

New versions of classes must generate the same serial UID as older versions in order to be able to exchange data. But changing the class changes the serial UID. To avoid this problem, a class can define the serialVersionUID class variable. When present in a class, the value of the variable is used instead of a calculated UID.

The serialver command provided by the JDK calculates the serial UID for a class and prints it. A new version of a class must define the serialVersionUID variable and set its value to the UID of the original version of the class. Both versions of the class will then use the same serial UID. In order to be able to use the correct UID, `serialver` must be run before the new version of the class is defined. This is the output for the serializable version of `SimplePepper`:

```
C:\serial>serialver SimplePepper
SimplePepper: static final long serialVersionUID =
7835202140011595704L;
```

The `serialver` command has a graphical interface that can be displayed using the `-show` option. The functionality is the same as the text-only version. The name of the target class is entered in the "Full Class Name" entry field. Pressing the `Show` button displays the serial UID of the class.

```
C:\serial>serialver -show
```

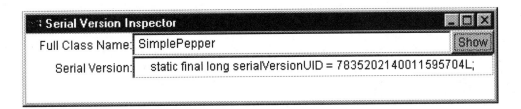

Using cut and paste, the UID can be copied to the `serialVersionUID` variable of the new version of a class.

Let's look at a complete example using `SimplePepper`. A new version defines a new property, `price`. It defines the `serialVersionUID` variable in order to be able to read/write compatible information with older versions. The `SerPepper` class is also updated to display the new property.

```
public class SimplePepper implements java.io.Serializable {
    static final long serialVersionUID = 7835202140011595704L;
    private String iKind;
    private int iPrice;
```

The new class definition contains the `serialVersionID` variable and the new property `price`. The value was obtained by using `serialver` as shown above.

```
    public String getKind() {
        return iKind;
    }

    public void setKind(String aKind) {
        iKind = aKind;
```

```
  }

  public int getPrice() {
    return iPrice;
  }

  public void setPrice(int aPrice) {
    iPrice = aPrice;
  }
```

Get and set methods are added for the price property.

```
import java.awt.*;
import java.awt.event.*;
import java.io.*;

public class SerPepper extends Frame implements ActionListener {
  private  TextField iFileNameTextField = new TextField(0);
  private  TextField iKindTextField = new TextField(0);
  private  TextField iPriceTextField = new TextField(0);
  private  Button iBrowsePushButton = new Button("Browse");
  private  Button iWritePushButton = new Button("Write");
  private  Button iReadPushButton = new Button("Read");
```

The updated class definition for SerPepper contains an additional entry field for the price.

```
  public static void main(String[] args) {
    SerPepper aSerPepper = new SerPepper();
    aSerPepper.setVisible(true);
  }

  public SerPepper() {
    super("Pepper (De)Serializer");
    setLayout(null);
    setBounds(20, 20, 360, 224);
    setBackground(Color.lightGray);

    Label lbl1 = new Label("File");
    Label lbl2 = new Label("Kind");
    Label lbl3 = new Label("Price");
    lbl1.setBounds(12, 25, 47, 27);
    lbl2.setBounds(14, 94, 27, 29);
    lbl3.setBounds(14, 125, 30, 30);

    iFileNameTextField.setBounds(67, 24, 271, 28);
```

```
iKindTextField.setBounds(67, 94, 271, 28);
iPriceTextField.setBounds(67, 133, 271, 28);

iWritePushButton.setBounds(204, 181, 104, 30);
iBrowsePushButton.setBounds(268, 55, 70, 27);
iReadPushButton.setBounds(50, 180, 104, 30);

this.add("LabelFilename", lbl1);
this.add("iFileNameTextField", iFileNameTextField);
this.add("iBrowsePushButton", iBrowsePushButton);
this.add("LabelKind", lbl2);
this.add("iKindTextField", iKindTextField);
this.add("LabelPrice", lbl3);
this.add("iPriceTextField", iPriceTextField);
this.add("iWritePushButton", iWritePushButton);
this.add("iReadPushButton", iReadPushButton);

iBrowsePushButton.addActionListener(this);
iWritePushButton.addActionListener(this);
iReadPushButton.addActionListener(this);

this.enableEvents(AWTEvent.WINDOW_EVENT_MASK);
}
```

The new entry field is added to the layout; everything else remains unchanged.

```
public void actionPerformed(ActionEvent anEvent) {
  toggleButtonState();
  if (anEvent.getSource() == iBrowsePushButton)
    selectFile();
  if (anEvent.getSource() == iWritePushButton)
    serializePepper();
  if (anEvent.getSource() == iReadPushButton)
    deserializePepper();
  toggleButtonState();
}

private void selectFile() {
  String fileName;
  FileDialog iFileDialog = new FileDialog(this);
  iFileDialog.setVisible(true);
  if (iFileDialog.getFile() == null)
    fileName = "";
  else
    fileName = iFileDialog.getDirectory() +
          iFileDialog.getFile();
    iFileNameTextField.setText(fileName);
```

```
            iKindTextField.setText("");
            iPriceTextField.setText("");
        }
```

The `actionPerformed()` method is not changed; `selectFile()` must initialize the new entry field to an empty string.

```
        private void serializePepper() {
           SimplePepper pepper = new SimplePepper();
           pepper.setKind(iKindTextField.getText());
           pepper.setPrice(Integer.valueOf(
                   iPriceTextField.getText()).intValue());
           try {
              FileOutputStream fos = new
   FileOutputStream(iFileNameTextField.getText());
              ObjectOutputStream oo = new ObjectOutputStream(fos);
              oo.writeObject(pepper);
              oo.flush();
              fos.close();
           } catch (Exception e) {}
           iKindTextField.setText("");
           iPriceTextField.setText("");
        }

        private void deserializePepper() {
           try {
              FileInputStream fis = new
   FileInputStream(iFileNameTextField.getText());
              ObjectInputStream oo = new ObjectInputStream(fis);
              SimplePepper pepper = (SimplePepper)oo.readObject();
              fis.close();
              iKindTextField.setText(pepper.getKind());

   iPriceTextField.setText(Integer.toString(pepper.getPrice()));
           } catch (Exception e) {}
        }
```

The `serializePepper()` and `deserializePepper()` methods must be updated to read and write the `price` property.

```
        private void toggleButtonState() {
           boolean newState = !iBrowsePushButton.isEnabled();
           iBrowsePushButton.setEnabled(newState);
           iWritePushButton.setEnabled(newState);
           iReadPushButton.setEnabled(newState);
```

```
    }

    protected void processWindowEvent(WindowEvent anEvent) {
        if (anEvent.getID() == WindowEvent.WINDOW_CLOSING) {
            dispose();
            System.exit(0);
        }
    }
}
```

The `toggleButtonState()` and `processWindowEvent()` methods remain unchanged; they are simply included for completeness.

Once again, create a new directory for this version of `SimplePepper` and `Ser-Pepper`. The output of the new version is shown below. Create a file named `Habanero.ser` and set the properties as shown.

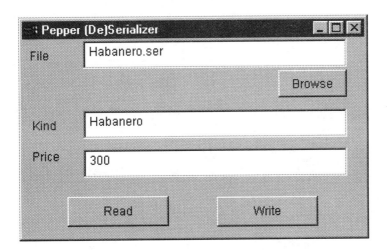

Now try to read the `Bell.ser` file from the first serialization example. It will present the `kind` property and set the price to zero. `Price` is not defined in the stream for the old version, so it is initialized to the default value of zero for an `int`. Compare the byte stream generated by the new version shown below with the byte stream generated by the original version of the example.

Pepper (De)Serializer

File	..\serial\Bell.ser
	Browse
Kind	Bell
Price	0

Read   Write

The serialization process will store the data as shown in the next figure.

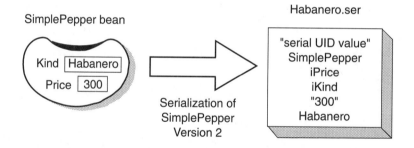

SimplePepper bean

Kind Habanero
Price 300

Serialization of
SimplePepper
Version 2

Habanero.ser

"serial UID value"
SimplePepper
iPrice
iKind
"300"
Habanero

Using the old version of the example, try to read the Habanero.ser file produced using this version of the example. The kind property is shown, but the
price property will be discarded because it is not used by the older version of
SimplePepper.

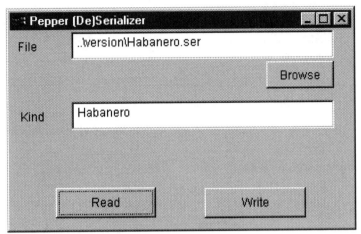

Reading new objects with the old version

Conclusion

In this unit, we have examined four possibilities for serializing and deserializing beans:

- Default serialization using the Serialization interface
- Customized serialization using the Serialization interface
- Customized serialization using the Externalizable interface
- Serialization using version control

The four possibilities are quite straightforward. However, as we have tried to show in the explanations and examples, numerous combinations and permutations of the techniques are possible. The results vary widely depending on what is combined. We have tried to show a representative sample of the more typical possibilities.

Serialization is most typically used by builder tools to keep track of customized beans during development. It is also used for Remote Method Invocation when sending data across a network. However, when making the state of an application persistent at runtime, serialization is a lightweight option at best. Serialization must be initiated explicitly, and there is no concept of concurrency or rollback. Later in the book, we come back to serialization when we talk about making applications persistent.

But in the meantime, let's take a break from all the theory. Joe's Tex-Mex Heaven is short on chili peppers and we are hungry. It is time to implement the chili pepper application using the concepts we have examined so far.

Jalapeño Poppers
KK22

The usual way to make poppers is to fry the peppers. But in this recipe, we only cook them in the oven.

The Market Basket:

Pickled jalapeños. Cheddar cheese. 1 fresh habanero (optional)

How to:

Open the jalapeños by making a cut from the top to the bottom. If you want a mild version, you can take away the seeds and stems; otherwise you can leave them as is.

Fill the jalapeños with the cheese, as much as you can get into the chili.

Also, to make the poppers more snappy, you can slice a habanero and put it in the jalapeño together with the cheese. This is only recommended if you want a really hot dish. Also, remember to protect your skin when you handle the habanero.

Cook them in the oven at 350 degrees Fahrenheit for 15-20 minutes.

These poppers are perfect together with a *Jalapeñorita*!

Chapter **4**

The Chili Pepper Application

▼ MAPPING THE STORY TO CLASSES

▼ MAPPING THE CLASSES TO BEANS, DEFINING THE INTERFACES

▼ BUILDING AND CONNECTING THE BEANS

▼ ADDING THE GUI

The purpose of this chapter is to take the reader step by step through the development of an application using beans. The idea is to provide the reader with an example that applies and integrates the ideas and concepts discussed in the previous chapter. The beans that will be built are non-visual beans. They represent business knowledge. We do not discuss the building of visual beans, or widgets. However, the principles are exactly the same as those for building non-visual beans. The GUI for the application was built using VisualAge for Java, a development environment which provides a large number of visual beans. As the GUI is relatively simple, there was no need to build custom, visual beans. The visual beans provided by VisualAge are used to define an applet which displays the GUI and starts the application.

We start by mapping our chili pepper story to a model. This is not intended as an exhaustive explanation of object-oriented analysis, design and modeling techniques. There are numerous books available for more information on this fascinating topic. Rather, it is included for completeness. The next step is to map the classes that were defined to beans. A bean may be something as simple and small as a simple class or as large as an entire subapplication or application. As a result, a key step is the actual definition of the public protocol of the beans, their interfaces. Not every public event, method or member of a class automatically becomes part of the public interface of the resulting bean. There may be very good reasons for hiding some of the inner workings of the bean. Once the beans have been defined, they can be connected to form the logic of the application. The last step is to provide a GUI in the form of an applet for the application. This step will not be covered in great detail, as it is not the intention of this book to focus on the use of a single tool. There are various tools which provide support for this step. Chapter 6 provides an overview of the various application builder tools currently available.

A note about the implementation of the application. The application is not intended to be an example of "the perfect oo-application." It is perhaps more appropriate to refer to it as a prototype. We have not followed the model-view-controller convention. The GUI of the applet is linked to the model, albeit using events. Ideally, the application logic should be decoupled from the presentation logic. However, the book is not intended to be a guide to oo-programming, nor is it a guide to visual programming per se. The "perfect oo-application" is to a certain extent a matter of taste and common sense. Along with oo-methodology, it is a topic that has a tendency to become religious. We would like to skirt these issues and focus on our primary goal. Above all, the application is meant to illustrate different possibilities when working with beans.

Unlike the other examples in the book, the source code for the application has not been placed directly in the text. There is simply too much code. However, the entire source code is provided on the accompanying CD-ROM for easy reference.

Mapping the Story to Classes

The first step in the development of our little application using beans is to map the story (see the Introduction) to a hierarchy of objects that together provide the necessary functionality for the application. This first step is not beans specific or, for that matter, even Java specific. It involves object-oriented design, analysis and modeling. The result is an object model. The object model is not a must. It is possible to model using other techniques and then develop using an object-oriented language. However, such an approach is neither desirable nor recommended. Non object-oriented modeling techniques impose too many restrictions to be practical or even usable.

There exist a number of object-oriented modeling paradigms. The word modeling in the context of this chapter is used in the broader sense. It includes the analysis and design as well. Sadly enough, the issue of the "correct" object-oriented modeling paradigm has become a very religious issue. In fact, almost all the current modeling paradigms provide good results. Some are more encompassing than others, and some even offer integrated tool support. It is, however, beyond the scope of this book to discuss the various paradigms in detail. It is also not the intention of the authors to recommend any particular method.

For the purposes of this book, the following pragmatic methodology is used. It represents a mixture of UML (the unified modeling language) and IBM-internal methodology. Please refer to the Appendix for the actual end products. The individual steps of the methodology are listed in the sections of this chapter to which they apply.

1. The bounds of the application are laid out. In other words, what belongs in the scope of the application and what does not belong is defined.

2. A use case is drawn up for the application. The use case contains a main success scenario as well as failure scenarios to capture the things that could go wrong. Not all of the failure scenarios are explicitly modeled into the application. They are provided in the use case for completeness.

3. Objects are found by examining the problem statement, the use case and by using CRC cards.

4. Classes corresponding to the objects are defined. They are then fleshed out and verified using object-interaction diagrams.

The following classes are defined as a result of these first steps. Once again, please refer to the Appendix for the use case and the class hierarchy.

- `Pepper extends Object`
- `Person extends Object`
- `PersonRole extends Object`
- `Agent extends PersonRole`
- `Broker extends PersonRole`
- `Grower extends PersonRole`
- `Inspector extends PersonRole`
- `Shipment extends Object`
- `ShipmentState extends Object`
- `Order extends Object`
- `OrderItem extends Object`

- `Policy extends Object`

- `Rule extends Object`

- `InspectionResult extends Object`

Perhaps a note is needed here about the implementation of the four individuals (`Agent`, `Broker`, `Grower` and `Inspector`) found in the story. The implementation may seem rather complicated at first glance. Why not just make four subclasses of `Person`, one for each of the four individuals? The answer is quite simple. Yes, it is possible to place all four individuals under `Person`. However, we want to go one step further. The book is about using beans in the enterprise. Since people who play roles can be found in numerous business situations, we want to provide a more elegant and flexible solution. The key is to think of the above individuals as roles that can be played by a person. If we think about it, it is possible to imagine one person playing more than one of the roles. For instance, perhaps an agent is moonlighting as a grower. This type of situation is difficult to model when each of the classes for an individual is a direct subclass of `Person`. The instance that represents the agent must point to the instance that represents the grower and vice-versa. This is not necessarily elegant code. We model a class for the person and create a separate hierarchy for the roles a person can play. The roles simply point to the instance of the person who is playing the role. If a person plays several roles simultaneously, then each instance of a role points to the same instance of `Person`. The `Agent` instance and the `Grower` instance each point to the same `Person` instance as their role player.

Once the classes are defined, we document them using Object Interaction Diagrams (OIDs). Please see the Appendix for the actual OIDs. The OIDs help visualize the interactions between the classes. The next step is to map the classes to beans. As we have already seen at several points in the book, there does not have to be a one-to-one mapping between classes and beans. A bean may encompass the functionality of one or more classes. At the same time, other classes may exist solely to provide information about the beans.

Mapping the Classes to Beans, Defining the Interfaces

Having defined the classes and their interactions, the next step is to map the classes to beans. In defining the beans, we go back to the characteristics of beans described in Chapter 2. Using the characteristics, we examine the application. We can ask ourselves the following questions:

- Is there a potential for reusing parts of the application?

- Can we leverage the frameworks provided for beans?

- Which parts of the application, if any, can benefit or profit from being programmed visually?

Let's reread the chili pepper story and look at the list of classes defined in the previous unit. Doesn't the way the individuals interact with each other seem to be a typical example of objects communicating through events?

"Hi Gary, I need some peppers for a customer. Do you have any in stock?"

"Well Betty, I'll have to go take a look. I'll call you back."

or:

"Good morning, Isabelle, I have an urgent shipment of peppers for a customer. How soon could you have them inspected?"

"I will try to take them to the lab this afternoon. I will call you when I am finished."

In order to realistically model the way individuals interact in the real world, we implement each of the four individuals by using beans. In other words, the broker, the grower, the inspector and the agent are all mapped to a corresponding bean. In addition, the shipment is also implemented as a bean. We need to know when and how the state of a shipment has changed. The broker can react according to what has happened by listening on the events generated by a change in the state of the shipment.

The beans communicate using events, so we need to define the events and the event listener interfaces. A ShipmentChangeEvent is generated by changes in a Shipment that is the responsibility of a Broker. ShipmentChangeListener is an interface that allows interested objects to listen on ShipmentChangeEvents. PepperApplet will implement the interface. The applet needs to know when the shipment has changed so it can update the GUI. A BrokerActionEvent is generated by Broker when it needs to initiate actions such as having the shipment inspected or insured. The BrokerActionListener interface allows objects to listen on events generated by the broker and react appropriately. Grower, Inspector and Agent all should implement the BrokerActionListener interface. In addition, the current instance of Broker must listen on the button clicked event generated by the OK pushbutton of the applet's GUI in order to know when to begin processing a new shipment. The ActionEvent and the ActionListener interface already exist; they do not need to be defined.

Since we plan to link the events and their listeners using VisualAge, we must define the methods we want to connect with the events we just defined. We define a method, handleOrders() in Broker to accept a collection of Orders and begin processing them as Shipments. The handleOrders() method is called when the OK button of the GUI is pressed. We define an additional method in Broker, propertyChange(), to handle the ShipmentChangeEvent() generated by `Shipment`. In `propertyChange()`, the `Broker` examines the event and decides what is to be done next. The broker action events can lead to any one of the following, depending on the exact event:

- load - `loadShipment()` in `Grower` is invoked.

- inspect - `inspectShipment()` in `Inspector` is invoked.

- insure - `insureShipment()` in `Agent` is invoked.

In order to show a mix of Java classes and beans, we implement the remaining classes as standard Java classes.

Let's verify what we have so far before starting to code to make sure that we have not forgotten anything. The story in graphical form is shown again as a refresher.

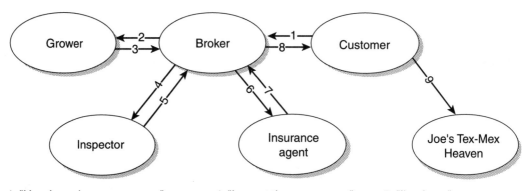

1. "Hey, I need some peppers."
2. "Hey, I need some peppers."
3. "Here's them peppers."

4. "Inspect these peppers."
5. "I'm done."
6. "Insure this shipment."

7. "I'm done."
8. "Here's your peppers."
9. "Now this is good food!"

Let's take all the classes and events we have defined to see if we can cover the story as it is shown above. The numbers in the list correspond to the numbers in the diagram.

1.   The customer (the user) enters an `Order` on the applet's GUI. An `Order` contains `OrderItems`. Each `OrderItem` specifies a kind of `Pepper` and the amount desired. The customer specifies the mode of transportation desired (Truck, Air) and the destination (Texas, World). Both are attributes of the `Order`. When the `OK` pushbutton on the GUI is pressed, the event is caught by the applet, and the `handleOrders()` method on the `Broker` is called with the `Order` as the parameter.

2. The `Broker` opens a `Shipment` using the information from the `Order` and adds the `Shipment` to its collection of `Shipments`. The default state of the `Shipment` is "Initialized." The `Broker` generates a load shipment `Broker-ActionEvent` that is caught by the `Grower`. The `loadShipment()` method on the `Grower` is called with the `Shipment` as the parameter. The `Broker` also generates a `ShipmentChangeEvent` that the applet catches to display the `Shipment` and its status on the GUI.

3. The `Grower` checks to see if it has enough `Peppers` in stock of the kind desired. If so, the amount of `Peppers` of the kind desired are instantiated. The instances of `Pepper` are loaded into the `Shipment`, and the `shipmentState` is set to "Loaded." If not enough `Peppers` of the kind desired are in stock, the `shipmentState` is set to "Not Loaded."

4. In either case, setting the `shipmentState` generates a `PropertyChangeEvent` since `shipmentState` is a bound property. The `Broker`, who is listening on the `PropertyChangeEvents`, examines the event and decides what to do. If the current state of the `Shipment` is "Not Loaded," the `Shipment` is canceled. Otherwise, the `Broker` generates an inspect shipment `BrokerActionEvent`, which is caught by the `Inspector`. The `inspect()` method on the `Inspector` is called with the `Shipment` as the parameter. The `Broker` also generates a `ShipmentChangeEvent` that the applet catches to update the status of the `Shipment` on the GUI.

5. The `Inspector` passes the `Peppers` contained in the `Shipment` through its collection of `Rules` to see if any apply. If no `Rules` apply, the `shipmentState` is set to "Inspected" and `inspectionResult` is set to OK. If any of the `Rules` apply, the `shipmentState` is set to "Inspected," and `inspectionResult` is set to "Not OK."

6. Once again, setting the `shipmentState` generates a `PropertyChangeEvent` since `shipmentState` is a bound property. The `Broker`, who is listening on the `PropertyChangeEvents`, examines the event and decides what to do. Since the current state of the `Shipment` is "Inspected," the `inspectionResult` is checked to see if the `Shipment` is OK. If not, the `Shipment` is canceled. Otherwise, the `Broker` generates an insure shipment `BrokerActionEvent`, which is caught by the `Agent`. The `insureShipment()` method on the `Agent` is called with the `Shipment` as the parameter. The `Broker` also generates a `ShipmentChangeEvent` that the applet catches to update the status of the `Shipment` on the GUI.

7. The `Agent` insures the `Shipment` with a `Policy` that corresponds to the mode `iTransportation` and the destination `iDestination` of the `Order` for the `Shipment`. The `shipmentState` is set to "Insured."

8. Once again, setting the `shipmentState` generates a `PropertyChangeEvent` since `shipmentState` is a bound property. The `Broker`, who is listening on the `PropertyChangeEvents`, examines the event and decides what to do. Since the current state of the `Shipment` is "Insured," the `Broker` calls its own `deliverShipment()` method, which simply sets `shipmentState` to "Sent." The `Broker` also generates a `ShipmentChangeEvent` that the applet catches to update the GUI one last time.

9. This is the most important step. Unfortunately, it lies outside the scope of the application, as we have not defined a cooking robot. Time to take a break and enjoy.

In this unit, we have gone through the following steps of the methodology:

1. Beans were defined using the classes and their interactions as a starting point. Some of the classes from the previous step were mapped to beans; the rest were left as classes.

2. Interaction diagrams were drawn up for the beans in order to verify the design of the beans and to ensure that the use case could be fulfilled.

Having now defined everything, we can continue with building and connecting the beans.

Building and Connecting the Beans

Having defined which classes are to be implemented as beans and which are to be left as is, we continue by writing the code. Once the code has been written, we connect some of the beans by hand. Using the graphical editor in VisualAge, we connect the remaining beans with the tool. We want to compare the generated event-handling code with the code we have written using the concepts we examined earlier.

The event-handling code we write by hand is the code to handle the events generated by a `Shipment` when its state is changed. In implementing the `Shipment` class, we make `shipmentState` a bound property, and we set `Broker` to listen on the `PropertyChangeEvents` that `Shipment` generates. When a `Broker` receives a `PropertyChangeEvent`, its `propertyChange()` method, the method which examines the event and decides what to do next, is called. The `Broker` also fires a `ShipmentChangeEvent`. This will allow the GUI to update itself. When the state of a shipment changes, we want to send additional information. We want to send not only the source, the `Shipment` object, we also want to send the old and new state of the shipment.

In the previous unit, we defined a `ShipmentChangeEvent` and a `Ship-mentChangeInterface` to handle updating the GUI when the `shipment-State` changes. We will generate the code for this connection in the next unit when we define the GUI for the applet.

We now want to go ahead and define the connections between the `Broker` and the `Grower`, the `Inspector` and the `Agent`. In the graphical editor for `Pepper-Applet`, we drop a `Broker`, a `Grower`, an `Inspector` and an `Agent`, and we define three connections. We connect the `BrokerActionEvent` of `Broker` with the `loadShipment()` method of the `Grower`, with the `inspect()` method of the `Inspector` and the `insureShipment()` method of the `Agent`. The result is shown here:

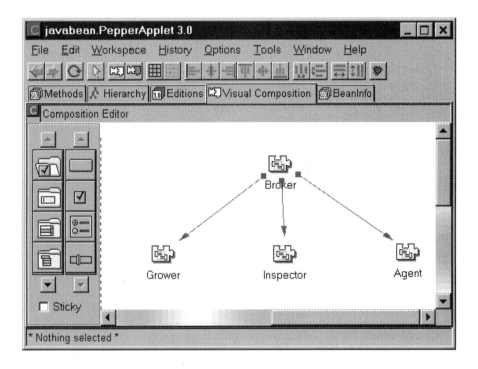

The result in the generated code is unexpected and unusual. The editor does not change the definitions of `Grower`, `Inspector` and `Agent` to allow them to implement the `BrokerActionListener` interface, which would enable them to listen for the `BrokerActionEvent`. Instead, the editor changes the definition of `PepperApplet` to allow it to implement the interface. Why? The reason is quite simple. The editor has been opened on the `PepperApplet` class; it is the main class in the current editor. Any connections defined on the editor will be defined by the code generator as passing through the main class of the editor.

The point is not included to provide a how-to for working with VisualAge. Rather, it is included as a word of warning about the potential risks associated with using visual development tools. It is important to understand exactly how a code-generation tool works before using it. The code that was generated is not "wrong." The tool has worked as designed, and it has been designed correctly. A tool is only as "stupid" as its user. Here, we have been "stupid" to make a point.

In this unit, we covered the following steps of our methodology:

1. The individual classes and beans were implemented.

2. The beans were connected.

Having now implemented and connected the logic of the application, we can continue with building and connecting the GUI.

Adding the GUI

As stated in the introduction to the chapter, VisualAge was used to build the GUI for the applet. It would have been possible to do this by hand. However, we wanted to illustrate the use of both visual and non-visual beans in a graphical editor. Once again, the implementation shown here is not complete. The application logic has not yet been completely separated from the presentation logic. A more refined implementation of the applet would perhaps show the GUI communicating with a controller for the `Broker`. The application logic seen below in the form of the connections between the `Broker` and the other three individuals would be found on a separate graphical editor for the `Broker` class. Our goal here is to provide an implementation which illustrates all the visual connections used to connect our beans on a single graphical editor.

The edited GUI is shown on the following page. An explanation follows:

The GUI is defined in the graphical editor for the `PepperApplet` class. Let's examine what we see from top to bottom. The GUI contains an entry field for the name of the customer. Selecting a type of pepper enables the corresponding entry field, allowing an amount to be entered. The next section contains two check boxes for the destination (Texas, World) and two check boxes for the mode of transport (Truck, Air). The next section displays the status of the shipment as it is processed. The pushed event of the OK pushbutton is connected to the `handle-Orders()` method of the `Broker`. The `ShipmentChangeEvent` of the `Broker` is connected to the shipment status display of the GUI. The connections within the GUI between the various components define the tabbing order. The destina-

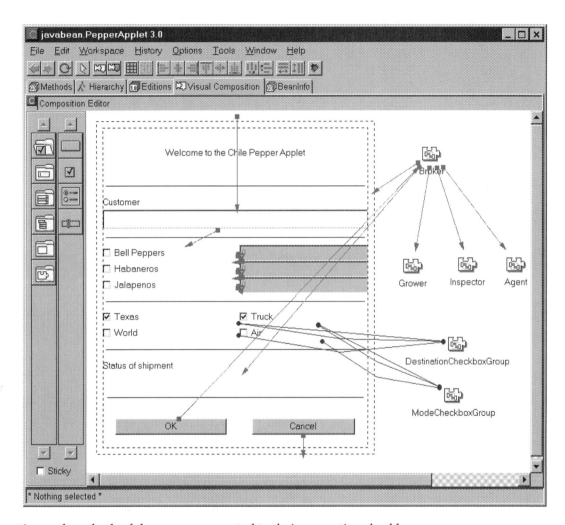

tion and mode check boxes are connected to their respective checkbox groups, essentially allowing the groups to manage their individual checkboxes. The Cancel pushbutton stops the applet.

The completed applet is shown below, after Joe's Tex-Mex Heaven has finally received its long-awaited shipment of peppers.

In this unit, we have completed the last step of the methodology:

- A GUI was added to visualize the functionality of the application.

Having now completed the application, we can sit back and take a well deserved break before looking at some additional features such as printing, remote and distributed objects, database access, and internationalization, which are very important when developing applications for the enterprise environment.

Empanaditas al Chorizo (Sausage Turnovers)

The Market Basket:

2 tablespoons chopped green chili. 5-6 ounces chorizo (Mexican sausage). 1 chopped onion. 1 fresh garlic clove. Pastry for 9-inch, double crust pie. 3 tablespoons sour cream. Olive oil.

How to:

Roll pastry to a 1/8-inch thickness on a lightly floured board.

Cut pastry into circles that are 3 inches in diameter. Set aside.

Remove casings from chorizo. Fry chorizo in a small skillet at medium heat. Drain.

Fry the onion in olive oil until brown; add the crushed garlic at the end.

Combine chorizo, onion, sour cream, and chile in a small mixing bowl.

Place a spoonful of mixture, off center, on each pastry circle.

Fold pastry in half over filling, and pinch edges together to seal.

Pierce top of turnovers with tines of a fork.

Place empanaditas on an ungreased baking sheet and bake in a 450 degree oven for 10-12 minutes or until golden.

<space>Chapter</space> **5**

Enterprise Functionality

▼ INTERNATIONALIZATION

▼ DISTRIBUTION / REMOTE METHOD INVOCATION

▼ PERSISTENCY / ACCESSING LEGACY DBs

▼ PRINTING

The purpose of this chapter is to introduce additional functionality that is useful in an enterprise environment. Features like printing, database access, remote or distributed processing, and availability in different languages are central in the enterprise. Java provides a number of frameworks for implementing such features. Each unit in this chapter discusses one of these features. Detailed examples illustrating the use of the frameworks are provided for each topic.

Internationalization

Being able to write global programs is a not just a nice-to-have feature; it is becoming a must-have feature for programs running on the Internet as well as those running on intranets of multinational companies. It is becoming a must because both developers and users are representing an ever increasing variety of languages and cultures. What exactly is meant by a global program? A global program is one that can be tailored or tailor itself to a user's language and conven-

117

tions. Writing global programs involves two distinct steps: internationalization and localization. Internationalization can best be defined as the ability to develop software independently of the conventions or languages of its users. Once it is developed, the code can then be localized for any number of countries, or even regions. Localization means that it is possible to adapt text, numbers, dates, currency and user-defined objects to the specific conventions of a country or region.

In implementing internationalization, the following design goals were followed by Sun:

- **International by default**. Internationalization should not be a feature that can be added on at will at some point in the development effort; rather, Java code should be internationalized by default. This will ensure that internationalization is an integral part of the code. Ideally, it should result in making it easier to write internationalized code than to write non-internationalized code.

- **Object-oriented design**. Instead of relying on a traditional global state to set a locale-dependent environment, it should be possible to use a more dynamic and extensible object-oriented design. A global state must be accessible throughout an application. This creates interdependencies between objects that could be reduced if not eliminated using a more flexible approach. In addition, a more object-oriented design allows locale-sensitive classes to store the information they need, rather than getting it from a central state object.

- **Multilingual support**. In addition to providing support for a wide variety of individual languages, Java must be able to provide multilingual support to support those users who communicate with each other using more than one language.

- **Platform independence**. Internationalized Java code should not restrict its ability to be executed on any number of different platforms. In other words, internationalization should be strictly platform independent.

- **Support for Unicode**. Unicode should be fully supported. In fact, Java has fully achieved this goal in choosing Unicode as its primitive, built-in character type. Unicode is a 16-bit international character encoding standard. It can represent over 65000 individual characters.

- **Backwards compatibility**. Alternate classes, interfaces and methods should be provided to allow internationalization in previous implementations that could not support internationalization because of design limitations.

We stated above that writing global programs involves two distinct steps: internationalization and localization. The first step in localization is to define the locales that will be supported.

Defining Locales

A locale represents a distinct combination of a language and a country. Examples include English/United States or German/Switzerland. When using locales, it is possible to provide support for various language groups within a particular country. For instance, English/Canada and French/Canada are two distinct locales. In the same way, dialects can be accounted for. French/Canada and French/France are represented as two distinct locales.

Locales are represented in Java by using instances of the class `java.util.Locale`. A new instance of `Locale` can be created as follows:

```
Locale swissGerman = new Locale("de", "CH")
```

The constructor accepts two strings. The first represents the language, and the second represents the country. The strings are ISO codes. The language string is a two-letter lowercase ISO 639 code, and the country code is a two-letter uppercase ISO-3166 code. There are a number of predefined locales in the class, such US and UK. The predefined locales can be accessed as constants.

```
Locale unitedStates = Locale.US
```

The full list of predefined locales is visible in the JavaDoc of the `Locale` class.

The second possibility for constructing a locale is to take into account vendor- or browser-specific components. This is done by using the following constructor:

```
Locale winTurkish = new Locale("tr", "TR", "WIN")
```

In this case, the third parameter represents a variant; it is a vendor- or browser-specific code such as WIN, MAC or POSIX.

Unlike other languages, a Java locale is not used as a container for locale-specific information. Rather, it can be used as a parameter for accessing locale-specific information in special containers. These containers are discussed in detail in the next section. A locale can, however, return useful information such as its language or country in a displayable format. The class `Locale` is capable of returning a default locale. In most cases, this is the platform locale.

Resource Bundles

Once the locales have been defined, it is necessary to define resource bundles for all the locale-specific information. A resource bundle is a container for locale-specific information. Information can be grouped or bundled in instances of a class from the `ResourceBundle` hierarchy. Information is typically not just separated by locale; it is further subdivided into logical groupings such as numbers, dates and time, error messages, labels for GUI elements, and so on. Information is stored in resource bundles by using key-value pairs. The key is the same across all the related bundles; the value is different for each locale.

In the example below, we see two bundles. One is for the locale United States, and one is for the locale Germany. Both bundles have the same structure. They are subdivided into GUI labels, error messages and so on. The key for a specific item, for instance, a specific error message, is the same for each resource bundle; however, the value is different for each bundle.

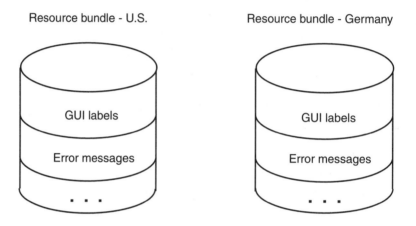

Java provides a hierarchy of three classes for creating resource bundles as shown below.

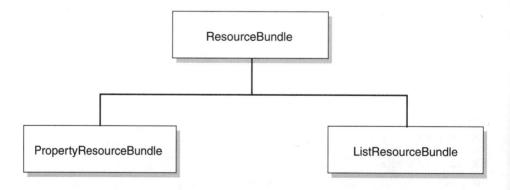

All three classes are abstract classes; they are not meant to be instantiated. Sub-classes of `ListResourceBundle` store key-value pairs in a two-dimensional array and instances of `PropertyResourceBundle` manage a properties file that contains key-value pairs. There are three possibilities for creating resource bundles. The first is to subclass `ListResourceBundle` and provide key-value pairs for the new instance to manage. The second is to subclass `PropertyResource-Bundle` and provide a properties file to manage. The third is to create a new subclass of `ResourceBundle` with appropriate behavior.

In the example above, each bundle represents a logical grouping. Each subdivision within a bundle maps to a subclass of `ResourceBundle` or one of its subclasses. Related subdivisions share a common base class name. They differ, however, in their suffixes. For example, if GUI labels in the resource bundle for the United States maps to a class called `GuiLabels`, GUI labels in the bundle for Germany might map to a class called `GuiLabels_DE`. The common base class name the two share is `GuiLabels`. The convention of a common base class name must be followed in order for the loading of resource bundles to function correctly. It is not necessary to subdivide a bundle into different groups or classes. A resource bundle can be a single class if desired. Whatever format is chosen, it must remain the same across all resource bundles for the application.

Let's go through an example to highlight the two possibilities. Let's assume we have an applet that displays the following information.

GOOD MORNING FROM AUSTIN, TEXAS	
Date:	3.12.1997
Weather:	Warm, rain
	OK Cancel

The applet should be able to reconfigure itself for German users as follows:

```
              GUTEN  TAG AUS AUSTIN, TEXAS


    Datum:        12.3.1997


    Wetter:       Warm, Regen


                                    OK          Abbrechen
```

We can identify two groups of elements. The first group contains all the labels such as OK, Cancel, and so forth. The second group contains the date display. We also have two locales we need to handle: English/US and German/Germany.

We start by creating a base resource bundle for the United States locale. This will contain the English values. This bundle will be referenced if we are asked to provide information for a locale we have not specifically encoded or which simply cannot be located. It acts as a default bundle. We define a class, GuiLabels, as a subclass of ListResourceBundle to hold our GUI labels.

```java
import java.util.ListResourceBundle;

public class GuiLabels extends ListResourceBundle {

  public Object[][] getContents() {
    return contents;
  }

  static final Object[][] contents = {
    {"labelGreeting", "GOOD MORNING FROM AUSTIN"},
    {"labelDate",     "Date:"},
    {"labelWeather",  "Weather:"},
    {"labelWarm",     "Warm"},
    {"labelRain",     "Rain"},
    {"okButton",      "OK"},
    {"cancelButton",  "Cancel"},
  }
}
```

The class `GuiLabels` is the default resource bundle. It contains the values for the United States locale. It is used for other locales when no locale-specific information is found. We can define a second class, `GuiLabels_DE`, for the German locale.

```java
package morning;

import java.util.ListResourceBundle;

public class GuiLabels_DE extends ListResourceBundle {

  public Object[][] getContents() {
    return contents;
  }

  static final Object[][] contents = {
    {"labelGreeting", "GUTEN TAG AUS AUSTIN"},
    {"labelDate",     "Datum:"},
    {"labelWeather",  "Wetter:"},
    {"labelWarm",     "Warm"},
    {"labelRain",     "Regen"},
    {"okButton",      "OK"},
    {"cancelButton",  "Abbrechen"},
  }
}
```

Combining Locales and Resource Bundles

Now that we have defined a resource bundle for each locale that we intend to support, we can access the localized information in the code. Two steps are required in order to be able to access the localized information for a specific locale. The first step is to load the resource bundle that corresponds to the current locale, in this case Germany.

```java
Locale currentLocale = Locale.GERMANY;
ResourceBundle guiLabels = ResourceBundle.getBundle
("morning.GuiLabels", currentLocale);
```

Once the resource bundle is loaded, the information in it can be accessed as follows:

```java
Label labelGreeting = new
Label(guiLabels.getString("labelGreeting"));
Button okButton = new Button(guiLabels.getString("okButton"));
Button cancelButton = new
Button(guiLabels.getString("cancelButton"));
```

We have not described in detail how to extract the strings from the code and replace them with keys from the resource bundles. This is either done manually by the developer or with support from a development tool. In any case, this step, known as internationalization, is a prerequisite for localization to work.

Conclusion

The internationalization framework provides a simple two-step process for writing global programs. The first step, localization, leads to the definition of locales and pools of locale-specific information. The second step, internationalization, replacing strings in the code with keys from the pools, is not supported. At most, a development tool can be counted on to provide support in the form of editors and viewers. As development tools for Java mature, such features are more likely to be found.

Distribution/Remote Method Invocation

Currently, there are two possibilities for implementing distributed processing in Java. Remote Method Invocation is an object model for making Java objects distributed. It is specifically designed for the Java environment, unlike CORBA (Common Object Request Broker Architecture) which is more language neutral. CORBA is not discussed here in detail. However, the Java IDL (Interface Definition Language) for CORBA is introduced at the end of the unit. The java.net package provides support for using TCP/IP socket communication between Java programs. TCP/IP is not covered in this unit since it is not by itself a means of implementing distributed processing.

RMI

RMI is designed to make remote objects look and act as if they were local to the caller. A remote object is one that can be invoked from a Java Virtual Machine (JVM) other than the JVM of the calling object (local object). The second JVM can be on the same host or on a separate host.

Remote execution of an object differs from local execution in several ways:

- When a local object is passed as an argument to a method in a remote object, a copy of the object, not a direct reference, is passed.

- A remote object passed as an argument to a method in a local object is passed by reference. Remote objects are never used directly by the local object.

- All objects that may potentially be used as remote objects must be subclasses of `java.rmi.server.RemoteObject`. It extends `Object` and overwrite `toString()`, `hashCode()` and `equals()`. These methods have a different implementation because they have to reference the object in the other JVM. Once an object has been defined to be a candidate for being used as a remote object by having it subclass RemoteObject, its behavior changes slightly.

- Remote objects need to handle situations which are not typical of local execution. For example, network availability and state is not a typical issue during local execution conditions. All the remote public methods may throw `java.rmi.RemoteException`.

The syntax for working with remote objects is the same for local objects. So, before starting to work with remote objects, the local object needs a reference to it. The local object has to ask a server for a reference to the desired remote object. The server keeps a list of remote object names and a reference to all remote objects it has. The RMI bootstrap registry is the server-side process that is responsible for maintaining the list of registered remote objects and for returning a reference of remote objects to clients.

After receiving a reference to the remote object, the local object works with it as any other ordinary object. The use of remote objects is completely transparent for the client besides the fact that all the methods of a remote object can throw a `RemoteException` exception. The local object needs to be prepared for these exceptions because they reflect network and server problems. A proxy (or stub) is used by the local object to simulate the presence of the remote object. It is also responsible for sending the methods invocations and data across the network and receiving any resultant data or exception from the remote object.

The remote object uses a skeleton object to receive all the incoming invocations and transform them in normal method calls. It is also responsible for transforming the data sent across the network in objects. The skeleton is also capable of sending exceptions generated by the remote object to the local object.

The stub skeleton objects use serialization to send objects across the network. Default Java classes (for instance, String, Date) and primitive data types already support serialization. User-defined classes that are to be sent to remote objects or received as result of a remote method invocation must support serialization (through the `Serializable` or `Externalizable` interfaces).

An object that is to act as a remote server has to define which methods it will allow to be called from a remote VM. Not all the methods of a remote object need to be exposed for a remote invocation. The remote object uses a remote interface to define which of its methods can be called remotely. Before being available for remote invocations, a remote object must be instantiated and registered with the RMI bootstrap registry.

The following graphic shows how all the elements of RMI interact.

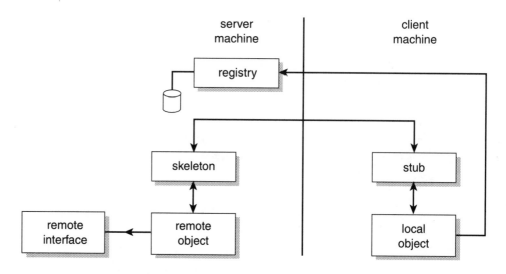

RMI Bootstrap Registry

The RMI Registry handles the mapping of server alias names to objects. It is a separate process that runs on the server machine. To start the RMI registry, type:

```
start rmiregistry (for Windows)
rmiregistry &     (for UNIX)
```

The RMI Registry uses the TCP/IP port 1099 by default. To use a different port, just pass the desired port number as a parameter for the `rmiregistry` command. The `rmiregistry` process does not generate any output and can run safely in the background.

Each remote object has to register itself with the RMI Registry. The section Remote Objects explains how to register an object with the RMI Registry.

The registry is a runtime only directory. As soon as you stop the `rmiregistry` process, the directory of the remote servers will be lost. After restarting the registry, the directory will be empty, and the remote objects will have to rebind to the registry.

The RMI Registry needs access to the skeleton object of each registered remote object. Make sure the `CLASSPATH` points out the actual directories where each skeleton is located before running the `rmiregistry` command.

Remote Interface

The Remote Interface is used to specify which methods of a remote object may be called through remote invocation. Not all public methods are automatically available for remote invocation, nor do all the methods of the remote object have to be included in this interface. The Remote Interface is used to specify a subset of a remote object's public methods.

All the Remote Interfaces must extend `java.rmi.Remote` and all the methods defined in the interface have to throw `java.rmi.RemoteException`. Other exceptions may also be included in the throw list, but `RemoteException` has to be present.

Remote Interfaces have to be declared public.

There is no convention for the name of the Remote Interface. This is an example of a Remote Interface:

```
import java.rmi.RemoteException;

public interface PepperRI extends java.rmi.Remote {

    public String getPeppers() throws RemoteException;
    public void willFail() throws RemoteException, Exception;

}
```

Remote Object

A remote object is an object that acts as remote server waiting for calls from objects from another VM. A remote object needs to implement the Remote Interface and extends the `java.rmi.server.UnicastRemoteObject` class. The `UnicastRemoteObject` class defines a remote object that runs in a single machine (without copies) and that is valid only while the server process is alive.

Before being available for remote invocations, a remote object has to be instantiated and registered with the RMI bootstrap registry. The registration method receives a name that will identify the object in the registry and a reference to the actual remote object. Different instances of the same class can be registered under different names. This is an example call of a registration:

```
Naming.rebind("PepperServer", new Pepper());
```

Remote objects have to have a constructor, and this constructor has to list the `RemoteException` exception in its throw list even when no action is performed (remember that an empty constructor has an implicit call to the superclass constructor). The constructor does not need to be defined in the Remote Interface.

Remote objects may implement an additional interface, the `java.rmi.server.Unreferenced` interface. Implementing the `Unreferenced` interface allows remote objects to be notified when the object is no longer referenced by any clients. The notification is done by calling the remote object's `unreferenced()` method. This method allows the remote object to define what it should do when it is no longer referenced.

The remote object always references the Remote Interface and the skeleton object. These two objects needed are loaded by the remote object. Make sure the `CLASSPATH` is correctly defined, or put these files in the same directory.

Following is an example of a remote object. It uses the Remote Interface presented above. You can compile and run this example. It will register itself in the registry.

```
import java.rmi.server.UnicastRemoteObject;
import java.rmi.*;

public class Pepper extends UnicastRemoteObject implements
PepperRI {

    public Pepper() throws RemoteException {}

    public String getPeppers() throws RemoteException {
        return "Bell, Jalapeno, Serrano, Habanero";
    }

    public void willFail() throws RemoteException, Exception {
        throw new Exception("Exception thrown by the remote
object!");
    }

    public static void main(String args[]) {
        try {
            Naming.rebind("PepperServer", new Pepper());
            System.out.println("PepperServer bound in registry");
        } catch (Exception e) {
            System.out.println("Pepper error: " + e.getMessage() );
            e.printStackTrace();
        }
    }
}
```

Stubs and Skeletons

Remote objects are always referred to through proxies. The reference to the remote object is called a proxy or a stub. The stub contains all the public methods defined in the remote interface. It is the object responsible for forwarding method calls to the server. The skeleton is the object on the server-side that is responsible for invoking the desired methods on the target object. Both the stub and the skeleton are generated by the framework after compiling the remote object class using the `rmic` command. They are not developer defined classes. An overview of the process of remote method invocation is presented below:

1. The client locates the reference to a remote object and invokes a method on it.

2. The method is invoked on the stub.

3. The stub forwards the request. If any parameters are specified, they are serialized and sent to the skeleton.

4. The server skeleton receives any parameters and deserializes them. Then it invokes the method on the real remote object.

The class `java.rmi.server.RemoteStub` is the superclass of all the stubs. The stub contains the same methods as the actual class. The skeleton contains a method, `GetOperations()`, that returns all the operations for the remote object. An operation is a description of a method. It also contains a dispatch method that is used to invoke the target method of the remote object.

RMI Stub Compiler. Stubs and skeletons are automatically generated by the `rmic` command. Input to `rmic` is a remote object class. So the remote object needs to be compiled before running the `rmic` against it.

The output for the `rmic` compiler is the class files for the stub and the skeleton. Use the `-keepgenerated` option to see the generated temporary source files. These files are deleted by default when the compiler exits.

To specify which directory `rmic` uses as starting point for compilation, use the `-d` option. For example, if the package name is `javabean`, and all the files are in the `x:/pepper/javabean`, you can specify:

```
rmic -d x:/pepper
```

and the files will be searched for in the `javabean` subdirectory.

To see detailed information from compilation, such as what classes are being loaded, use the `-verbose` option.

```
rmic -verbose Pepper
```

This will use the current setting of CLASSPATH, print out all the classes that are loaded during compilation, and print the classes that the Pepper class is referring to. Output from the compilation is the stub and skeleton; in our case it will be the files Pepper_Stub.class and Pepper_Skel.class.

Local Objects

Local objects are the ones that use remote objects. The syntax for working with remote objects is the same as working with ordinary local objects.

The local object has to obtain a reference to the remote object before it starts working with it. The java.rmi.Naming class is used to get references to remote objects. URLs are used to locate the object in the network and describe the host machine name, optional port number and the name of the remote object. The protocol is rmi. The general form for an RMI URL is:

```
rmi://hostname[:port]/RemoteObject
```

To get a reference for the PepperServer of the example above that is registered in a machine called hj7006e, a local object should call:

```
Naming.lookup("//hj7006e/PepperServer")
```

If you look up a remote object on your local machine, you can omit the hostname, and in that case only use Naming.lookup("PepperServer").

The type of the remote object must be the type of the Remote Interface, not the remote object. After receiving a reference to the remote object, the local object works with it as with any other local object. Communication or server problems are reported by RemoteException exceptions. The local object needs to be prepared for these exceptions.

The java.rmi.registry.LocateRegistry can be used by local objects to perform queries to a remote registry. This example gets all the registered object names from a server and displays them.

```
import java.rmi.registry.Registry;
import java.rmi.registry.LocateRegistry;

public class Lookup
{
    public static void main(String argv[]) {
        System.out.println("Simple RMI Registry Lookup
Application\n");
        if(argv.length != 1) {
            System.out.println("\nusage: Lookup <hostname>.\n");
```

```
            System.exit(1);
            }

        try {
            Registry registry =
LocateRegistry.getRegistry(argv[0]);
            String[] list = registry.list();
            System.out.println("\nList of names in registry on
            host " + argv[0]);

            for(int i=0; i < list.length; i++) {
                System.out.println(" - " + list[i]);
            }
        }
        catch (java.rmi.UnknownHostException e) {
            System.out.println("Cannot find the host " + argv[0]);
            System.exit(1);
        }
        catch (java.rmi.RemoteException e) {
            System.out.println("No registry found on host " +
            argv[0] + " port 1099");
            System.exit(1);
        }
    }
}
```

To be able to run, a local object needs access to the Remote Interface and to the stub classes. If the local object is part of an applet, these two classes can be served by an HTTP server. If the local object is part of an application, these files need to be local and accessible through CLASSPATH.

This is an example of a local object that uses the remote object presented earlier. It uses Naming.lookup() to get a reference to the remote object. It also shows what happens when the remote object raises a regular exception.

```
import java.rmi.*;

public class PepperApp {
    private PepperRI iPepper;

    public static void main(String[] args) {
        if (args.length != 1) {
                System.out.println("usage: PepperApp <hostname>");
                System.exit(1);
        }
        PepperApp pa = new PepperApp(args[0]);
```

```
     }

   public PepperApp(String aHost) {
     try {
        PepperRI aPepper = (PepperRI)Naming.lookup("rmi://" +
               aHost + "/PepperServer");
        System.out.println("The kind of this pepper is: " +
               aPepper.getPeppers());
        aPepper.willFail();
         System.out.println("Normal end.");
     } catch (Exception e) {
        System.out.println("Pepper exception: " +
   e.getMessage() );
     }
   }

 }
```

Testing the Distributed Application

It is possible to test a distributed application in just one machine, even if the machine is not part of a network. The TCP/IP support must be installed for the application to run.

Compile the Remote Interface (PepperRI), the remote object (Pepper) and the local object (PepperApp). Generate the stub and skeleton for the remote object. Start the registry with the rmiregistry command. Start the remote object to create an instance and register it with the registry. Then start the local object by passing the hostname of the host machine for the registry. The output will look like this:

```
The kind of this pepper is: Bell, Jalapeno, Serrano, Habanero
Pepper exception: Exception thrown by the remote object!
```

After receiving the reference for the remote object, the local object calls getPeppers() on the remote object. The remote object returns a string that is printed on the screen. Then the willFail() method is invoked. This method raises an exception that is caught by the local object, and the message of the exception is displayed on the screen.

Distributed Applet

This section presents an applet that uses the same remote object and Remote Interface defined earlier, the PepperApplet.

This is the applet version of the last application (local object). It works in a very similar way. The only important difference is in the way the URL is created. An applet can only communicate with the server it came from; so we use the `getCodeBase().getHost()` method defined in the applet to find the host-name. And we get the name of the remote object from a parameter on the applet tag.

```java
import java.awt.*;
import java.rmi.Naming;

public class PepperApplet extends java.applet.Applet {
    String iKind;

    public void init() {
        String pepperServer = getParameter("PepperServer");

        try {
            String distURL = "rmi://" + getCodeBase().getHost() +
                "/" + pepperServer;
            PepperRI iPepper = (PepperRI)Naming.lookup(distURL);
            iKind = iPepper.getPeppers();
        } catch (Exception e) {
            System.out.println("Pepper exception: " +
                e.getMessage() );
            e.printStackTrace();
        }
    }

    public void paint (Graphics g) {
        if(iKind != null) {
            g.drawString("The peppers on the server are:", 25,
90);
            g.drawString(iKind, 25, 105 );
        }
    }
}
```

Create the HTML for the applet, and, for example, call the file PepperApp.htm. The `PepperServer` parameter is used in the applet code to locate the server.

```html
<applet code="PepperApplet" width=500 height=300>
<param name="PepperServer" value="PepperServer">
</applet>
```

Do not forget that the registry must be running, and the `Pepper` object needs to be registered. Run the example:

```
appletviewer PepperApp.htm
```

The output should be like this:

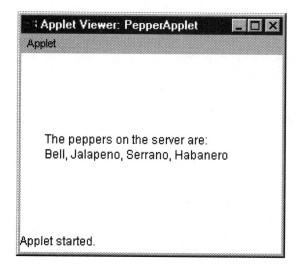

A Short Description of CORBA

CORBA is a standard defined by OMG (Object Management Group). It specifies how to define remote objects by using IDL (Interface Definition Language). The IDL is compiled into language-specific bindings, and the output is server stub files. To these stubs you add your program logic. The output from the IDL compiler can also be client-side include files. The client does not need to be written in the same language as the server object. The language mapping is done by the bindings.

At the time we were writing this book, is an alpha version of the Java IDL was available. This means that you can create server-side objects in Java that can be reached from other language implementations using CORBA. You can also create client-side mappings that make it possible for a Java client to reach a CORBA server object.

Persistency

Persistency, the ability to store the current state of the system and restart the system at a later date by retrieving the stored state, is one of the central requirements of enterprise computing. Not only will Java applications require databases of their own for new applications, it will also be necessary to access and manipulate a wide variety of existing databases. Java provides a number of possibilities for accessing existing and new application-specific databases. These options include:

- Accessing relational databases using the Java Database Connectivity (JDBC). This is currently the most viable alternative for accessing both existing and new relational databases. JDBC is a DBMS-independent API. It is a low-level API that supports basic SQL functionality. It requires the use of database-specific drivers. All databases that provide JDBC drivers can be accessed directly by using JDBC. Databases such as object-relational databases or even non-relational databases such as IMS from IBM can be also be accessed if a JDBC driver is available. Other databases for which ODBC (Open Database Connectivity) drivers are available can be accessed by using a JDBC-ODBC bridge.

- Accessing relational databases using embedded SQL for Java (JSQL). At this point, the JSQL is still under development by IBM, Oracle and Tandem.

- Accessing object-oriented databases using the standard API for object databases from the Object Database Management Group (ODMG). The standard API is still under development. However, several vendors of object databases, such as POET, are developing databases for Java.

- Writings objects to files and retrieving them using the byte streams produced by serialization. This is a very primitive method of making objects persistent. There is no locking or any of the other features typically associated with databases. It can be an option for small applets or applications where concurrency is not an issue. It is typically used in a development environment to store the current state of a customized bean. Serialization is covered in detail in Chapter 3.

We discuss each of these options in turn through the course of this unit. It is important to note that at this point in time, only JDBC presents a viable option for making an application persistent. JSQL and the ODMG standard are still under development, and serialization cannot really be seen as a true option for making an entire application persistent for reasons explained above. Although these options are features of Java itself, they apply equally well to beans. In addition, we provide a detailed example of how to use JDBC to access IBM DB2.

JDBC

JDBC stands for Java Database Connectivity. It is the Java API for client access to relational databases. JDBC provides classes for accessing databases in a uniform manner, similar in concept to Microsoft's Open Database Connectivity (ODBC). Both implementations are based on the same specification, the X/Open SQL Call Level Interface. JDBC support can be used in both applications and applets.

The JDBC drivers work as a database abstraction layer. Java programs can access different database engines only by changing the JDBC driver. However, some vendors may provide additional features in their JDBC drivers to take advantage of database-specific functions. It is important to be aware of the database-specific functions supported by the driver being used, especially when writing database independent applications.

An application or applet using JDBC can communicate with databases from different vendors only by using the vendor-specific database driver. Multiple database connections are allowed. All the necessary drivers must be loaded. Multiple connections to the same database are also possible.

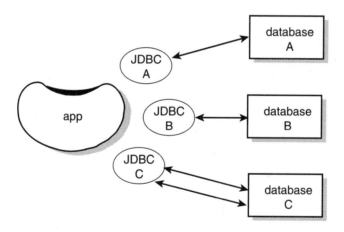

Java programs that access databases go through a common flow of events to get access to database resources:

- Load the target database JDBC driver.
- Connect to the database.
- Execute SQL statements.

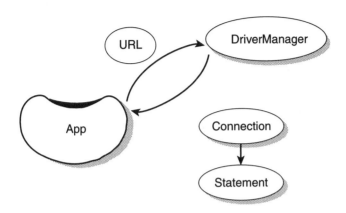

Mapping Beans to Relational Database Tables

A common problem when using an object oriented language like Java with relational databases is how to read and write objects to and from relational tables. The problem becomes more intricate when the object has references to one or more different objects.

One solution to this problem is to directly map each object's field into a column in a table. Relational databases require a column (or combination of columns) to be unique identifiers for each line. It is necessary to provide each object with a unique identifier, stored in a new attribute. The identifier requires an additional column in the table in the database.

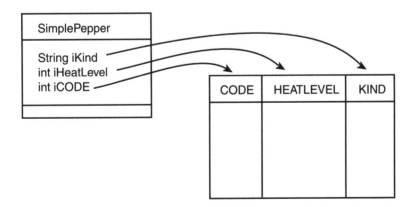

When an object references other objects, for example an `Order` object that references its `Item` objects, it must be possible to maintain the relationship between the objects when storing them in the database. A table is created for each object, and the object's references are maintained by table relationships. The referenced object table must include a column for the identifier of the object that refers to it.

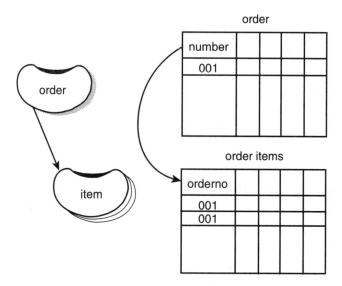

There is no default method for writing an object (with or without references to other objects) to a relational database table and retrieving it. The behavior must be implemented for each object that is to be stored in the database. A typical way of dealing with this problem is to define a class or an interface `PersistentObject` that all the objects that need to be stored in the database can either extend or implement. The class or the interface would contain the basic behavior for making an object persistent to the database in question.

An alternative method for storing objects in databases is to use the capability of the database to store binary information. Serialization can be used to create a stream representation of an object. The resulting byte stream can then be stored in a database. See Serialization at the end of this unit for more information.

Loading JDBC Drivers

The Java virtual machine maintains a reference to each JDBC driver that has been loaded. If two applications that run on the same virtual machine use the same database driver, the driver is not loaded again when the second application needs it. It is passed a reference to the driver by the virtual machine. The virtual machine uses an object called `DriverManager` to maintain the references to each available driver.

The `DriverManager` looks for the `jdbc.driver` system property when it is initialized. The `jdbc.driver` property, if present, must contain a list with the available JDBC driver names separated by semicolons. All the JDBC drivers listed are loaded by the `DriverManager`. They are then available for all of the applications and applets that run on the virtual machine to use. The way properties are saved varies for each virtual machine implementation and platform. It is usually possible for the developer to edit the file containing the properties. The documentation of the virtual machine being used should specify how the properties are saved.

An application or applet can load any additional JDBC drivers that it needs. It must simply call `Class.forName()` and pass the fully qualified name of the driver (for instance, COM.ibm.db2.jdbc.app.DB2Driver) as the parameter. This loads the driver into the virtual machine.

Independent of the method used to load it, the JDBC driver automatically registers itself with the `DriverManager` when it is loaded. No additional action need be taken by the application in order to use the driver once it has been loaded.

The following example illustrates a simple method to find out which drivers are available for an application or applet. The example application loads several JDBC drivers. It then asks the `DriverManager` for a list of the registered drivers. An easy way of testing the example is to make one of the drivers be loaded automatically by the `DriverManager` by defining its name in the `jdbc.driver` property. Run the example to see if the driver is available. If any other driver is automatically loaded, it will be listed as well.

Some JDBC drivers are needed to make the examples in this unit work. The DB2 JDBC drivers are provided in the CD-ROM that comes with this book. Copy the file db2java.zip to your local disk and add it to your `CLASSPATH` environment variable. This will make the drivers available for local applets and applications.

```
import java.sql.*;

class DrvLister {

  public static void main(String argv[]) {
    try {
      Class.forName("COM.ibm.db2.jdbc.app.DB2Driver");
      Class.forName("COM.ibm.db2.jdbc.net.DB2Driver");
      Class.forName("sun.jdbc.odbc.JdbcOdbcDriver");
    } catch (Exception e) {
      e.printStackTrace();
    }
    System.out.println("JDBC drivers loaded:");
```

```
        java.util.Enumeration enu = DriverManager.getDrivers();
        while(enu.hasMoreElements())
          System.out.println(enu.nextElement());
    }
  }
```

Note that loading a driver does not make it automatically available. A driver may have external dependencies and check for certain conditions before registering itself with the `DriverManager`. This is the case of the local JDBC driver for DB2. If the database client software (or the server) is not installed on the same machine where the driver is being loaded, it will not be available for use. See the JDBC local driver section below for more information.

Connecting to Databases

To connect to a database, a connection can be requested from the `DriverManager` using `DriverManager.getConnection()`. This is an overloaded function with three different signatures.

```
DriverManager.getConnection(String url)
DriverManager.getConnection(String url, String user, String
password)
DriverManager.getConnection(String url, Properties info)
```

In each of the three implementations, the first parameter is a database connection URL. The second method accepts the user name and password to set the connection. The last method uses a `Property` object to send multiple parameters to the driver. The `Property` class inherits from Hashtable. It is used to save parameter names (the keys) and values.

The database connection URL specifies the target database and its location. It can also provide information to help the driver set the desired database connection characteristics, when possible (for example, cache size). The format of the database connection URL is:

```
jdbc:<subprotocol>:<subname>
```

The subprotocol is the name of the connectivity mechanism which can be supported by more than one driver (for example, db2, odbc). The subname syntax depends on the subprotocol.

The `DriverManager` receives the connection URL and passes it to all the loaded drivers. The first driver which accepts the URL as a valid connection string will be used to connect to the database. If no driver accepts the URL, an SQLException exception (no suitable driver) is thrown.

When the connection is successfully established, a Connection object is returned by calling getConnection() on DriverManager. A Connection object is responsible for transaction control. The transaction control methods that Connection implements are: commit(), rollback() and setAutoCommit(). The default behavior is to commit changes after each statement which is executed. The behavior can be changed by calling setAutoCommit(false) on the desired Connection object. The Connection object also provides information about the tables and stored procedures in the destination database and about the connection itself. The getMetaData() method describes all the information that a Connection object can provide.

Executing SQL Statements

Before executing an SQL statement, an application or an applet must call a method on the Connection object to obtain the correct Statement object for the action it wants to perform in the database. The table below describes the three methods which return a Statement.

Return Object Type	Method	Description
Statement	createStatement()	used to execute regular SQL expressions like SELECT, INSERT, DELETE and DDL
PreparedStatement	prepareStatement()	used for executing pre-compiled SQL statements
CallableStatement	prepareCall()	used to make calls to stored procedures

A discussion of stored procedures is beyond the scope of this book. The CallableStatement class will neither be presented nor discussed in the examples below.

Two methods are provided by both Statement and PreparedStatement to execute SQL statements. The executeUpdate(String sql) receives an SQL string containing an INSERT, DELETE or UPDATE statement and returns the number of rows updated. This method is also used to execute DDL statements. The executeQuery(String sql) method is used to run a SELECT statement against the database. This method returns a ResultSet object containing the resultant rows from the database query.

Using the PreparedStatement Class. Precompiled SQL statements are statements defined at compile time (in the source code) with values that can be set at runtime. An example of a precompiled statement is:

```
SELECT * FROM pepper WHERE heatlevel = ?
```

The question mark can be replaced with the desired value at runtime, but the statement is fixed in the code.

The `PreparedStatement` class provides all the necessary methods to set values in a pre-compiled statement with the correct SQL type. The correct method from the list shown has to be used to set the parameter value with the correct SQL data type. See the JDBC specifications for all the data type conversions.

- `setBigDecimal()`
- `setBoolean()`
- `setByte()`
- `setBytes()`
- `setDate()`
- `setDouble()`
- `setFloat()`
- `setInt()`
- `setLong()`
- `setNull()`
- `setObject()`
- `setShort()`
- `setString()`
- `setTime()`
- `setTimeStamp()`

The following code excerpt demonstrates how to execute a precompiled SQL statement:

```
...
PreparedStatement statement = connection.prepareStatement(
    "UPDATE peppers SET heatLevel = ? WHERE kind = ?");
statement.setInt(1, 10);
statement.setString(2, "Bell");
int updatedRows = statement.executeUpdate();
...
```

Using the Statement Class. Statement objects are used to send a string containing an SQL statement to the database.

The following code excerpt demonstrates how to execute a regular SQL statement:

```
. . .
Statement statement = connection.createStatement();
ResultSet rows = statement.executeQuery("SELECT * FROM
peppers");
. . .
```

Database Literals. The JDBC specification defines the use of database literals. JDBC follows the ISO standard format. The following table shows the supported database literals and their format.

Type	Literal
date	{d 'yyyy-mm-dd'}
time	{t 'hh:mm:ss'}
timestamp	{ts 'yyyy-mm-dd hh:mm:ss.f...'}

The JDBC driver converts the database literals to the database-specific format. This is an example of database literal use:

```
aStatement.executeQuery(
    "SELECT name FROM customer WHERE birthday >
            {d '1971-09-30'}");
```

Reading Query Results. The executeQuery() method returns the selected rows in a ResultSet object. The selected rows are accessible in sequence using the next() method. It is not possible to go back to a line after having left it. The first call to next() will return the first row in the ResultSet object.

The columns in the current row can be retrieved by number or by name. Retrieving columns by number is more efficient than retrieving columns by name; however, it is less flexible. Column indexes start at 1.

The ResultSet provides a complete set of get methods to read column contents. These methods try to convert the SQL type to the desired Java type. Consult the JDK documentation for the ResultSet get methods and the JDBC documentation for all the possible conversions. All data types can be converted to a String using getString().

The `ResultSet` provides the `wasNull()` method to determine if the content of a table field retrieved from the database was null. The field must first be read. Calling `wasNull()` will determine if the value represents a SQL null. The get methods always return a compatible Java value for SQL null values; null for objects, zero for numeric values and false for boolean values.

When the `Statement` object used to create a `ResultSet` is closed, all of the associated `Statement` objects are closed as well.

Working with Large Parameters. If the database contains a field with very large data, it is possible to read or write the contents of the field in data chunks. It is possible to attach a stream to a database field and then read or write the field data in small pieces. It is useful for manipulating multimedia information such as pictures, sound, large texts, and so forth.

The `ResultSet` provides three types of streams for reading fields. The following table lists the different streams and the methods that return them. All of the methods can receive a column name or number as a parameter.

Stream Type	ResultSet Method
byte	getBinaryStream()
ASCII	getAsciiStream()
Unicode	getUnicodeStream()

Any call to a get method while reading the stream will close the stream. It is necessary to read all the contents of a table field before reading the value of another field.

Streams for writing to database fields are provided by `PreparedStatement` objects. They can be from the same type as the get streams. When using a stream to write to a table field, the total number of bytes must be specified before starting to transfer the data.

JDBC Drivers

There are three different types of JDBC drivers that Java applications and applets can use:

- *local drivers,* drivers that rely on the database client software to communicate with the database

- *net drivers,* drivers that use a database independent protocol or a proprietary protocol to talk directly to the database server

- *JDBC-ODBC bridge,* which provides support for accessing any database that is accessible through ODBC

The local and net drivers are provided by the database vendor of each different database server. The JDBC-ODBC driver comes with the JDK. However, the JDBC-ODBC bridge needs database-specific ODBC drivers in order to access a database.

Creating a Sample Database. Access to a database server is needed to be able to run the examples described here. Any database for which JDBC drivers exist can be used to run the examples. We will use IBM DB2 in the examples in this chapter. A trial version of the IBM DB2 server and the IBM DB2 JDBC drivers can be found on the CD-ROM that comes with this book. The IBM DB2 JDBC drivers are used to show how JDBC drivers work. All drivers of the same type (local or net) work in a similar way; the explanation is valid for any JDBC driver. In order to run the examples, a few modifications of the source code may be needed in order to use the correct driver for your database. Load the correct driver (local or net) and change the connection URL to correspond to the syntax specified in the database manual. If you do not want to install the IBM DB2 server, you need to create the sample database and the sample table used in the examples in your own database.

Install the IBM DB2 database server for your platform. Follow the post-installation instructions to correctly configure the database.

For UNIX machines, you will have to create a new instance of the database for the user you want to work with. Type db2instance <username>. This will create a new database instance under the target user directory. The ~/sqllib/db2profile contains a set of environment variables that allow the user to access the database (for instance, path information). The information in this file is needed to update your environment. If you are using korn shell, add the following line to your ~/.profile:

```
. ./sqllib/db2profile
```

After the installation, type db2start to start the database server. Open the IBM DB2 Command Line Processor (type db2 for UNIX machines). This is a window where you can enter database commands and SQL strings to be executed by the database server. Create the database by typing the command: CREATE DATA-BASE pepper. We provide a PEPPER.BAT file which can be used by OS/2 and Windows users to create and populate the sample table. If you are using OS/2 or Windows, run PEPPER.BAT and skip to the next section. If you are using another operating system or another database, follow these steps:

1. Connect to the Pepper database. Type `connect to pepper`.

2. Create the Pepper table. Use the following DDL statement to create the pepper table: (\ is used by the IBM DB2 command processor to describe a command that continues on the next line. Leave at least one space between the last character in the line and \)

```
create table pepper (              \
     code       integer not null, \
     kind       varchar(15),       \
     heatlevel  integer,           \
     price      decimal(4,2),      \
     primary key(code))
```

3. Populate the Pepper table.

```
insert into pepper values (0, 'Habanero', 300000, 1.45)
insert into pepper values (1, 'Serrano' , 10000 , 1.25)
insert into pepper values (2, 'Jalapeno', 5000  , 0.99)
insert into pepper values (3, 'Bell'    , 0     , 0.75)
```

4. Close the connection with the database with the command: `connect reset`.

5. Quit the command line processor: `quit`.

JDBC Local Drivers. The JDBC local driver is a thin layer that relies on the database client software to communicate with the database server. JDBC local drivers require the prior installation and configuration of the database client software in each workstation. Other languages (like C, C++, Smalltalk) access databases in a similar way. JDBC local drivers use the API provided by the database client software to access the database. The network protocol used for communicating between the database client software and the database server is, in many cases, proprietary. Java applications can use the local drivers to access existing databases using the same protocols used by older applications.

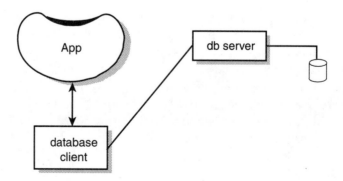

The connection URL for the IBM DB2 JDBC local driver is:

```
jdbc:odbc:<database name>
```

The only parameter needed to establish the connection is the database name. All the information needed to locate the database server is provided by the database client software.

The following example application runs a `select` statement and prints the result data in the screen. If you did not create the sample database and the sample table, you can see how to create the sample database above. The `userid` and `password` variables may need to be changed to match the values defined in your system. The example will run without any further configuration if you are testing the application on the same machine where your database is installed.

```
import java.net.URL;
import java.sql.*;

class DbApp {
  private final int ALIGNLEFT  = 0;
  private final int ALIGNRIGHT = 1;
  private Statement stmt;
  private ResultSet rs;

  public static void main(String argv[]) {
    DbApp db = new DbApp();
  }
```

The class `DbApp` is a subclass of `Object`. It contains variables for the statement and the result set. The `int` instance variables are used to align the display of results of queries on the database. The `main()` method starts the example application by creating a new instance of `DbApp`.

```
  public DbApp() {
    try {
      // Register the driver
      Class.forName("COM.ibm.db2.jdbc.app.DB2Driver");
      connectDB();
      runQuery("SELECT kind,heatlevel,price FROM pepper");
      displayData();
      stmt.close();
    } catch (Exception e) {
      e.printStackTrace();
    }
  }
}
```

The constructor registers the IBM DB2 driver and connects to the sample database. A query is run on the database to select all the `kind`, `heatlevel` and `price` properties for each pepper in the Pepper table.

```
private void connectDB() throws SQLException {
   // Prepare the connection URL
   String db  = "PEPPER";
   String url = "jdbc:db2:" + db;
   // Set the user and password
   String userid = "mkomis";
   String password = "ncc";
   System.out.println("Connecting to the DB");
   Connection con = DriverManager.getConnection(url, userid,
password);
   stmt = con.createStatement();
 }
```

The `connectDB()` method establishes a connection to the sample database. An `SQLException` is generated if the connection cannot be established. The URL of the database, the user ID and the password are sent to the `DriverManager` to establish the connection. The `createStatement()` method returns an instance of `Statement` that can be used to execute regular SQL expressions like `SELECT`, `INSERT`, `DELETE` and DDL. The `Statement` object is assigned to the `stmt` instance variable.

```
private void runQuery(String aSQLStatement) throws
SQLException {
    System.out.println("Running the query: " + aSQLStatement +
"\n");
    rs = stmt.executeQuery(aSQLStatement);
 }
```

The `runQuery()` method accepts a `String` representation of an SQL statement and passes it to the `Statement` object obtained earlier to execute against the database. The `ResultSet` object that is returned is assigned to instance variable `rs`. If the query cannot be executed, an `SQLException` is generated. A line listing the SQL statement is written to the console.

```
private void displayData() throws SQLException {
    System.out.println("Kind       Level  $/lb");
    System.out.println("--------  ------  -----");
    while (rs.next()) {
      String kind  = rs.getString("kind");
      String level = rs.getString("heatlevel");
```

```
    String price = rs.getString("price");
    System.out.print(padString(kind, 8, ALIGNLEFT) + " ");
    System.out.print(padString(level, 6, ALIGNRIGHT) + " ");
    System.out.println(padString(price, 5, ALIGNRIGHT) + " ");
  }
}
```

The displayData() method displays the data contained in the result set of the last query on the console. The int variables defined at the beginning are used to size and adjust the display. The individual Strings are accessed from the result set by using getString() and passing the name of the variable as the key.

```
  private String padString(String aString, int aLength, int
anAlignment) {
    if (aString.length() == aLength)
      return aString;
    else if (aString.length() > aLength)
      return aString.substring(0, aLength);
    else {
      char[] dstArray = new char[aLength];
      if (anAlignment == ALIGNLEFT)
        aString.getChars(0, aString.length(), dstArray, 0);
      else if (anAlignment == ALIGNRIGHT)
        aString.getChars(0, aString.length(), dstArray, aLength-
aString.length());
      return new String(dstArray);
    }
  }
```

The padString() method pads a String to a desired length in the direction specified using blanks. The getChars() method copies characters from a string starting at the position specified into the destination character array starting at the position specified.

The example can be run by compiling the source and executing: java DbLocal. The result is shown below:

```
C:\db\app>Java DbLocal
Connecting to the DB
Running the query: SELECT kind,heatlevel,price FROM pepper

Kind      Level  $/lb
--------  ------ -----
Habanero 300000  1.45
Serrano   10000  1.25
Jalapeno   5000  0.99
Bell          0  0.75
```

Common Errors. There are two errors which may occur if a database service is not available. They may be seen when trying to run the example. These are exceptions sent by the IBM DB2 JDBC driver and are easy to avoid. A description and a solution for each follows:

Problem:

```
java.sql.SQLException:
[IBM][CLI Driver] SQL1032N No start database manager command
was issued.
SQLSTATE=57019
```

Solution:

The database server is not running. Type db2start to start the IBM DB2 server.

Problem:

```
java.sql.SQLException:
[IBM][CLI Driver] SQL1402N Unable to authenticate user due
to unexpected system error.
```

Solution:

The security server is not started. This can happen only in the Windows NT version of IBM DB2 because Security Server is a different service. You need to open the Services window to start the Security Server. You can also start the IBM DB2 server from this window.

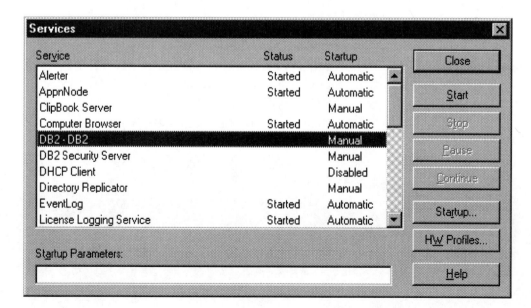

JDBC Net Drivers. JDBC net drivers provide a way for applications to access the database without using database client software on the workstation. This configuration supports thin clients, where it is not desirable or possible (network computers) to install the database client software. This solution also helps minimize the burden of maintaining large client/server applications because no database client software needs to be installed on the workstation, nor is a database-specific configuration of the workstation necessary.

Because the workstation has no previous database information when an applet starts running, the connection URL for a net driver must include the address of the database server machine to be able to establish communications. The port number of the database server that is waiting for incoming calls also needs to be provided. The connection URL for the IBM DB2 JDBC net driver is:

```
jdbc:db2://server:port/database name
```

The solution on the server-side varies with the type of database server that is used. The IBM DB2 server uses a separate process to listen for Java application calls. This process, the Java client listener, receives the database request from Java client applications and passes it to the database server. This process is also responsible for giving the resulting information back to the client. To start the IBM DB2 Java client listener, issue the following command on the database server machine:

```
db2jstrt <port number>
```

The `<port number>` is the TCP/IP port used for listening for incoming calls. This can be any free port in the system.

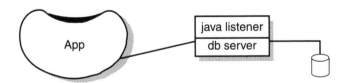

Change the `DbApp` application to use the JDBC net driver. Load the JDBC net driver and change the connection URL to use it. The port parameter must specify the port number used by `db2jstrt`. Start the IBM DB2 Java client listener before running the application. The output will be the same as that of the previous example.

From:
```
...
Class.forName("COM.ibm.db2.jdbc.app.DB2Driver");
...
String url = "jdbc:db2:" + db;
```

To:
```
...
Class.forName("com.ibm.db2.jdbc.net.DB2Driver");
...
String server = "hj7006e";
String port = "1300";
String url = "jdbc:db2://"+server+":"+port+"/"+db;
```

The complete example using the JDBC net driver is on the distribution CD-ROM. The example is called DbNet.

Common Errors. A common error is to forget to start the IBM DB2 Java client listener. This will cause the following exception:

```
java.sql.SQLException:
[IBM][JDBC Driver] CLI0616E Error opening socket. SQLSTAT
E=08S01
```

Use the command `db2jstrt <port number>` to start the IBM DB2 Java client listener.

JDBC-ODBC Bridge. A large number of database servers come with ODBC drivers. The JDK includes a JDBC-to-ODBC bridge driver to enable a Java application or applet to access any database for which an ODBC driver exists. This is a good migration path and can be used while no JDBC drivers are available for a specific database server.

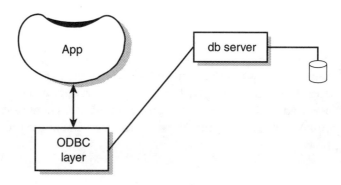

The connection URL for the JDBC-ODBC bridge driver is:

```
jdbc:odbc:<odbc database name>
```

ODBC drivers support a number of configurable parameters. If any other parameters need to be sent to the ODBC driver, they may be added after the database name. The parameters must be separated by semicolons. For example:

```
jdbc:odbc:pepper;UID=mkomis;PWD=ncc
```

The example presented uses a simple connection string. Refer to the ODBC manual for further information on parameters used by ODBC drivers.

Before using an existing database as an ODBC data source, it must be included in the ODBC resource list. The IBM DB2 server comes with a program that can register a IBM DB2 database as an ODBC data source, the IBM DB2 CLI-ODBC Administrator. Open the CLI-ODBC Administrator and select the database you would like to access through ODBC (Pepper in this example) and push the `Add as ODBC` button. The database selected can now be accessed through ODBC.

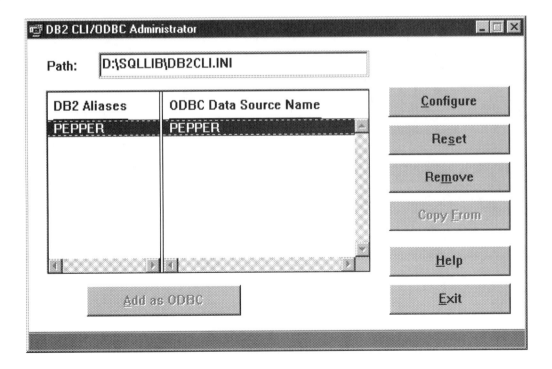

Change the `DbApp` application to work with ODBC databases. Load the JDBC-ODBC bridge driver and change the connection URL to use it. The output will be the same as that of the previous example.

```
From:
...
Class.forName("COM.ibm.db2.jdbc.net.DB2Driver");
...
String url = "jdbc:db2://"+server+":"+port+"/"+db;

To:
...
Class.forName("sun.jdbc.odbc.JdbcOdbcDriver");
...
String url = "jdbc:odbc:" + db;
```

The complete example using the JDBC-ODBC driver can be found on the CD-ROM. It is called DbODBC.

Applets

Applets that can access databases make perfect database client programs. They require no proprietary database client software installed on the workstation. They automatically make any machine with a Java-enabled browser a database client, extending the Java concept of write once, run everywhere to database client applications. No database-specific configuration is required on the client to allow it to access the database. Any intranet or Internet client can access the data in the database.

The applet must use JDBC net drivers to access the database. It is necessary to check with the database provider if JDBC net drivers are available for the database server. Nothing prevents an applet from using the local client drivers used in Java applications. In this case, the database-enabled applet would only run on clients with the proprietary database client software correctly installed and configured. This is probably not the most common scenario for applets.

Database connections from applets underlie the same security restrictions as applets; they can only be made to the server where the applet was downloaded from. This can be a problem for some Internet servers as the same machine will have to act as both a database server and an HTTP server.

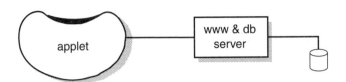

A solution to this problem is to configure the HTTP server as a database client and use the database facilities to access the database server on any other machine. It is possible to implement a solution like this using IBM DB2. The database server can be any supported IBM DB2 platform. The Client Application Enabler (CAE) must be installed on the HTTP server.

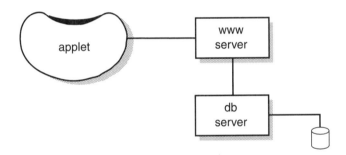

The security restrictions are important in the Internet environment, but may not be convenient for intranet networks where access to different databases is needed. Signed applets are able to access different database servers on different machines and can be used in intranet environments.

Loading JDBC Drivers from Applets, Using an HTTP Server. In order to access the database, an applet needs to use JDBC drivers. It has to load the drivers the same way applications do, using the command:

```
Class.forName(<driverName>)
```

When an applet tries to load another driver, it first searches the local library (specified by the CLASSPATH environment variable in the client) to see if the desired class is present. If not, the applet sends a request to the same server from where it was downloaded for the missing driver classes. This request is a normal HTTP GET command. For example, if an applet needs the IBM DB2 JDBC net driver (COM.ibm.db2.jdbc.net.DB2Driver) and it is not found on client machine, the following http command is sent to the server:

```
GET /com/ibm/db2/jdbc/net/DB2Driver.java
```

Each package level has been translated into a subdirectory in the server, but many Java packages are usually found in a single zip file (the IBM DB2 JDBC drivers are distributed using a single zip file). For the http server be able to find and send the drivers, they must be extracted from the zip file and placed in the http server root directory. The directory structure must match the structure for the packages (directory names are case sensitive for most http servers). The directory structure is normally recreated when exploding the packages file. If the directory /www/html is the root directory for the http server, the IBM DB2 JDBC net driver should be in /www/html/com/ibm/db2/jdbc/net/DB2Driver.java.

Storing the applet and the JDBC drivers on the server is the desired method for clients who require casual access to the database, for example Internet clients. For clients who frequently access the same database or use the same driver to access different databases, the JDBC drivers can be stored locally to minimize the applet load time and the network traffic.

Database Enabled Applet Example. This is a modified version of the previous example that reads the Pepper table and displays the results. This applet works the same way the application does, but it stores the ResultSet data in a local vector to support the screen repainting necessary for applets. It runs the query against the database and copies the ResultSet data to a local vector before closing the Statement. The paint() method uses the local vector to display the query results whenever it is necessary, even after closing the Statement and any associated ResultSets.

The source code of the applet is the same regardless of whether the drivers are stored locally or on the http server.

```
import java.net.URL;
import java.sql.*;
import java.awt.Graphics;
import java.util.Vector;

public class DbAptNet extends java.applet.Applet {
  private ResultSet iResultSet;
  private Connection iConnection;
  private Vector iQueryData = new Vector();
```

The applet DbAptNet defines an instance variable for the ResultSet, the Connection and for the Vector which holds the data from the ResultSet.

```
static {
  try {
    Class.forName("com.ibm.db2.jdbc.net.DB2Driver");
```

```
  } catch (Exception e) {
    e.printStackTrace();
  }
}
```

This piece of static code is executed only once, when the class is loaded. It tries to load the appropriate driver. If the load fails, the exception that is generated is caught and a stack trace of it is printed.

```
public void init() {
  resize(300,300);
  try {
    connectDB();
    Statement stmt = iConnection.createStatement();
    iResultSet =
        stmt.executeQuery(
          "SELECT kind,heatlevel,price FROM pepper");
    saveQueryData();
    stmt.close();
  } catch (Exception e) {
    e.printStackTrace();
  }
}
```

The init() method sets the size of the applet to 300 x 300 pixels. It then connects to the database and creates an instance of Statement for accessing data in the database. The Statement is then used to retrieve the kind, heatlevel and price of all the peppers in the Pepper table. The query data is saved, and the Statement is closed. Once again, if something fails, the exception generated is caught, and a stack trace of it is printed.

```
public void paint(Graphics g) {
  int line;
  int kindColumn  = 10;
  int levelColumn = 85;
  int priceColumn = 135;

  g.drawString("Kind", kindColumn, 30);
  g.drawString("Level", levelColumn, 30);
  g.drawString("$/lb", priceColumn, 30);

  g.drawLine(kindColumn, 45, kindColumn+65, 45);
  g.drawLine(levelColumn, 45, levelColumn+40, 45);
  g.drawLine(priceColumn, 45, priceColumn+25, 45);
```

```
    line = 60;
    for (int i=0; i<iQueryData.size(); i++) {
      String[] row = (String[])iQueryData.elementAt(i);
      g.drawString(row[0], kindColumn, line);
      g.drawString(row[1], levelColumn, line);
      g.drawString(row[2], priceColumn, line);
      line += 15;
    }
  }
```

The paint() method is used to draw the applet. The information retrieved using the previous method is displayed.

```
private void saveQueryData() throws SQLException {
  while (iResultSet.next()) {
    String[] row = new String[3];
    row[0] = iResultSet.getString(1);
    row[1] = iResultSet.getString(2);
    row[2] = iResultSet.getString(3);
    iQueryData.addElement(row);
  }
}
```

The saveQueryData() method goes through the ResultSet of the query sequentially and the values of each kind as a separate String in an Array of Strings. Each Array is added to the Vector that stores the query data. The method generates an SQLException if something fails.

```
private void connectDB() throws SQLException {
  // Prepare the connection URL
  String server = "hj7006e";
  String port = "1300";
  String db  = "PEPPER";
  String url = "jdbc:db2://"+server+":"+port+"/"+db;
  // Set the user and password
  String userid = "mkomis";
  String password = "ncc";
  System.out.println("Connecting to the DB");
  iConnection = DriverManager.getConnection(url, userid,
password);
  }
}
```

The connectDB() method connects to the database. The server name, port ID and database name are used to put together the URL. The URL, the user ID and

the password are then used to access the database. The method generates an
SQLException if the connect fails.

The following must be placed in an HTML file in order to test the applet.

```
<applet code=DbAptNet.java width=300 height=300>
</applet>
```

Either a Java-enabled browser or the Applet Viewer can be used to test the applet.
The output when using the Applet Viewer is shown below.

Kind	Level	$/lb
Habanero	300000	1.45
Serrano	10000	1.25
Jalapeno	5000	0.99
Bell	0	0.75

Applet Viewer: DbAptNet.java

The example concludes the discussion of the possibilities that exist when using
JDBC.

JSQL

Embedded SQL provides a second possibility for accessing relational databases.
Embedded SQL, also known as static SQL, allows SQL statements to be placed
directly in the code, whereas the JDBC, also known as dynamic SQL, is essentially

an interface for passing strings to a database as SQL commands. There are advantages and disadvantages to both.

Dynamic SQL is more flexible than embedded SQL because an application can generate the strings at runtime. However, for those applications that do not need the flexibility of being able to generate SQL at runtime, embedded SQL offers some important advantages. Since the SQL statements are fixed in the code, they can be error-checked at development time. In addition, the statements can be pre-compiled at runtime for faster execution. The JSQL source is smaller than corresponding JDBC code, and it offers more possibilities for optimization. In addition, variables and methods in Java can derive their types from SQL queries and tables, potentially removing the need for code that parses object keys and casts data from a database to a type based on those object keys.

JSQL is essentially a set of clauses that allow SQL statements to be placed in the Java source code as expressions and statements. Examples of SQL statements that are supported include (the list is not meant to be exhaustive):

- Queries: SELECT statements

- Data manipulation: INSERT, UPDATE and DELETE statements

- Transaction control: COMMIT and ROLLBACK statements

- Data definition: CREATE and DROP statements

- Stored procedures

- Stored functions

- Session commands

A JSQL translator generates Java code from the SQL clauses. The code that is generated allows the application to access a database through a call interface. During translation, the SQL statements are analyzed. Syntax-checking is performed on the SQL statements. Type-checking is done to ensure that the data exchanged between Java and SQL is type compatible and converted correctly. Schema-checking is done to ensure that the SQL statements are valid in the database schema where they are run. The translation can be done in different ways. A JSQL translator can be integrated directly into the a Java development environment; the translation can also be done by a standalone JSQL translator. For the special case where Java is supported as a stored procedure language on an RDBMS, the JSQL translator can be integrated with the Java and SQL compilation.

Embedded SQL already exists for languages such as C, FORTRAN, COBOL, and ADA. Java differs from other "host languages" in various ways.

- Java is portable across a wide range of platforms. Thus, database applications written in Java that make use of JSQL automatically benefit from being portable to a range of platforms.

- A JSQL translator written in Java can be written in such a way that code can be generated that is optimized for specific databases by making use of reusable code specific to the database.

- Java provides automatic memory management known as garbage collection. As a result, it is no longer the developer's responsibility to manage the memory for data retrieved from a database. This eliminates a common source of errors in other languages.

Currently, JSQL is still in the proposal stage. The goal is to have an ANSI definition for JSQL. It is being developed by IBM, Oracle and Tandem.

Standard API for Object Databases

The standard API for object databases is currently under development by the ODMG, the Object Database Management Group. The idea is similar to the one that led to the creation of the SQL standard for relational databases. The goal is to produce a set of specifications which will enable applications to access and manipulate information stored in object databases in a uniform manner. However, the task is made more difficult by the lack of a de facto language for object databases. As part of the API, an object database standard for Java is planned. The overriding goal in providing the ability to connect to object databases from Java is that "the programmer should perceive the binding as a single language for expressing both database and programming operations, not two separate languages with arbitrary boundaries between them." Although the entire API is only expected to become available sometime in 1997, the Java standard will be released earlier.

The ODMG has established the following principles for an object database standard for Java:

- *Transparency*: No changes to the Java source code are required to make instances of existing classes persistent.

- *Reachability*: Any objects that can be reached from the root objects in the database are automatically made persistent on transaction commit.

- *Multiple possible implementations*: A binding from Java to an object database can be implemented by preprocessing Java source code, by postprocessing Java byte code, or by using an enhanced Java interpreter.

- *Consistency*: Binding to an object database from Java is consistent with established Java syntax, practice and style. Java and the object database share a single, unified type system. The binding respects the automatic memory management implemented by Java. Objects become persistent when they are referenced by other persistent objects in the database and are removed from the database when they are no longer referenced by persistent objects.

- *Full support for ODMG object model*: The ODMG is adding classes to the Java environment such as collections, relationships, transactions, and databases in order to be able to fully support the ODMG object model.

The current definition includes a Java Object Definition Language, a Java Object Manipulation Language and a Java Object Query Language.

Serialization

An alternative method for storing objects in databases is to use the capability of databases to store binary information. Serialization can be used to create a stream representation of an object. The byte stream can be stored in a table in the database. The table that will contain the object only needs the identifier column and a binary column long enough to keep the stream representation of the object. This approach is valid for objects with or without references to other objects because relationships are automatically maintained by the serialization process. The implementation is easier than directly mapping each object field to a column because serialization is used to create a representation of the object and restore all the objects and relationships. The ability to attach a stream to database binary fields makes the use of the serialization mechanism very simple. Since it needs a stream to read from and write to, it can use the stream attached to the database field in order to access the field directly.

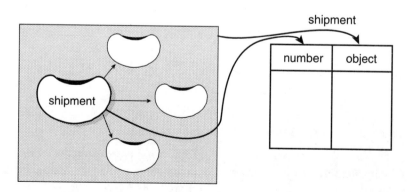

Only Java applications will be able to use the information stored in this table. If other programs, written in other languages, need to access the information, a Java bridge needs to be written just to load the rows and provide the information in a format that the other application can understand.

Serialization provides an additional "lightweight" alternative for making beans persistent. When a bean is told to serialize itself, a byte stream representation of the current state of the bean is produced. The byte stream can be written to a file for example. The file can be read in order to recreate the object. Serialization must be initiated by the programmer in the application. Serialization used in this way offers no support for concurrency, locking, rollback, and similar features typically associated with databases. Serialization has been covered in detail earlier in the book. Please refer to Chapter 3 for more information.

Conclusion

In this unit we have covered the four types of possibilities for making a Java application or applet persistent and/or for accessing legacy databases. Of the possibilities discussed, JDBC offers the most concrete approach. The other options are not yet fully developed, or in the case of serialization, they are not an "equal" alternative.

Printing

Printing is another functionality that is commonly used in the enterprise environment. Printing from Java is very straightforward. Java makes use of the operating system resources in order to print. Because of the security restrictions on untrusted applets for accessing operating system resources, it is currently not possible to print from an untrusted applet. However, applications and signed applets are able to print. In this unit, we discuss how to print using the operating system resources. As an example, we will show how to print the `HelloPepper` bean that was developed at the end of Chapter 2.

Printing Framework

Printing in Java is very similar to drawing images, graphics and text on the screen. In general terms, a `PrintGraphicsContext` object replaces the `GraphicsContext` used when rendering to the screen. Objects can render transparently to the printing device or to the screen by using their `print(Graphics aGraphics)` or `paint(Graphics aGraphics)` methods. Depending on the type of graphics context that is passed as a parameter when one of the above methods is called, an object will render either to the screen or to the print device. This is a very elegant solution, particularly if true WYSIWYG (What You See Is What You Get) is an issue. Those objects that want to profit from true WYSIWYG need only define `paint(Graphics aGraphics)`, for example, which can be used to render to the screen or to the print device. Those objects that want or need to know where they are rendering to can simply ask the graphics context which was passed as a parameter if it implements the `PrintGraphics` interface. If it does, then the print device is the current rendering target; otherwise the screen is the target. The `PrintGraphics` interface provides a graphics context, an object from the `Graphics` hierarchy, with the ability to communicate with the operating system printing resources.

The most important object in the printing process is the `PrintJob`. `PrintJob` is an abstract class that initiates and executes the printing. Instances of `PrintJob` provide access to the print graphics context mentioned above. An instance of `PrintJob` is obtained from the toolkit using `getPrintJob(Frame f, String jobTitle, Properties props)`. All three parameters are optional. The parameter `jobTitle` is a string that describes or names the print job. The `Properties` parameter `props` can be used to pass in platform-dependent property values for the print job, such as a printer name, page orientation or page order. When a print job is initiated, any operating system-specific print dialogs for configuring the print job are displayed. It is currently not possible to extend the native print dialogs or to override them with custom print dialogs. When the `getPrintJob()` method returns, the print job has been configured to the user's input. A print graphics context can be obtained by sending `getGraphics()` to the print job. In addition to providing the print graphics context, the `PrintJob` also provides access to the current printing properties such as the dimensions of a page in pixels or the resolution of the page in pixels.

The print graphics context returned by the print job represents a single page. However, it is the application's responsibility to handle pagination. The application can use the parameters that are available from the print job to determine the size of a page and decide when it is necessary to start a new page. When the current page is complete, sending `dispose()` to the print graphics context will flush the page to the print device. In order to render an additional page, a new print graphics context must first be obtained by using the method `getGraphics()`.

Once a print graphics context has been obtained, the actual rendering can be done by sending the component to be rendered the message `print(Graphics aGraphics)` or `paint(Graphics aGraphics)` as described above. A hierarchy of components such as a window containing numerous widgets can be rendered by sending `printAll(Graphics aGraphics)` to the root of the hierarchy. The hierarchy is traversed, and each descendant is sent the `print(Graphics aGraphics)` method in turn. The default implementation of `print(Graphics aGraphics)` simply calls a component's `paint(Graphics` aGraphics) method. If the print() method has not been overridden, then the component will render itself on the print device in the same way that it renders itself on the screen.

Printing Example

In order to illustrate the concepts presented above, we now show how to print the simple HelloPepper bean we created in Chapter 2. We create a window containing the bean and a pushbutton. When the button is pushed, the bean is printed.

The first step is to create the window containing the bean and the pushbutton. We begin by defining the class PepperPrint as a subclass of Frame. Using our favorite editor, we write the following:

```
package HelloPepper;

import java.awt.*;
import java.awt.event.*;
/**
 * The PepperPrint class displays the HelloPepper bean along
 * with a pushbutton "Print". When the button is pressed, the system
 * printing resources are used to print the bean.
 */
public class PepperPrint extends Frame implements
ActionListener {
private  HelloPepper pepper;
```

We implement the ActionListener interface in order to be able to react when the print pushbutton is pressed. When the button is pressed, an Action event is generated. By registering itself as a listener for events generated by the pushbutton, the window is able to react when an event is detected. We have defined an instance variable pepper of type HelloPepper to hold on to the bean. We have placed the PepperPrint class in the same package as the HelloPepper bean for the sake of convenience.

The next step is to define a constructor for our window. We will build a simple window using a BorderLayout layout manager to arrange the components. A BorderLayout works by positioning four components against the four edges of the container and positioning another component in the center. The component in the center receives the remaining space. The default layout manager for a Frame is BorderLayout; so we do not need to set it explicitly.

```
/**
 * Create an instance of a PepperPrint object.
 */
public PepperPrint() {
    this.super("Print a Pepper");
    HelloPepper hPepper = new HelloPepper();
    hPepper.setSize(300, 300);
    this.setPepper(hPepper);
    this.add("Center", this.getPepper());
    Button printButton = new Button("Print");
    printButton.setActionCommand("print");
    printButton.addActionListener(this);
    this.add("South", printButton);
    this.pack();
}
```

We first instantiate a `HelloPepper` bean and set it to the desired size of 300 x 300 pixels. We then set the instance variable `pepper` to point to it. We add the bean to the window and place it in the center position. The pushbutton is instantiated with the label "Print." The command name of the action event generated by the pushbutton is set to "print." We add the window as a listener on the pushbutton in order to catch the action event when it is fired by the pushbutton. The pushbutton is placed along the lower edge of the window. The `pack()` method simply tells the frame to take advantage of all the available space by packing its components together as tightly as possible.

The next step is to define what happens when the action event fired by the pushbutton is received by the window. We would like the window to react by telling the bean to render itself to the current print device.

```
/**
 * The actionPerformed method is invoked when the print button
 * is depressed. The system printing resources are used to print
 * the pepper.
 * @see #PepperPrint
 */
public void actionPerformed(ActionEvent event) {
    String command = event.getActionCommand();
    PrintJob printJob;
    Graphics printGraphics;
    if (command.equals("print")) {
        printJob = this.getToolkit().getPrintJob(this, "Print a
Pepper", null);
        if (printJob != null) {
            printGraphics = printJob.getGraphics();
            if (printGraphics != null) {
```

```
            this.getPepper().printAll(printGraphics);
            printGraphics.dispose();
        }
        printJob.end();
      }
   }
}
```

We begin by defining local variables for the command contained in the action event for the print job and for the print graphics context. We then check to make sure the command is actually the print command. If it is, we ask the toolkit for a print job with the name "Print a Pepper." If the print job is valid, we get a print graphics context for a new page. If the print graphics context is valid, we tell the bean to render itself and all its components on the print graphics context that we pass along as the parameter. We do this by sending the bean the `printAll(Graphics aGraphics)` message. As described above, `printAll(Graphics aGraphics)` sends the bean the `print(Graphics aGraphics)` message. Since the print method is not overridden in `HelloPepper`, the `paint(Graphics aGraphics)` method is invoked as in the Chapter 2. We then send the print graphics context the message `dispose()` in order to flush the page to the print device. The print job is informed that we are finished by using `end()`.

The following methods are included for completeness. The get and set methods for the `pepper` instance variable are self-explanatory. The `main()` method is called when the code is run. It creates an instance of the `PepperPrint` window, sets it to 350 x 400 pixels and tells it to display itself.

```
/**
 * Return the value of the pepper variable.
 * @see #setPepper
 */
public HelloPepper getPepper() {
    return pepper;
}

/**
 * Start the PepperPrint object.
 * @see #PepperPrint
 */
public static void main(String args[]) {
    PepperPrint aPepperPrint = new PepperPrint();
    aPepperPrint.setSize(350, 400);
    aPepperPrint.show();
}
```

```
/**
 * Set the value of the pepper variable to an instance of
HelloPepper.
 * @see #getPepper
 */
public void setPepper(HelloPepper aPepper) {
    pepper = aPepper;
}
```

The resulting window is shown below.

Conclusion

The printing framework is a very straightforward framework which makes use of the platform printing resources. Printing is very much like drawing on a screen. For applications and applets that do not want to worry about printing, the process can be made transparent. The same methods which are used to render the object on the screen can be used to render the object on the print device.

Chili Con Carne
(Chili with Meat)

Market Basket:

1/2 cup chopped onion. 1/2 teaspoon garlic salt. 1 pound ground beef. 1/2 teaspoon salt. 2 cups tomato sauce. 1/4 cup red chili powder. 2 cups pinto beans. 2 cups water, approximately. One black chocolate square. 1/2 teaspoon cumin. Olive oil.

How to:

Fry onion and beef in a medium-sized skillet at medium heat until beef is browned. Add the cumin, mix it. Drain.

Add remaining ingredients and simmer at low heat for approximately 30 minutes.

Additional Topics

▼ PACKAGING BEANS, APPLETS AND APPLICATIONS

▼ SECURITY AND BEANS

▼ VISUAL DEVELOPMENT ENVIRONMENTS

The purpose of this chapter is to introduce the reader to additional topics that could be of interest in an enterprise environment. Most of these topics are not directly integrated or applied to the application. We discuss how to build and use compound beans, beans that are themselves made up of other beans. We also discuss the reuse of beans, how to make beans available to others and accessing and using third-party beans. In discussing special purpose beans, we provide an example of a bean that was instrumental in the making of this book. It does not contain any "business knowledge"; rather, it is a bean that converts text written in HTML format to a BookMaster format. In addition, an overview will be provided of the various builder tools currently available that support the use of beans.

Packaging Beans, Applets and Applications

By now you know how to create class files and beans and run them as applets and applications. It is time to learn how to package your beans. You could, of course, distribute all your different class files and resource files, but that might not be the best way to do it.

In the JDK 1.1 one of the new features introduced was JAR files. JAR is short for Java Archive, and in that file you can bundle all the files used by your beans.

JAR Files

The JAR file is a way to bundle class files and resources needed by applets. It has the same format as a zip file, and the files in it are compressed. A JAR file might contain class files (`.class`), serialized beans (`.ser`), images (`.gif`), or any other type of file that will be used by the applet.

Suppose that an applet needs image files and sound files. The developer of the applet can put all these resource files into one single JAR file. When a Web browser downloads the applet, it gets the whole JAR file in one http transaction. Later on, when the applet is referring to other classes or resources, the browser will check the JAR file before doing another http `GET` from the Web server. This improves download time, and it makes it easy to distribute an applet with the corresponding resources as one file.

```
<applet code=Pepper.class
              archive="PepperJar.jar"
              width=200 height=200
<param name=pepper value="Habanero"
</applet>
```

In the sample above, you can see that the name of the applet is `Pepper`, just as you specify it without a JAR file. The archive parameter is where you point to the JAR file containing the `Pepper.class`. The `param name=pepper` is a parameter we send to the `Pepper` class. So in this case, when the applet is downloaded from the Web server to your Web browser, you get the `PepperJar.jar` file. This JAR file contains the `Pepper.class` and all the files that are needed by the Pepper applet, all in one transaction from the Web server.

When the Pepper applet refers to a resource that is not in the JAR file, the browser will open a connection to the Web server and try to load it from the relative `codebase` of the `Pepper.class`. If the `codebase` is not specified in the applet tag, the directory from which the HTML page was loaded will be used. Below you see a sample where we specify the `codebase` for our classes and resources.

```
<applet code=Pepper.class
              codebase="../PepperCode"
              archive="PepperJar.jar"
              width=200 height=200
<param name=pepper value="Habanero"
</applet>
```

You can also include more than one JAR file in the archive parameter. This is done by comma-separating each entry.

```
<applet code=Pepper.class
            codebase="../PepperCode"
            archive="PepperJar.jar, Habanero.jar,
            Serrano.jar, Jalapeno.jar, Bell.jar"
            width=200 height=200>
<param name=pepper value="Habanero">
</applet>
```

There are classes in Java that will assist you in exploring zip and JAR files. You find these classes in the `java.util.zip` package. Note that there is no need for you to use these classes in your applet to benefit from the JAR files. The applet loader automatically looks into the JAR files that are specified in the `archive` statement.

A JAR file also consists of one manifest file, and it may also contain signature files. Signed applets are shipped in JAR files. Let us start with how you create the JAR file; then we will talk more about manifest and signature files.

If you think of a bottle of vodka as the JAR file, and a habanero as a bean, you are on your way to the *Traditional Swedish Habanero Vodka*. It is very easy to make. Choose your favorite kind of vodka and pick your favorite habanero, preferably a red or orange one, since they look very nice in the bottle. Slice the habanero and put the slices in the bottle; do not remove the seeds. Let the habanero stay in the bottle as long as needed, but after a week or two, you will find a very nice tropical smell when you smell the contents. You can leave the habanero in the bottle until the vodka is finished. In Sweden it is used to handle long cold dark nights during winter. It works very well during bright summers also.

The JAR Command

The command used to create a JAR file is `jar`.

The command

```
jar -cf Pepper.jar Pepper.class iconpepp.gif
            habanero.gif serrano.gif jalapeno.gif bell.gif
```

will create a JAR file named `Pepper.jar`. It will contain the `Pepper` class and the five GIF files that are listed. To check the contents of a JAR file, you can enter the command

```
jar -t < peppsec.jar
```

It will return the list of files to the screen. For example:

```
Pepper.class
iconpepp.gif
habanero.gif
serrano.gif
jalapeno.gif
bell.gif
```

Adding the v parameter will cause the `jar` command to generate verbose output; so

```
jar -tv < peppsec.jar
```

will display:

```
 919 Tue Apr 08 18:19:56 CDT 1997 META-INF/MANIFEST.MF
3215 Tue Apr 08 18:19:54 CDT 1997 Pepper.class
1711 Wed Apr 02 15:33:16 CST 1997 iconpepp.gif
3081 Fri Apr 04 18:18:08 CST 1997 habanero.gif
1989 Fri Apr 04 18:18:30 CST 1997 serrano.gif
1711 Wed Apr 02 15:33:16 CST 1997 jalapeno.gif
1254 Fri Apr 04 18:03:18 CST 1997 bell.gif
```

When we want to add manifest file information for our JAR file, we add the m parameter and specify the file containing manifest information as the third parameter. The first parameter is still the options for the `jar` command, and the second parameter is the target JAR file.

```
jar -cfm PepperJar.jar Pepper.mf Pepper.class iconpepp.gif
              habanero.gif serrano.gif jalapeno.gif bell.gif
```

The content of the manifest file, `Pepper.mf`, is as follows:

```
Manifest-Version: 1.0

Name: Pepper.class
Java-Bean: True
```

We will explain more about manifest files a little later.

Here we summarize the command line options for the `jar` command that we use.

c   Create a new JAR file.

f   Specify the name of the JAR file.

m   Include manifest information from a manifest file.

t   List the contents of the JAR file.

v   Generate verbose output.

Manifest Files

We do not intend to cover all the details about manifest files and the specifications and standards that relate to them. Instead we choose to give you enough information so you can get started with packaging your applets into JAR files and using your beans in the Bean Box and with other such tools.

There is one manifest file in each JAR file. The file name for the manifest file is META-INF/MANIFEST.MF. In the beginning of that file, we add the version number.

```
Manifest-Version: 1.0
```

Information in the manifest file is grouped in what is called *name: value* pairs. You separate each 'name: value' with an empty line. This grouping is called *sections*.

In our examples we use manifest files to tell the Bean Box which class files that are beans in the JAR file. Each file is put in a separate section. The name of the file should include the relative path within the archive. So in the example below, you see the relative path to our `Security.Pepper.Pepper.class`.

```
Name: Security/Pepper/Pepper.class
Java-Bean: True
```

A file name may not appear twice in the manifest file. If you want to add more information about a file, you put all information in the same section. Note that we use forward slashes, and not backslashes, in the file name.

Signature Files

In the JAR file you may also find signature files. Like the manifest file, they are stored with the relative path META-INF, and they have the extension .SF. So, for example, a signature file may be called META-INF/JALAPENO.SF. It is a binary file, generated by the `JavaKey` command. You can read a little more about `JavaKey` in the Security and Beans section and the signed applet example.

Signature files are used to validate files in the archive. We will not go into detail about either cryptographic algorithms or signature files. But since these sections

may appear in a manifest file, we will talk about them briefly. They may look like the following example for the `Pepper.class` entry in the manifest file.

```
Name: Security/Pepper/Pepper.class
Digest-Algorithms: MD5
MD5-Digest: C2iY7XFrKwNJgMpnU6NfKA==
```

The `Digest-Algorithms` tell you which algorithms to use when calculating the value. In this example we use the `MD5` algorithm. This in turn points to the `MD5-Digest`, followed by the calculated value to which the checksum of our file is compared. Please note that you don't have to enter the MD5-Digest information by yourself. It is put there by the `JavaKey` command.

In the next chapter, we provide a signed applet sample, and in that sample we make use of these algorithms (all generated by the `JavaKey` command).

We should also tell you that there is a non-alcoholic version of our Traditional Swedish Habanero Vodka, and in this recipe you simply leave the vodka out of the picture. Just slice the habanero, and eat it as it is. It has a wonderful taste! And it is guaranteed to take away potential colds or flus. And remember that after slicing the habanero, you need to be very careful about which parts of your body you touch! The authors are talking from their own experience in this matter.

Conclusion

In this chapter you have learned that a JAR file is the preferred way to package an applet. All the resources needed by an applet can be put into one JAR file. It has the same format as a zip file, but in addition a JAR file contains a manifest file with information about its contents, and a JAR file may also contain signature files if you want to turn your applets into signed applets.

JAR files are loaded by the applet loader when the archive parameter is specified in the HTML applet tag.

Security and Beans

Security is a wide topic and could mean many different things depending on the view of the reader or the author.

In this book, we talk about applet security that is implemented in a Web browser. Applet security provides mechanisms to protect the resources from being manipulated on the client machine. That could mean reading or writing files, opening socket connections with other hosts and so on. This chapter covers signed applets. Using signed applets releases some of the security protection mechanisms that are used when running your Java code as an applet.

Security could also be the way to provide access control to different functions or resources in beans. This is called authentication. Usually, you provide a user ID and a password in order to get access to these kinds of protected resources.

There are three different packages in the JDK 1.1 that are related to security.

1. The `java.security` package contains classes and interfaces for handling certificates, principals, keys, signers, and so on. The functionality of these classes and interfaces are related to the functions you will see later on when we turn an applet into a *signed applet*.

2. The `java.security.acl` package contains interfaces for handling group, owner and permission relationships mostly on files and directories.

3. The `java.security.interfaces` package contains interfaces for handling DSA (Digital Signature Algorithm). DSA is defined in NIST's FIPS-186.

In the JDK, you will find an abstract class called `java.lang.SecurityManager`. The purpose of the `Security Manager` class is that in your application you can add security checking before doing certain operations. You might want to check in which environment your Java code is running and act based on that. There is one security manager involved when running applets and another one when using Remote Method Invocation (RMI).

In this chapter, we talk about how you can remove some of the security mechanisms that are provided by the security managers for applets. You do this by telling the security manager that you trust the source from which the applet is downloaded. That is, in other words, a signed applet.

Signed Applets

A signed applet is an applet that is loaded from a source that you consider as trusted. A signed applet has fewer restrictions in accessing the file system, network ports or other resources in the client.

Signed applets are useful when you want to remove some of the security mechanisms that are used by web browsers for applets. The security manager provided for applets is more strict than when you run your Java programs standalone on the client as applications loaded from the file system of the client. The Java Virtual Machine will, by default, not let you load your applet from one Web server and let it connect to another server, for instance. This is a feature you might miss when using database servers, transaction servers and so on. You do not want to be forced to run a transaction or database server on the same physical machine as your Web server just to bypass that restriction with applets.

You might also want to be able to read or write files on the local disk of the client. This is not permitted for a standard applet, but by making the applet signed, you will be able to do it.

So in order to let the applet be more free, there is a way to relieve the applet from these constraints. In a simple way, this is done by telling the Web browser that this specific applet came from a trusted source. This allows the applet to access these restricted resources in our local client.

The Signed Pepper Applet

In this example, we will introduce another version of the `Pepper` class. It needs to be able to write a file on your local disk. It will write a message to you in the file that you specify as a parameter to the applet. The HTML file that loads the applet looks like this:

```
<applet code=Pepper.class
                codebase="./."
                archive="PeppSec.jar"
                width=200 height=200>
<param name=file          value="/Pepper.Dat">
<param name=pepper value="Habanero">
</applet>
```

As you see, to this Pepper applet you can specify the *filename* as a parameter. We also specify the *kind* of Pepper as a parameter. So in this case, the file `Pepper.Dat` will be created in the root directory of your current drive. The kind of Pepper will be a habanero. We have not provided any error handling in our Pepper if you write the wrong names, so please be aware of that.

If you read this book online, you find the full source code of the example here. Some of the code is similar to the other examples we provide. We have done this example in a very simple way. When the `init()` method is invoked, we try to write a message to a file. If we succeed, we write a message to a `String` to inform the user about our successful operation. This string will be used later when we paint the window. If we catch an exception, we put the exception text in the string that will present the message to the user. The two exceptions we are checking for are the `java.lang.SecurityException` and the `java.io.IOException`.

```
        try {
                iDataOutputStream = new DataOutputStream(
                        new BufferedOutputStream(new
                           FileOutputStream(iFile)));
                iDataOutputStream.writeChars(
                        "Hello!" +
                        "This is the Pepper applet that is
                        writing to a file!" +
                        "The kind of Pepper is: " + getKind() );
                iDataOutputStream.flush();
                iMessage = "File " + iFileName + " written to
                        disk.";
        }
        catch (SecurityException e) {
                iMessage = "Security exception - " +
                              e.getMessage();
        }
        catch (IOException e) {
                iMessage = "I/O exception - " + e.getMessage();
        }
```

When we paint the Pepper, we first check the size of the window, then we draw a graphic that represents the kind of pepper. Together with the graphics, we draw the message in the window. Here is the code for that.

```
public void paint(Graphics g) {
        Dimension d = getSize();
        g.drawImage(iImgCurrent, 0, 0,
                                d.width, d.height - 15, this );
        g.drawString(iMessage, 10, d.height - 5);
   }
```

If the applet is not signed, you will catch the security exception. The window will then look like the following one.

The Security exception is thrown by the applet security manager. Web browsers do not let applets write files to the local drive. In order for the applet to write files to the disk, we need to make the applet trusted. That is, we need to make it a signed applet.

If we are trying to write to a file that is not writable, we get the I/O exception. The I/O exception could be because you specified a directory that does not exist. It can also be that a file already exists, and it is marked read only. Note that you can not get the I/O exception until the applet is trusted. That is because you need to pass the security check done by the applet security manager before being able to open the file. Not until then will you be able to reach the file system and catch possible error situations.

If we succeed in writing to disk, we notify the user by writing a line at the bottom of the applet.

File /Pepper.Dat written to disk.

To succeed in writing the file to the disk, you need to have the *certificate* that will be delivered by the authors of the applet. By importing this certificate into the identity database of the client, you consider the source of the applet to be trusted. Before understanding how to use the certificate, we explain some basic concepts you need to know in order to use this certificate file.

The Identity Database, Identities and Signers

If you look in your JDK directory, you will see a file called identitydb.obj. This is the Identity Database where information about identities and certificates is stored. It is in a binary format, so don't waste time looking into it. A system administrator can change the location of the Identity Database. That is done by editing the properties file, java.security, that is found in the lib/security directory in the relative path from where your JDK is installed. Add the property named identity.database, and specify the new location of the Identity Database. For example:

```
identity.database=/hot/peppers/are/good/for/you/pepper.obj
```

An *identity* is like a user ID. It could be a company name, a department name, or a user ID. In the example that we provide, we use the identity jalapenoteam. The identity is created in the Identity Database by using the command:

```
javakey -c jalapenoteam true
```

The c parameter tells JavaKey to create a new identity. The true parameter means that the identity is trusted. Trusted means that any applet signed by that identity has full access to your system once a certificate file with that identity is registered in the Identity Database. Specifying false, or omitting this parameter means that the identity is not trusted. An identity has one or more certificates that authenticates its public key. A public key is used to verify the signature of a JAR file.

A *signer* has more rights than an identity. In addition to public keys, it has private keys. A private key is used for signing applets. That means you do not want to expose your private keys to anybody. Keep them in a place with restricted access. The signer is created in the Identity Database by using the command:

```
javakey -cs jalapenoteam true
```

To list all the identities and signers in your Identity Database, you use the command:

```
javakey -l
```

The output will be something like this:

```
[Signer]jalapenoteam[identitydb.obj][trusted]

habaneroteam[identitydb.obj][not trusted]
```

Here you see that jalapenoteam is a signer that is trusted. On the second line, you see that habaneroteam is an identity that is not trusted. The output shows that habaneroteam is not a signer; it is an identity.

The Certificate File

The certificate file is the file you will distribute to the users of your applet. It needs to be registered in the Identity Database of the client system. Also, to be able to register the file, there needs to be an entry with the identifier that is used for the certificate file. The name of the identifier might be provided at the same time as the certificate file since it is needed before you can import the certificate file into the database. For details, see further on in this chapter in the next section, Step by Step to a Signed Applet.

When a user is downloading the signed applet, the applet security manager will check if the applet comes from a trusted source. That is, it checks to see if an entry exists in the Identity Database and if there is a certificate associated with that entry. The security manager will also calculate the checksums from the keys to check that they validate OK.

The certificate directive file in our example looks like this:

```
#
# Certificate directive file. Used to create certificate file.
#

issuer.name=jalapenoteam
issuer.cert=1

subject.name=jalapenoteam
subject.real.name=The Jalapeno Team
subject.org.unit=ITSO
subject.org=IBM
subject.country=Texas

start.date=1 Apr 1997
end.date=31 Dec 1999
serial.number=0001

signature.algorithm=DSA

out.file=jalapeno.cer
```

The `issuer` section contains information about the identity and which certificate to use. The `issuer.name` points to the name of the signer/identity. The `issuer.cert` points to the certificate number. To get a list of the all the certificates in the database, you can use the `javakey -ld` command. If you know the identifier you are looking for, you can use `javakey -li` identifier. For example: `javakey -li jalapenoteam`.

The `subject` section contains information about the subject: name, real name, organization, organization unit, country, and so on.

There is also a section related to the certificate. That section contains the start date, end date and serial number.

One section specifies which security algorithm to use. The `signature.algorithm` tells you that. In our case above, we use the default algorithm.

Notice the last statement of our sample certificate directive file. There you find the name of the certificate file that you distribute to clients so they can update their Identity Database.

Let's start the journey to creating the necessary files so users can make use of our signed applet.

Step by Step to a Signed Applet

Here is a step by step guide that will explain the different tasks you need to do before you can ship your signed applet. We explain which files that are used and how they relate to each other.

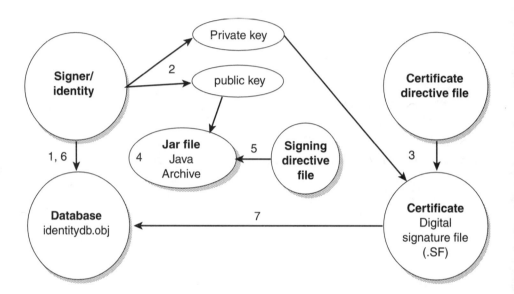

1. Create the `jalapenoteam` signer. Run the command:

    ```
    javakey -cs jalapenoteam true
    ```

    This will create an entry in the database file `identitydb.obj`. The output from the command will be:

    ```
    Created identity [Signer]jalapenoteam[identitydb.obj][trusted]
    ```

2. Create the public and private keys for the `jalapenoteam`. We call the files `jalapenoteam_pub` and `jalapenoteam_priv`. A public key is used to **verify** the signature of a JAR file, and a private key is used to **sign** the JAR file. Run the command:

    ```
    javakey -gk jalapenoteam DSA 512 jalapenoteam_pub
        jalapenoteam_priv
    ```

This tells the javakey to generate DSA (Digital Signature Algorithm) keys. The length of the key will be 512 bits. Once again, keep an eye on the file that contains the private keys! Store it in a safe place because in the wrong hands, it will be possible for bad guys to ship contaminated applets.

Successful execution will result in the following message:

```
Generated DSA keys for jalapenoteam (strength: 512).
Saved public key to jalapenoteam_pub.
Saved private key to jalapenoteam_priv.
```

3. The certificate file is needed by our users since they will import it into their Identity Databases. The file is created using the command:

```
javakey -gc jalapenocert
```

Check the certificate directive file to have a look at the format of it. Please note that the statement out.file in the certificate directive file specifies the filename of the certificate file you want to create. In our example, the name of the file will be jalapeno.cer.

After executing the command, and if everything went fine, JavaKey will tell you this:

```
Generated certificate from directive file jalapenocert.
```

It is the jalapeno.cer that you ship to the users of your applet.

4. Create the JAR file.

```
jar cfm PeppSec.jar pepper.mf Pepper.class *.gif
```

This will add the Pepper.class, the manifest file pepper.mf, and the graphics to the JAR file. Note that at this time, the archive is not signed. It is still an ordinary JAR file.

5. To sign the JAR file, you need a sign directive file.

The sign directive file we use in this example looks like this:

```
#
# JAR signing directive file. Used to sign a JAR file.
#

signer=jalapenoteam
cert=1
chain=0
signature.file=JALAPENO
```

In this file you need to specify at least four parameters.

- The identity of the `signer`. In our case it is `jalapenoteam`. This identity needs to be in the Identity Database.
- The `cert` parameter tells the number of the certificate. When you generate or import a certificate, you get a number assigned. You can view the certificate numbers by using the `javakey -ld` command. If you want to see certificates only for a specific signer, you use `javakey -li jalapenoteam` (in our case).

Generated certificate from directive file jalapenocert.

```
javakey -li jalapenoteam
Identity: jalapenoteam
[Signer]jalapenoteam[identitydb.obj][trusted]
                public and private keys initialized
                certificates:
                certificate 1
                  for  : CN=The Jalapeno Team, OU=ITSO, O=IBM,
                  C=Texas
                  from : CN=The Jalapeno Team, OU=ITSO, O=IBM,
                  C=Texas

                No further information available.
```

- The `chain` parameter is not used yet. It is reserved for future use, and should be set to 0.
- The `signature.file` parameter tells the name of the signature file. We specify JALAPENO here, which means that we will have a META-INF/JALAPENO.SF and a META-INF/JALAPENO.DSA file in the JAR file. The .SF is the signature file, and the .DSA is the file with the keys.

That is all the information that is needed in the file. To sign the JAR file, issue the command:

```
javakey -gs jalapenosign PeppSec.jar
```

This will create a file named `PeppSec.jar.sig`.

The output from the command:

```
Adding entry: META-INF/MANIFEST.MF
Creating entry: META-INF\JALAPENO.SF
Creating entry: META-INF\JALAPENO.DSA
Adding entry: Pepper.class
Adding entry: iconpepp.gif
```

```
Adding entry: habanero.gif
Adding entry: serrano.gif
Adding entry: jalapeno.gif
Adding entry: bell.gif
Signed JAR file PeppSec.jar using directive file jalapenosign.
```

Since the applet class loader works on *archive* files with the extension `.jar`, rename the file to `PeppSec.jar`.

Now you have your signed archive containing your applet, and you have a certificate file you can register in the Identity Database of the clients that will use your applet.

Steps to Do at the Client

1. Create identifier in the Identity Database. This is done by issuing the command:

```
javakey -c jalapenoteam
```

If this command executes without errors, the output is:

```
Created identity jalapenoteam[identitydb.obj][not trusted]
```

2. To import the certificate into your Identity Database, run the command:

```
javakey -ic jalapenoteam jalapeno.cer
```

Doing this results in this message:

```
Imported certificate from jalapeno.cer for jalapenoteam.
```

Having followed these steps, the clients where you have created the identity and imported the certificate file should now be able to run the signed applets. The signed applets should now have the same access as if they were executed locally as applications.

Having all these chili pepper-related names makes us feel hungry for a green *Tomatillo Salsa*. Grab a bunch of tomatillos, remove the husks and rinse them in water. Get some cilantro and chop it. Find a couple of green serranos. Mix the tomatillos, cilantro and serranos in a food processor. Add lime juice, and you might want some extra salt to taste. This is a very nice salsa to use with chips.

Conclusion

In this chapter we described what a signed applet is and how it can be used. You have also learned about how to use certificate files at the client.

Visual Development Environments

As stated at the beginning of the book, beans are defined as reusable software components that can be manipulated visually by using a visual development environment. The visual development paradigm has become more and more popular. Visual programming allows the developer to focus more on the business problem at hand. Visual programming allows the developer to assemble applications by manipulating and connecting reusable components visually. A code-generation engine within the environment generates the code corresponding to the connections that the developer has made visually. The code generation saves time and minimizes a potential source of bugs. Automatically generated code is rarely performance tuned. The emphasis is on stability and ease of generation, not on flexibility and speed. In those cases where performance is critical, automatically generated code may need to be performance tuned or replaced by something else. However, visual is not to be confused with easy. Contrary to much of the marketing brouhaha, visual programming cannot be used effectively without a solid working knowledge of the underlying programming language. Used properly and judiciously, visual programming is a promising and fascinating development paradigm. Visual programming allows a useful division of labor according to developer skills. Highly skilled and experienced developers can build and make available reusable components such as beans for other developers with more business knowledge and fewer technical skills to use to assemble into applications.

Visual development environments exist for a number of popular languages such as Smalltalk, C and C++, Basic and others. These environments vary widely in their features. Some are nothing more than enhanced GUI builders while others offer a full range of components and support for building complex and sophisticated client server applications. Although Java is still very new, there already exist a number of visual development environments for it. Some vendors have started from scratch while others have modified or extended existing products. Visual development environments for Java are not to be confused with tools that generate Web pages, even though such features may be integrated into certain environments. The purpose of this unit is to provide an overview of the products available at this time. The list is by no means exhaustive, nor is it intended to be used as a rating of the products currently available.

Java Workshop

Java Workshop is a Web-centric Java development environment from Sun written entirely in Java. The user interface is similar to existing Web browsers, so it is easy to understand. The user interface supports Web browser functions, including support for URL addresses. When Java Workshop is started, a Web page with a tool bar containing icons representing the tools in the environment is displayed. Each icon on the tool bar is actually a Java applet. When a tool is selected, a new Web page containing the tool is loaded into the browser.

Java Workshop is a complete toolset. It includes:

- Project Manager.

- Visual Java, a graphical GUI builder.

- A Source Editor for writing and viewing Java source code easily. It also supports automatic Java applet tag insertion into HTML pages.

- Build Manager, an easy-to-use make-and-compile facility. It supports automatic error location for faster debugging.

- A graphical Debugger which supports threads, variable evaluation, and breakpoint debugging.

- Source Browser, including a convenient hypertext-linked class hierarchy tree.

- Project Tester.

- Portfolio Manager, for creating, sharing and publishing Java projects, including applets across intranets and the Internet.

- Online hypertext-enabled documentation including tutorials.

Java Workshop is available for Wintel and Solaris platforms.

JBuilder

JBuilder from Borland is an application development environment for building Java applets and applications visually by using its Visual Designer (modeled after Delphi from Borland). It allows the development of projects ranging from content-rich, Web-delivered applets and applications that require client/server database connectivity to enterprisewide distributed computing solutions. It brings together visual development tools, support for JavaBeans and scalable database connectivity, including InterClient, the first JDBC/Net implementation from a major database vendor, thus giving developers a complete toolset for Internet/intranet development. It is an open and extensible environment.

JBuilder includes editing and browsing tools, easy-to-use Experts, fast compilers, a graphical debugger and extensive class libraries. Access to InterBase, Oracle, Sybase, SQL Server, Informix and Object Design ObjectStore PSE for Java, a high-performance object-oriented database, are supported. It also supports JDBC.

Borland is supporting key industry technologies for Java. It will include Open Environment's scalable middleware technology.

VisualAge for Java

IBM VisualAge for Java is the latest addition to the VisualAge family of visual development environments. In its current form, VisualAge for Java is very similar to VisualAge for Smalltalk. ENVY, the unmatched source code management tool for team development found in the Smalltalk version, forms the core of the Java version as well. VisualAge for Java can be used to develop 100% Pure Java-compatible applications, applets and JavaBeans. It can connect Java clients to existing server data, transactions and applications. This enables developers to extend server-based applications to communicate with Java clients on the Internet or intranet, rather than having to rewrite the application from scratch.

Currently, VisualAge for Java consists of two tools. The Interactive Development Environment (IDE) is the core. It contains the repository and source code management tools as well as a debugger and a visual development tool. Packages are grouped into projects. Numerous browsers are available for viewing and editing source code. The editors offer formatting and advanced error-checking facilities. Numerous wizards and templates aid in defining code. The repository and source code management tools make it virtually impossible to lose code. The version and change management tools are unequaled in their stability and ease of use. The debugger offers powerful capabilities for managing and debugging individual threads. It is possible to step through code at various levels of detail. Variable values and source code can be edited in the browser, and the thread being edited is automatically reset. Breakpoints can be set at the methods level. The visual development tool, the Composition Editor, is fully compatible with JavaBeans. Beans can be used to build applets as well as GUIs for applications. They can also be used to build non-visual beans containing program logic. Source code for instantiating the beans and the connections made between them is generated by the environment. A number of visual and non-visual beans are delivered with the product. The environment can be customized and extended using source code and beans from other developers and third-party vendors.

The second tool is Enterprise Access Builder (EAB). The EAB is a tool that uses and creates beans to provide access to enterprise data, transactions and applications. The beans can be incorporated into applets and applications using the IED. Currently, the EAB provides access to CICS transactions. Databases can be accessed using through ODBC by using a JDBC/ODBC bridge. A JDBC driver for DB2 is provided.

VisualAge for Java is currently available for Wintel and OS/2 platforms.

Visual Cafe Pro

Symantec was one of the first vendors to provide a visual development environment for Java. Symantec provides advanced Java debugging technologies, class and hierarchy browsing, fast Java and just-in-time (JIT) compilers, and visual design capabilities. With Visual Cafe, developers can quickly build sophisticated applications utilizing any of over 100 JavaBeans components. New technologies including two-way programming (round-tripping), live Java controls, and GUI layout management shorten the development process. Visual Cafe supports the industry standards, such as Sun's Java, JavaBeans, and JDBC standards. In addition, it supports Microsoft's Java Reference Implementation.

Visual Cafe contains a repository of components, the Component Library, that has its own built-in viewer, and a set of components including basic GUI elements and project templates (for example, applet, application, HTML file). Additional developer-built or third-party vendor components may be added as desired. For fast access to components, a Component Palette is provided in the form of a notebook. Visual Cafe provides three application templates: empty project, simple application, or simple applet. The latter two templates provide forms ready for filling in with controls, and prebuilt code for the About and Quit dialogs. A project and all its files get stored in a single directory. To prevent name conflicts, each project should be stored in a different directory. A project can be launched from within the IDE to test it.

For GUI building, Visual Cafe provides a Form Designer and a basic set of elements, such as buttons, scroll bars, text fields, and predefined dialogs. Elements can be dragged from the palette onto the form, and the necessary Java source code to instantiate the elements is generated. Events and listeners can be connected visually, and the code necessary for handling the connection is generated. Different types of forms, including applets, windows, message boxes and dialogs can be created. Properties of components are displayed in the Property List window. The property values can be dynamically modified in this window. Double-clicking on a component in the Form Designer, or selecting the Edit Source menu item from the pop-up menu for the component, will bring up a Source Editor window for the underlying Java source code. The Source Editor window is also used as the debugger window during project execution.

While debugging, it is possible to step over or into Java statements being executed. Breakpoints can be set on an expression. Individual threads can be executed, paused, or resumed. The calls, returns and variables for the current thread are visible. Variable values can be edited in the debugger. Remote debugging of an applet or application running on another machine is possible.

Visual Cafe incorporates database support. It uses Symantec's dbAnywhere technology to provide distributed database access from anywhere on the Web. dbAnywhere provides ODBC drivers as well as drivers for Sybase and Oracle databases. The JDBC API is supported and allows developers to connect Web pages to databases. Applets created by Visual Cafe communicate with the dbAnywhere server (through JDBC), creating a three-tier architecture (applet GUI client on the front end, dbAnywhere server in the middle tier, database server on the back end). At the moment, dbAnywhere is simply a translation layer between the JDBC and the native or ODBC database drivers. In upcoming releases Symantec plans to expand dbAnywhere to support business logic in the middle tier.

Visual Cafe is currently available for Wintel platforms.

Conclusion

The number of development tools available and the capabilities of those described above is sure to change rapidly. Almost all of the tools described offer a visual building tool together with beans that are ready to use. Most tools only provide visual beans. A few, such as VisualAge, even provide non-visual beans for enterprise features such as database and transaction access. Most offer integrated code browsing tools. The quality of the support provided ranges from very rudimentary to very professional. Some tools even offer support for team development, a very important feature for enterprise development projects.

Chicken and Sausage Jambalaya

The Market Basket:

1 pound sausage (sliced) or chorizo. 1 pound ground chicken. 2 medium onions (chopped). 1 bell pepper (chopped). 6 green onions (chopped). 2 garlic cloves (mashed). 1 small can tomatos (optional). 1 cup raw rice. 2 cups water. 1/2 cup wine (your choice). 1 medium can mushrooms (drained). 1 medium can green peas (drained). 2 tbs. olive oil. Salt, pepper, chili sauce.

Optional: Large prawns (gambas)

How to:

Brown chicken and sausage in oil in a large pot.

Remove meat and add onions, peppers, garlic, green onions to existing oil.

Cook until slightly browned and add salt, pepper, and hot sauce to taste. Cook for a few minutes longer, stirring in the seasoning.

Add chicken, sausage, water, wine, rice and bring to boil.

Add mushrooms, peas and tomato sauce and gambas.

Cover and simmer for approximately 45 minutes or until rice is tender.

Chapter 7

Examples Used
in the Book

The examples provided and discussed throughout the book are listed and summarized in this section for the sake of readers who would like to review, reuse or extend them, without going through the specific chapters with the introduction and progressive presentation of the concepts. After the simple "Hello Pepper" bean, the examples are grouped for the Events, the Property, the Serialization the Remote Method Invocation, the Introspection and the Signed Applet topics covered. Refer also to the specific chapter on the Chile Pepper Application and its associated artifacts for a wider sample of bean oriented development.

The Simplest HelloPepper Bean

Beans as Units of Reuse

This example shows usage of inherited behavior (from class `Canvas`) and interface implementation (of `Serializable`) for a bean named HelloPepper. The code described in the Build section for a simple bean is provided in the samples

directory HelloPepper. Unlike the other examples, this is not an applet or an application to run but simply a bean considered as a component to be manipulated in a graphical tool or a building tool (for instance, VisualAge for Java and the BeanBox).

This is the iconized form of the bean in the sample.

On the composition surface of a tool, the HelloPepper bean appears as in the figure below.

 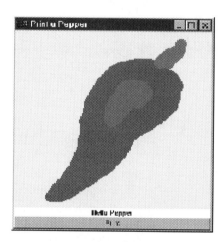

The view on the right is related to the printing functionality associated with the bean and is described in Chapter 5. The functionality extends the simple HelloPepper bean, and the related sample code is in the same directory.

Events or Notification Units

Intelligent Beans are Communicating with Each Other

This section summarizes the usages of events or notification units, for beans participating as event sources (Notifiers) and event listeners (Observers), with the examples from the Events section. The existing samples are distributed under subdirectories of the directory called Property, as follows:

1. In Events\PizzaExGUI: the first Events sample

2. In Events\PizzaExText: the second Events sample

Overview of the Two Events Samples

The first example (PizzaExText) shows the sequence of event observers (customers) notified when a pizza is available. At the availability of a pizza, the customers are notified, and if they are not currently eating a pizza slice already, they will start eating the new slice. These greedy customers are systematically eating the pizzas in four bites. The duration of each bite is implemented with a random value of less than three seconds.

The Pizza Events Sample Named PizzaExText

In this example the bakery has onepizza available every four seconds. Each customer eats four bites from a pizza and is then available to eat from another (new) pizza as soon as the availability of this new pizza is made known. When eating, they do not care about the availability (notification) of new pizzas. The four bites that each customer has of each pizza are counted and displayed here in the range of zero to three. A counter of the different pizza (shown as slice:) that each customer has eaten from is displayed (maybe for the final bill).

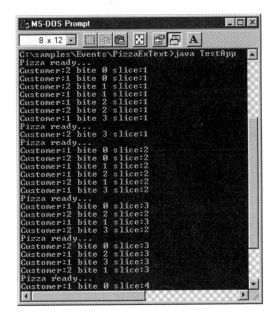

The Pizza Events Sample Named PizzaExGUI

The notification scheme of this sample is the same as the previous one (PizzaEx-Text): A PizzaEvent instance is sent to the instances of Customer (registered as listeners). What has been added is a Graphical User Interface (Panel) for a better perception of the concurrent activities of the notified customers. Here we have three concurrent customers. The bakery produces a pizza (read a pizza event) every six seconds. The next three captures of the application window will permit us to discuss the visual cues used. Refer to the Events section for the concepts and the code presentation.

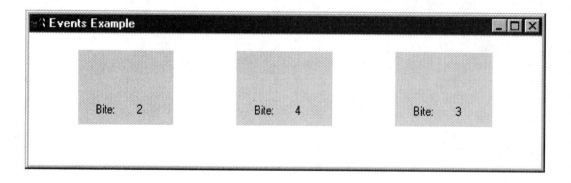

The three rectangles represent the three customers currently eating pizza. They each have four chances to take a bite of pizza (displayed in the range of 1 to 4). After the fourth bite, they want more, just like starving armadillos.

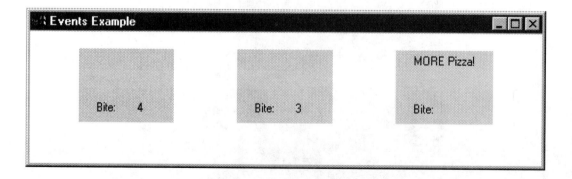

The "MORE Pizza!" label shows that a customer is waiting for a new pizza to be available in order to satisfy his/her appetite. When a new pizza event is notified, he/she will have a new first chance to take a bite at that fresh pizza.

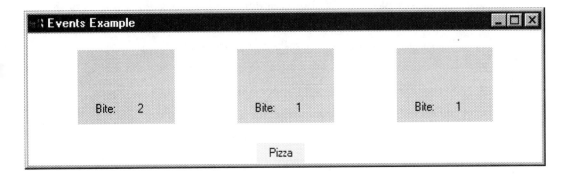

The availability of the new pizza occurs every six seconds and is displayed for less than two seconds as a yellow rectangle at the bottom so the user can see the event has occurred. At that moment, all the customers waiting for more pizza resume their meal.

Properties

This section summarizes the different types of views presented as examples throughout the Properties section. The Properties section is aimed at introducing to the reader the concepts of Property, their flavors, implementations and associated Property Editors. The examples used show how the two properties of the class Pepper are presented by default Property Editors and by specific Property Editors, both used by the PropertySheet component of the visual tool. Also, the BeanInfo role in this context is mentioned.

Here we will be presenting this example again, assuming the concepts are clearer, and focusing on the logical path through the four subsequent illustrations of Property Edition and through the associated sample code details. Each example is working with the same Pepper class presented as a bean. As for coffee, where a superior-tasting cup of coffee requires superior beans, a superior-handling visual tool of Java requires superior beans. Superior beans, which are high quality beans, have more than the appropriate accessor methods for their properties. They present specific BeanInfo-related classes, with specific Property Editors or specific Customizers.

For running the examples with the BeanBox, as illustrated, only the four .jar files are required. These do not contain the source code, which is kept separately in corresponding subdirectories. You may want to copy the JAR files (PeppDef.jar, PeppSimp.jar, PeppGUI.jar and PeppCust.jar) to your local BeanBox JARS directory (typically c:\BDK\jars).

The existing samples are distributed under subdirectories of the directory called Property, as follows:

1.   In Property\Default: the first Pepper bean sample

2.   In Property\Simple: the second Pepper bean sample

3.   In Property\GUI: the third Pepper bean sample

4.   In Property\Custom: the fourth Pepper bean sample

Overview of the Four Properties Samples

The first example (Default) shows the default behavior of properties when no Property Editor is specified and no `BeanInfo` or `Customizer` class is associated with the bean. A default PropertySheet appears with all the bean attributes that have a public getter or setter in the recognized format.

This second example (Simple) shows the default behavior of properties when elementary editors are provided for the two Pepper properties (`kind` and `heatlevel`) and are specified in the `BeanInfo` class (`PepperBeanInfo`).

The third example (GUI) shows the possibility of presenting a bean property in a specifically customized view referred to by the `BeanInfo` class associated with the bean and launched when clicking in the value of the property in the PropertySheet of the bean.

The fourth example (Custom) shows the possibility of presenting the properties in a fully customized way that can be separated from the PropertySheet. Control of synchronization of property values is illustrated as an example of the bean scope of the Customizer compared to the Property scope of individual Property Editors. The `PepperCustomizer` class provided for this behavior is referred to by the `BeanInfo` class (`PepperBeanInfo`).

The Pepper Bean Sample Named Default

This is the default case where no `PepperBeanInfo` class or Property Editors are written.

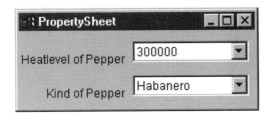

The BeanBox presents a PropertySheet for the Pepper class that shows kind and heatlevel and other properties that all have the right format of accessor methods. The right format makes them properties of the Pepper bean. The values set to attributes through the entry field are not controlled unless the application setter has the functionality.

The Pepper Bean Sample Named Simple

This simple case defines a PepperBeanInfo class with two property-specific editors: HeatEditor and KindEditor.

The BeanBox presents a PropertySheet with only the kind and the heatlevel properties both defined in property descriptors within the PepperBeanInfo class. The enhanced component layout (drop-down box) presenting the set of values for the property is due to the fact that the specific HeatEditor and KindEditor are provided with the getTags() method. Here, the entered values have the limited range provided with the choices visible in the drop-down box. Note that these specific editor classes are inheriting from the class java.beans.PropertyEditorSupport (which implements the Property Editor interface).

The Pepper Bean Sample Named GUI

This GUI-oriented case illustrates that Property Editors referred to in the PepperBeanInfo class can be fully customized widgets or widgets that extend other widgets.

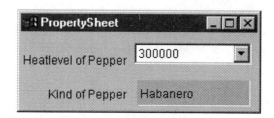

For example, the KindEditor for the kind property inherits from the AWT Panel. It also implements the Property Editor interface. The implementation of the Java-Beans Property Editor interface requires the support of specific features among which is the isPaintable() method meaning that the Property Editor is a graphical component.

This graphical component is the modal widget that shows up when clicking in the PropertySheet window on the value area of the "Kind of Pepper" property. It permits you to select the kind of pepper whose name is reflected in the PropertySheet and whose image is shown in the BeanBox. Note that the associated heatlevel remains unchanged and is not synchronized with the pepper selection. The responsibility for such synchronization between properties could be in the Pepper bean itself in a form of resetting heatlevel when setKind() is used. The scope of a Property Editor is to handle a single property; its role does not include property synchronization.

In fact, in this series of Pepper examples, the heatlevel is always bound to the specific type of pepper selected, and it is not really an independent attribute. Nevertheless, such a case where specific relationships or constraints have to be controlled in the interface, and not in the business object, may show up. The next sample (Property/Custom) shows that another component called a Customizer can be added for a wider control, global presentation and possible synchronization of the shown properties of a bean interface.

The Pepper Bean Sample Named Custom

This Customizer-oriented case illustrates the benefits of the `java.beans.Customizer` interface.

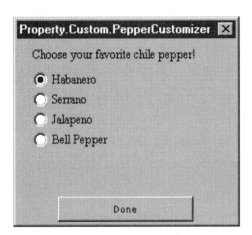

The sample shows again a default PropertySheet with no Property Editors for `kind` or `heatlevel`. The added functionality is not visible from the Property-Sheet, but is activated from the BeanBox Edit drop-down menu. When a Pepper bean of this sample is selected in the BeanBox, a new menu item named "Customize" shows up in the Edit drop-down menu. Clicking on this menu item opens the sample modal panel "Custom.PepperCustomizer" where a pepper selection can be made. The custom GUI layout of this example (Property/Custom) is identical to the one used in the previous example (Property/GUI).

The custom GUI layout or panel is called PepperCustomizer, and it also inherits from AWT Panel. As it can control all the relevant properties of a bean, it is the appropriate place to catch the events associated with a change of checkbox selection. When such a change event occurs, the PepperCustomizer sets the `kind` of the pepper to the one selected and sets the associated `heatlevel` to the corresponding value. Note that this setting of a secondary attribute does not have to be implemented here; this is just a convenient and reasonable place to put it. The other adequate place would be in the setter associated with the `kind` property. For example, this is done for the attribute `currentImage` of each pepper instance that is automatically updated when the `kind` of pepper is changing. Note that this attribute does not show up in the default PropertySheet because the accessor methods are kept private.

Serialization Styles

This section summarizes the different styles of serialization illustrated in the Serialization section.

The samples are parted under subdirectories of the directory called Serialization, as follows:

1. In Serialization\Serial: the default SimplePepper bean serialization

2. In Serialization\SerialControl: the second SimplePepper bean serialization

3. In Serialization\External: the third SimplePepper bean serialization

4. In Serialization\Version: the fourth SimplePepper bean serialization

Overview of the Four Serialization Samples

The next four examples show the conversion of a bean into a stream saved into a serialization file. The differences among these simple persistence examples are in the level of control needed in the serialization process. They progress from default to controlled or customized serialization, fully controlled externalization and versioning a class or bean.

The SimplePepper Bean Sample Named Serial

This SimplePepper bean implements the `Serializable` interface, and its serialization (by the method `serializePepper()` of the `SerPepper` class) is calling the default behavior for `writeObject(ObjectOutputStream)` invoked on the "serializable" `SimplePepper` instance.

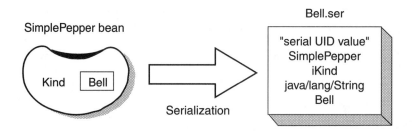

The SimplePepper Bean Sample Named SerialControl

This second SimplePepper bean implements the `Serializable` interface and its serialization (with the same method `serializePepper()` of the "serializable" `SerPepper` class) is calling the specific `writeObject(ObjectOutput-Stream)` of the `SimplePepper` class that additionally writes the date as a time-stamped value to the `ObjectOutputStream`.

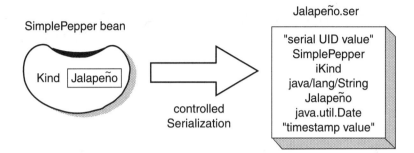

The SimplePepper Bean Sample Named External

This third SimplePepper bean implements the Externalizable interface. Here the serialization (with the same method serializePepper() of the SerPepper class) is calling the specific writeExternal(ObjectOutputStream) of the "externalizable" SimplePepper class that is in control of all that is written to the ObjectOutputStream after the Serial UID and the class name, which is the value ("Serrano") of the kind property.

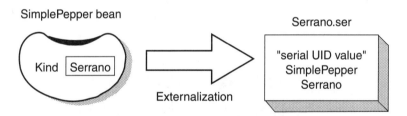

The SimplePepper Bean Sample Named Version

This fourth SimplePepper bean Serialization implementation illustrates the handling of the Serial UID value when a second version of a class has additional functionalities and needs to be compatible with serialized instances of the previous version and vice versa.

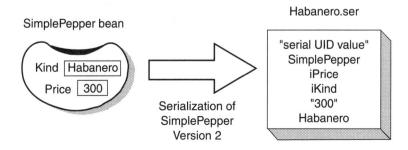

Persistency

As the armadillo collects pepper beans in a safe place for the winter, your application beans will need to be collected in a place to sleep at night. The type of place is your choice of persistency. This section summarizes the illustrations of file persistency covered in the Persistency section. You may want to refer as well to the file persistency aspects covered in the Serialization section.

The samples are parted under subdirectories of the directory called Persistency, as follows:

1.   In Persistency\drvlister: the first persistency-related sample

2.   In Persistency\Local: the second persistency-related sample

3.   In Persistency\Net: the third persistency-related sample

4.   In Persistency\DbODBC: the fourth persistency-related example

5.   In Persistency\applet: the fifth persistency-related example

The Persistency Sample Named DrvLister

This application helps to verify which drivers have become available for an application or applet. It loads some JDBC drivers, asks the `java.sql.DriverManager` class for the list of the registered drivers and displays their names as illustrated at the bottom line of the next figure.

The Persistency Sample Named DbLocal with a Local JDBC Driver

This example application loads the local DB2 JDBC driver
(COM.ibm.db2.jdbc.app.DB2Driver) and runs a SELECT statement on a DB2 sample Pepper database table. It then displays the output as presented next. The related exceptions that can occur are discussed in the Persistency section that also describes the configuration and runs of the example.

```
C:\Samples\Persistency\Local>java DbLocal
Connecting to the DB
Running the query: SELECT kind,heatlevel,price FROM pepper

Kind Level $/lb
-------- ------ -----
Habanero 300000 1.45
Serrano 10000 1.25
Jalapeno 5000 0.99
Bell 0 0.75
```

The Persistency Sample Named DbNet with a JDBC Net Driver

This is an example with no database client available on the local workstation. The local Java application relies on a specific DB2 Java client listener process on a port of the database server to be served. The output of the sample is identical to the previous sample (named DbLocal). Instead of loading the local DB2 JDBC driver, the Internet driver is to be used (COM.ibm.db2.jdbc.net.DB2Driver), and the connection URL, server and port must be set specifically as discussed in the Persistency section.

The Persistency Sample Named DbODBC with a JDBC-to-OBDC Bridge

This sample presents the simple connection string. The output of the sample is again identical to the previous samples (DbLocal and DbNet). Instead of loading a database-related driver, the JDBC-ODBC bridge driver is to be loaded (sun.jdbc.odbc.JdbcOdbcDriver). See the Persistency section for the needed change to the associated connection URL.

The Persistency Sample Named Applet

This sample illustrates the usage of a JDBC Internet driver for accessing the database. The applet first loads the JDBC driver (com.ibm.db2.jdbc.net.DB2Driver) from the local classpath or through an http get from the server, then issues the identical request on the Pepper table as in the previous three examples. For the applet implementation, there is a copy of the result in a local vector to support the

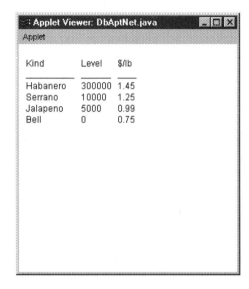

necessary screen repainting. The resulting applet view with the same information from the database is shown again.

Introspection

The introspection section provides an example branded the Descriptor application. The purpose of it is to use introspection on any available bean in order to display the bean's methods, properties and events.

The sample code is under the directory named Introspection.

The next screen capture shows the use of the Descriptor to view the Pepper bean features. The application requires only the `Pepper.class` to do the introspection.

The `PepperBeanInfo` class is not used for this default output. As soon as you compile the `PepperBeanInfo.java` into a `PepperBeanInfo.class` or as soon as a `PepperBeanInfo.class` is found according to the `CLASSPATH`, the output changes in function according to the specifications defined in the `Bean-Info` class. See the Introspection section for the sample output corresponding to the `BeanInfo`, which, for instance, hides the `kind` property.

Remote Method Invocation

The samples are parted under subdirectories of the directory called RMI, as follows:

1. In Rmi\App: the first RMI related sample

2. In Rmi\applet the second RMI related sample

3. In Rmi\Lookup: the third RMI related sample

Signed Applets

Authorized Beans Are to Be Trusted

In order for an applet to be granted more access rights and, for instance, to write on the local disk, it has to become a signed applet. This simple example from the Signed applets section that illustrates the security features (certificate, identity, signer) visualizes in the applet view the unsuccessful and successful operation of writing to a local file. The operation fails and raises a Security exception when the applet has not become trusted and does not present the appropriate credentials.

The sample code and files are under the directory named Signed.

Security exception - checkwrite

File /Pepper.Dat written to disk.

Chicken Curry with Apples

The Basket Market:

4-5 golden apples. 1 chicken cut in pieces. 2 onions. 1 tomato. 2 crushed garlic cloves. 1 cup of cooking cocomilk (without sugar). Cumin, pepper, salt, 3 teaspoons of curry paste. Olive oil. Fresh coriander leaves. Olive oil and butter.

How to:

Fry the chicken and chopped onions with a mix of olive oil and butter. Add cumin, pepper and salt. When cooked, add the garlic and the chopped tomato, mix. Add half a cup of water and the curry paste. When the liquid is starting to reduce add the cocomilk and the chopped apples. Cook until the apples are cooked. Top with the coriander leaves and serve with basmati rice.

Appendix A

Beans Coding Guidelines

We summarize in this section the Java and Beans Coding Guidelines used in the samples of this book. We present and motivate the conventions and requirements related to the usage of beans as used in the examples. The specific beans-related topics are labeled explicitly and explained in greater detail. For the Java-specific guidelines, we provide the commented series of the conventions we applied. At the end of the section, we refer to some specific coding guidelines documents currently available.

Comment Conventions

A JavaDoc comment (for automatic extraction by documentation generator) is present above each class and method.

```
/**

* Create the test instances and run the test.

*/

private static void test () {

... // This comment will not appear through JavaDoc
```

Naming Conventions

The general rule for all the names is to capitalize the first letter of each concatenated word (for instance, exampleOfCapitalizationOfConcatenatedWords). This applies to class, method and variable names written all together. The only names containing underscores would be the constant variables (fully capitalized) made up of several words.

Class and Method Name

- Class names start with a capital letter: `Broker`.

- No underscore used in class names. A capital letter starts a new word of a multiword name: `OrderItem`.

  - Method names start with a lowercase letter, and the starting letter of each new word is a capital letter with (no underscore): public void `handleOrders(Vector aVectorOfOrders)` of class `Broker`.

Variable Names

- Instance variables start with a prefix, `i`, and are accessed only by a getter and a setter with an explicit, respective, get and set prefix. `private int iAcceptedHeatLevel;`

```
instance variable public int getAcceptedHeatLevel(){

        return iAcceptedHeatLevel;

    }

    public void setAcceptedHeatLevel(int anAcceptedHeatLevel){

      iAcceptedHeatLevel = anAcceptedHeatLevel;

    }
```

- Class variables start with a prefix, c, and have for public access corresponding getter and setter with suffixes get and set.

```
private static Hashtable cHeatTable;
```

Pepper class variable: No example of class variable accesses with getter or setter in Chili Pepper Application.

- Parameter names start with an a or an an prefix.

```
public Pepper(String aKind);
```

Pepper constructor receiving a String as parameter:

```
public void loadShipment(Shipment aShipment) // Grower method
with an instance of Shipment as argument {...;
aShipment.becomeLoaded(); }
```

- Local temporary variables have no suffix.

- Constants are written in CAPITAL letters.

```
private static final String HABANERO = new String("Habanero");
```

Pepper constant variable: Another encountered convention for constant variable is the usage of a k prefix.

The four prefix-based conventions for the different class variables were selected because they help the reading of an individual line of code with a minimum of environment references. For instance, if a variable starting with an i is on the currently edited line, the reader immediately recognizes that he/she is reading a setter or a getter body section, as these are the only two methods that access the instance variable. When seeing a variable starting with an a, the reader knows this is a variable received as a parameter by the currently read method. If the name read does not start with one of the prefixes i, c, a or an, then this means that the variable is local to the method, and that it has to be initialized a couple of lines before. The readability advantage of these conventions has favored their usage.

Package Names

- Package names are made of all lowercase letters and are the same name as the directory name in which the group of classes resides:

```
package javabean;
```

Interface Names

- The used interfaces are imported explicitly:

```
import java.io.Serializable.
```

and then are used in the short-name version on the class definition line:

```
public class Agent extends, PersonRole implements Serializable
```

Access Conventions

The access conventions are the strict usage of getters and setters for the access of any class property (instance and class variables). Besides this common OO convention, it is also in the beans context, a specific bean's requirement for the proper recognition of the class as a bean by tools like the bean introspector.

- Instance variables are private. All their accesses, even from the same class, are done via the associated getter and setter.

```
private int iAcceptedHeatLevel; // Rule instance variable
public boolean check(Pepper aPepper) {
f(aPepper.getHeatLevel() < this.getAcceptedGeatLevel() ) ....
// this being the current instance of class Rule
```

- Instance variables are initialized in the class constructor by the setter method.

```
public PersonRole(Person aPerson) { this.setPerson(aPerson) );
// initializing iPerson in PersonRole constructor.
```

Construction Conventions

A default constructor is not required for the execution of the classes of the Pepper Broker Application. The reason for systematically having a (empty) default constructor is that the sample application BeanDescriptor.java of the book has been written with the assumed availability of this explicit constructor.

Initialization Conventions

- The variables of the class are initialized in the constructor of the class by using the corresponding variable setters.

```
Agent(String aName) {

setPerson( new Person( aName ) );

} // end of ctor
```

Class and Block Format Conventions

- The braces of the body of a class or a block should be aligned and on their own lines. Although, this becomes a matter of preference, code heritage, formatter, or edition. For traditional editing reasons, the code of the samples is presented as it is in the current majority of Java books with the opening curly brace at the end of the class, method or block name. See the following example:

```
public class OrderItem extends Object implements
java.io.Serializable {

private int iAmount;

private Pepper iPepper;

...

public OrderItem() {Pepper aPepper, int anAmount)

iPepper = aPepper;

iAmount = anAmount;

} // end of ctor

...

public String getAmount() {

return iAmount;

}

  } // end of class OrderItem
```

Import Conventions

- The writer has to be explicit with the import forms. Do not use the * forms.

Beanification Conventions

- As hard-wiring class (beans) relationships limit the possibilities of reuse, the reference to related beans should be implemented by defined interfaces and/or known implementations of Design Patterns. This opens the way to substitutions and facilitates shared understanding of the bean specifics.

  This will be with the Shipment class linking Pepper and Grower instead of a direct reference from Pepper to Grower that limits the generalization of the Pepper class as a Bean.

- Decide the scope of implementation of Cloneable and/or Serializable. All the classes of the sample are implementing java.io.Serializable. With a generalized decision, the advantage is that all the classes of the applications automatically inherit the same rich behavior of these parent interfaces.

As a summary of the beans tool-specific coding usages integrated above into our coding guidelines, we have seen:

1. The explicit presence of a default constructor for each class (only for the BeanDescriptor sample).

2. The explicit definition of a getter and setter with prefix get and set and the name of the property. This makes the encapsulated instance or class variable exposed to the JavaBeans introspection tools or calls.

3. The implementation of the `Serialization` interface by each class (implements `Serializable`).

Beans Events

- When using event objects, the name of a custom event that has to inherit from `java.util.EventObject` for implementing the notification is to be ended with the suffix "Event."

```
<DenominationOfTheEvent>Event (( == <EventStateObjectType> ))
```

Example:

```
public class PaintEvent extends java.util.EventObject

...== <EventStateObjectType> ))
```

- Event-handling methods:

  The method called when an event occurs is to be named:

```
void <eventOcurrenceMethodName>(<EventStateObjectType> anEvent);
```

- Event-handling methods with arbitrary argument list: (Note the usage restrictions of this guideline.)

  For the not-recommended and rare case where an `EventStateObject` is not passed:

```
void <eventOcurrenceMethodName>(<ArbitraryParameterList>);
```

- Multicast event delivery: (Probably needs to be synchronized.)

  The object that sends the event is responsible for the list of observers of its events. Its interface permits addition to the list with the method named:

```
public void add<ListenerType>(<ListenerType> listener);

public void remove<ListenerType>(<ListenerType> listener);
```

- Unicast event delivery: (Probably needs to be synchronized.)

  Same as the previous one for listener and constraint property:

```
public void add<ListenerType>(<ListenerType> listener)

    throws java.util.TooManyListenersException;

public void remove<ListenerType>(<ListenerType> listener);
```

Specific Coding Guideline References

Here are some more references for the construction of a more detailed set of coding guidelines.

- Doug Lea, Draft Java Coding Standard, 1996,
  (`http://gee.cs.oswego.edu/dl/html/javaCodingStd.html`).

- Also many C++ coding guidelines are perfect references for Java-style recommendations and coding standards.

JavaDoc Description

`JavaDoc` is the command used to generate documentation for your classes. The documentation will be in standard HTML; so you can use any browser to read it.

The generated documentation contains all the public and protected classes, methods and variables.

Text that you want to appear in the generated documentation is put within *doc comments*. A doc comment starts with `/**`, and ends with `*/`. For example:

```
/**

 * Jalapeno is usually not a very hot pepper.

 * But there are times when you are surprised!

 */
```

Documentation comments are only recognized when placed immediately before class, constructor, method, or field declarations.

You can use standard HTML in your doc comments in order to make the documentation more readable. We encourage you to use the simplest HTML tags, such as `<li>`, `<p>`, `<pre>` and such, since for example `<h1>` will change the structure of the document. For example:

```
/**

* <ol>

* <li>First line here

* <li>Second line here

* </ol>

* <p>New paragraph starts here.

*/
```

Of course, there is no need for you to include special doc comments. But they will make the generated documentation more readable. If you don't write anything, you will simply get a listing of your classes, methods and variables.

Options

There are special JavaDoc tags that will make the class documentation more readable. A JavaDoc tag always starts with an "@" sign. Tags always start at the beginning of a line.

JavaDoc Documentation Comment Tags. The tags who can be used are:

- @author
- @version
- @see
- @param
- @return
- @exception

The following example would print out the parameter and return value and the exception for this method.

```
/**

* Sets the kind of pepper.

* @see #getKind

* @param aKind is the name of the chili pepper.

* @return This method does not return anything
```

```
* @exception java.rmi.RemoteException This method throws

*                 a standard RemoteException

*/

protected void setKind(String aKind) throws RemoteException {

    iKind = aKind;

}
```

In the class description, the doc comments might contain the @author and @version tags. But remember to include the -version and -author options to the JavaDoc compiler in order to make them visible in the generated documentation.

```
/**

* This is the RMI version of the Pepper class.

* A pepper has a heatlevel, price and weight.

* @author Mats Pettersson

* @version 0.63

*/
```

JavaDoc Options

As parameters to JavaDoc, you can specify a single source file, multiple source files, or package names. If you specify a package name, you will get documentation for all the classes in the package, including a class hierarchy and an index. JavaDoc searches your CLASSPATH for the specified files. To include directories that are not in your classpath, you can specify the -classpath parameter to JavaDoc to add those.

- -classpath (Specify the classpath to use.)
- -sourcepath (Specify where the source files (.java) are, not the .class files.)
- -version (If a version tag is found, it will be included in the documentation.)
- -author (If an author tag is found, it will be included in the documentation.)

- `-noindex` (Do not generate an index.)
- `-notree` (Do not generate tree information.)
- `-d` (Specify the directory for the output files.)
- `-verbose` (Produce a detailed listing from the `JavaDoc` compilation.)

So, if we were to run `JavaDoc` for our sample code that is in the *javabean* package, we would issue the command:

```
JavaDoc javabean
```

If our `CLASSPATH` points to our package, the command would create all the documentation files in the current directory. If the `CLASSPATH` does not point to our package, we can include the `-classpath` parameter to the `JavaDoc` command. We can also specify a directory to put the output. Issuing the following command would find the package and put the generated documentation in the specified directory.

A note when using the `CLASSPATH` parameter: It overrides the `CLASSPATH` environment variable completely; so you need to include all the paths to your class references. For example, the path to where the JDK files are.

```
JavaDoc -classpath o:\rs7006\samples\pepper;

                  C:\JDK1.1\LIB\CLASSES.ZIP

         -d o:\rs7006\javadoc\pepper javabean
```

HINT! If you copy the images directory in \jdk1.1\docs\api\, and for this example place it in the relative path to your `JavaDoc`-generated documents, all the nice graphics for method descriptions and so on will be visible in the documentation.

The files generated by the command will be in the format packagename.classname.html. For example, we will have a javabean.Pepper.html, and a javabean.Grower.html and so on. There will also be a file called AllNames.html, that contains an index of all fields and methods. This file will not be created if you specify the `noindex` switch to `JavaDoc`.

Another file called Package-packagename.html will also be created, where `packagename` is the name of our package. So in our example, we will have a file called Package-javabean.html.

The file called packages.html will contain a list of all the packages for which we have generated documentation.

Tree.html shows the inheritance of the classes. If you specify the `notree` switch to `JavaDoc`, this file will not be created.

Chili Pepper Application Artifacts

The Chili Pepper application explained and referred to throughout this book is presented here in terms of a series of artifacts or work products. A minimum set of associated samples of the Requirements, the Analysis and Design, and the Implementation work products are provided in this section.

- Work product Introduction

- Problem Statement

- Analysis work products

- Design work products

- Implementation work products

- Chili Pepper Application Glossary

The Object Modeling Technique notation developed by James Rumbaugh is the style adopted as a base for the diagrams of the book. As the book, like maybe the reader, does not focus on the associated software development techniques, we will briefly describe the highlights of the notation used when they appear in the sequence of the work products selected. Also, the messages of this book in terms of Beans-Oriented Development are independent of this choice of notation.

Work Product Introduction

The series of artifacts developed for the Chili Pepper Application are the minimum set of deliverables the development team needed for the coordination, documentation and implementation of the sample application. This has been a lightweight experience of a work product-oriented development.

A work product is a concrete result of a planned project-related activity such as analysis, design or project management. work products include items delivered to customers and items used purely internally within a project. Examples of work products are Project Schedules, Object Model, Source Code, and even software products.

Our set of work products throughout this beans-oriented development, as collected in this section, has been divided into the following successively appearing groups:

1. The Requirements represented by our Chili Pepper story and its associated Problem Statement.

2. The Analysis work products, evolving from a draft list of candidate classes, and CRC exercise to an Analysis Object Model, Analysis Object Interaction Diagram and one Analysis State Transition Model.

3. The Design work products, describing initially the structure of the Java classes being built, and interactively the structure of the solution in terms of Beans. The set of work products was a Design Object Model, Design Object Interaction Diagrams and one Design State Transition Model. Through the experience of a Bean-Oriented Development, the idea came that it would be appropriate for a real and bigger project to document the solution also in terms of Bean Model and Bean Interaction Diagrams.

4. The User Interface Model documents the design of a prototype application user interface (for instance, Screen Layout work product). It can be grouped with the Design work products. For the Chili Pepper Application prototype, it has been drawn and composed with the Composition Editor of our building tool that has become the de facto work product.

5. The implementation groups of work products contain the Java source code, the associated Java documentation, the Coding Guidelines used to produce the code and the Glossary of the project.

The reader interested in further details about this work product-oriented approach for developing object-oriented applications and a full set of work products related to a Case Study should consult the book *Developing Object-Oriented Software, An Experience-Based Approach* written by members of the Object-Oriented Technology Center of IBM (mentioned in the bibliography).

Problem Statement

The Chili Pepper Broker and Insurance Co. is looking to increase market share. It needs to be highly competitive, scalable and responsive to customer demand. The company's management wants to see an implementation using a technology providing distributed objects as reusable components.

The purpose of the application is to convert an Order of Peppers into a Shipment to be delivered at a destination demanded by the Customer. The Actors involved in this process are the Customer who puts in an Order, the Grower who produces peppers, the Broker who creates and dispatches the shipment, and finally the Shipper who delivers the Peppers. Additionally, two types of operations occur before a shipment can be delivered. First, the Food Regulations conformance is controlled by an Inspector and second, an Insurance Policy is allocated to the shipment by an Insurance Agent.

The prototype of the application will implement the following business actions:

1. Broker arranges to sell peppers to customers.
2. Broker contacts growers to create shipments.
3. Inspector inspects shipment to make sure shipment meets rules.
4. Broker contacts agent to insure shipment (only if rules are met).
5. Broker contacts shippers to ship peppers from growers to customers.
6. Shipment is made.

Chili Pepper Analysis Work Products

The analysis work products presented are the Analysis Object Model, some Analysis Object Interaction Diagrams, and the Analysis State Model of the Shipment class.

- Analysis Guidelines
- Analysis Object Model
- Analysis Object Interaction Diagrams
- Analysis State Model

Chili Pepper Analysis Guidelines

Each work product presented in this section is shown with a similar template of subsections. The description presents what the work product is and the notation mentions the format in which the work product is presented. The traceability section shows the dependencies of the current work product with other work products that act as input (impacting ones) and the ones affected by the current one (impacted work products).

Analysis Guidelines are the set of rules intended to document the way in which analysis is to be performed on a particular project. The two kinds of Analysis Guidelines are the selection of the Analysis work products to be used in the project and the guidance on the way the analysis is performed. Then comes the section with the work product itself specific to the Chili Pepper Application.

Notation. Free-format text.

Traceability. This work product is not impacted here by other work products as the scope, scale and objectives of the project did not justify the production of formalized project management work products such as Intended Development Process, Project Workbook Outline, Quality Assurance Plan, Reuse Plan, Test Plan, and Issues.

This work product impacts the:

1. Analysis Object Model
2. Analysis Object Interaction Diagrams
3. Analysis State Model

Analysis Guidelines Work Product of the Chili Pepper Application. The analysis work products selected are: the Analysis Object Model (AOM), the Analysis Object Interaction Diagrams (AOIDs) for the scenario chosen and the Analysis State Model (ASM) of any class that would present a typical behavior of changing states related specifically with the problem at stake. Depending on the need, this does not preclude the usage of additional analysis tools like CRC classes and draft class specifications. These usages correspond to internal aids, but are not part of the documentation of the project.

The analysis uses the Rumbaugh OMT approach flavored with the Jacobson-based Requirements approach. The Analysis Object Model is drawn in agreement with the traditional Rumbaugh notations conventions for inheritance, aggregation and association. The notation section of each work product provides, as a courtesy to the readers unfamiliar with Rumbaugh's notation, the drawing conventions used in the work product diagrams.

Chili Pepper Analysis Object Model

The following AOM illustrates the structure of the Pepper business objects identified during the analysis phase.

The Analysis Object Model (AOM) is a static model of the part of the problem relevant to the Problem Statement. In common with the Design Object Model, it consists of classes and relationships between classes. The three kinds of relationships used are the association, the aggregation and the inheritance. The association is the simplest form of a relationship, also named the "knows-about" relationship, describing that one object uses another to complete a task. An association, like other relationships, has cardinality. The cardinality shows how many instances of the class can be associated with one instance of the other class. The aggregation is the second form of relationship. It means ownership and shows that a class is composed of one or several other classes. This relationship is synonymously called a containment, "whole-part" or "has-a" relationship, because an instance of the first class, the aggregator, contains or has instances of the second class, which are the owned components or aggregatees. The third form of relationship is inheritance (also called a generalization/specialization, or "is-a" relationship). It shows a hierarchical dependency between a supertype and a subtype, where the features of the supertype are inherited by all subtypes. In other terms, the child or derived class will inherit its properties, methods and events from its parent class.

Notation. An AOM is a class diagram presenting the relationships between the classes of business objects in the analyzed problem domain.

The class is drawn as a solid-outline rectangular box with the class name in it. Sometimes three-pane boxes are preferred, with the list of attributes in the middle pane and a list of services or operations in the bottom pane. Between the classes, drawn lines represent the relationships.

The endpoints of the static relationships show the cardinality or multiplicity with a black bullet (solid ball) for 0 to many, an empty bullet (hollow ball) for 0 or 1, an explicit 1+ for 1 to many. Exactly one is represented by a plain line ending with no mention (no marker). These notations are summarized in the next picture.

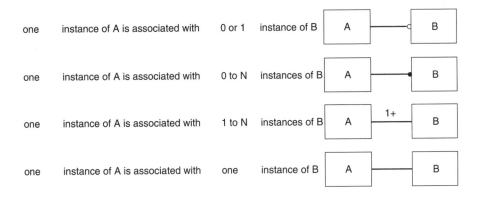

The notation for an aggregation relationship between a class C made of instances of a class B is illustrated again in the next picture for four different cases of cardinality, such as expressing how many instances of B can be contained by C.

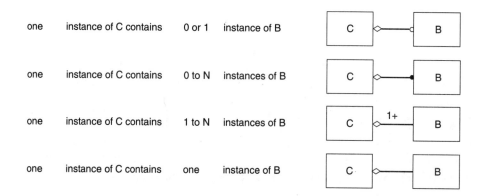

one	instance of C contains	0 or 1	instance of B
one	instance of C contains	0 to N	instances of B
one	instance of C contains	1 to N	instances of B
one	instance of C contains	one	instance of B

The OMT notation for inheritance is a triangle connecting a subclass to its parent class. For instance, in the AOM the parent class `PersonRole` has generic behavior and a containment that each of its derived classes, such as Grower and Broker, will inherit.

Traceability. This work product is impacted by the:

- Problem Statement
- Analysis Guidelines
- Analysis OIDs

and impacts the:

- Analysis OIDs
- Analysis State Model
- Design Object Model
- Glossary

Analysis Object Model Work Product of the Chili Pepper Application.

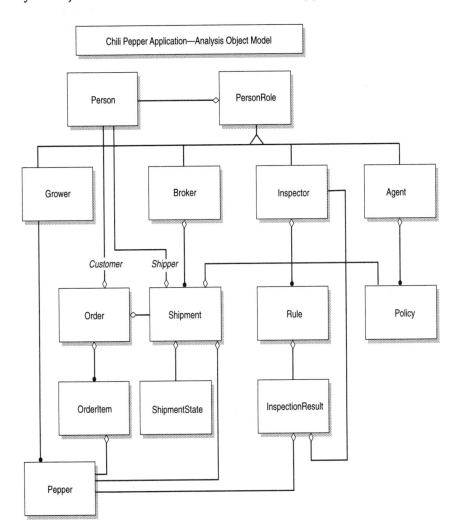

Chili Pepper Analysis Object Interaction Diagrams

The following AOIDs illustrate the collaboration between of the Pepper business objects for the success case of the main flow (scenario) of the application. The reader will recognize, in the Jacobson notation, the distribution of responsibilities and control among objects.

An Interaction Diagram shows the order in which requests between objects are executed. The Analysis Object Interaction Diagram (AOID) is a graphical representation of an Analysis Scenario expressed in terms of the interactions between real-world and analysis objects. The Analysis OID presents the dynamic of the Analysis Scenario by showing how the objects that participate collaborate in order to achieve the desired outcomes. AOIDs complete the link between the requirements work products and the AOM. They present the dynamics of the model focusing on understanding and abstracting the problem and business. The Design Object Interaction Diagrams will be the ones focusing on defining the solution to the modeled problem.

Notation. Each object is represented by a vertical timeline with the name of the object placed at the top of the line. The naming convention used in these AOIDs is to prefix the class name by "a" or "an." The solid portion of the line indicates the lifetime of the object. As long as the object is not instantiated, its vertical line is dashed. In Design OIDs, the additional convention of vertical rectangles showing that objects are in control, meaning active, will be used. Timelines are used as sources and targets of the chronological sequence of messages sent between objects. Messages represent object interactions. A condition within a pair of square brackets represents a decision point in the message sender object. If the message is true, the message attached is to be sent. The alternative to this condition is to use several AOIDs to present the options for a single scenario. A loop and a loop condition can be attached to an object timeline in order to represent repeated actions. Sometimes, even in Analysis, a specific internal activity is relevant to a timeline; this is represented by the name of the activity in curly braces.

Traceability. This work product is impacted by the:

- Problem Statement

- Analysis Guidelines

- Analysis Object Model

- Analysis State Model

and impacts the:

- Analysis Object Model

- Analysis State Model

- Design Object Interaction Diagrams

Analysis Object Interaction Diagrams of the Chili Pepper Application. The AOIDs are self-explanatory diagrams in a project when they are issued from associated Use Cases and Scenarios. In the scope of the Chili Pepper Application, that presents a single main use case and one scenario for the satisfactory load of a Shipment and one scenario for the cancellation of it due to unloadability. The commented AOID appears to be the only updated work product to prepare for Design. The summary of those comments have been reported after each of the following graphics.

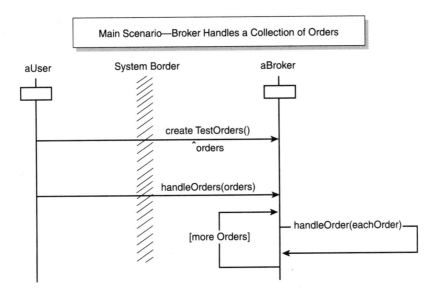

The User who acts upon the system triggers the creation of a series of TestOrders that are passed to the Broker of the application. The Broker is the key player in this Pepper business, here at the highest level, he/she receives a collection or orders and handles each of them as presented in the next AOID.

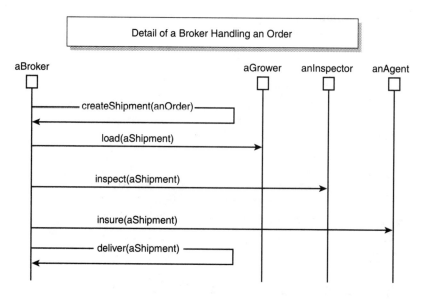

| | Detail of a Broker Handling an Order | | | |

Handling an Order means, for the Broker, the creation and preparation of one or several Shipments associated with that Order. Assuming the ordered peppers are originating from a unique source, there will be only one Shipment for each Order. When the Shipment is created, the Broker goes through a series of partners to fulfill that Shipment. Those business steps are dispatching the shipment to a Grower for loading, then to an Inspector for Food Regulations control, to an Agent for an Insurance Policy and finally to a Shipper for delivery to the destination demanded by the Customer. This last one is not seen as an Actor in the scope of the problem. The delivery information, in terms of associating the Shipper coordinates to the Shipments is the responsibility of the Broker and does not have to be delegated to a Shipper Object.

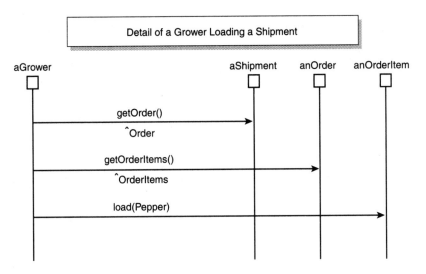

Detail of a Grower Loading a Shipment

The Grower is passed a Shipment by the Broker. That Shipment is created, but needs to be allocated the quantity of Peppers that are requested in the associated Order. As the Order may contain different kind of Peppers, different `OrderItems` may compose an Order, and each `OrderItem` kind is to be loaded by the Grower.

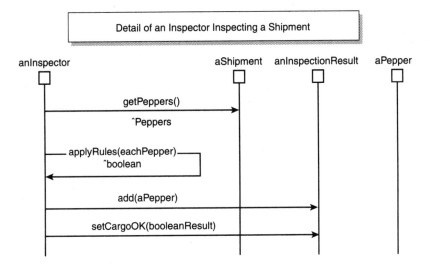

Detail of an Inspector Inspecting a Shipment

After loading, the Inspector receives the Shipment. For each kind of Pepper comprising the Shipment, the Inspector applies the appropriate inspection Rules. Then he/she creates the report of the inspection, which is named an

InspectionResult, and adds it to the Shipment. If the Shipment is approved, the Inspector finally labels the InspectionResult as OK.

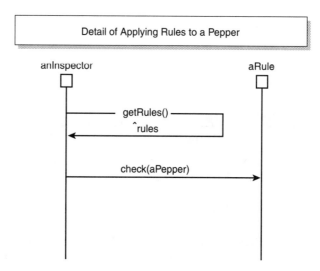

The detail of the business operation of inspection shows that the Inspector applies for the sort of Pepper into the consideration a checking operation confronting the Pepper to the corresponding rule to apply.

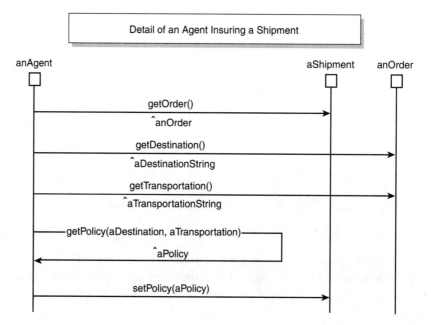

After inspection, the Shipment arrives in the hands of an Insurance Agent who reads the details of the Order associated with the Shipment in terms of Destination country and Transportation mode. As a function of this data, the Agent defines the Insurance Policy to be applied and associates the selected policy to the Shipment.

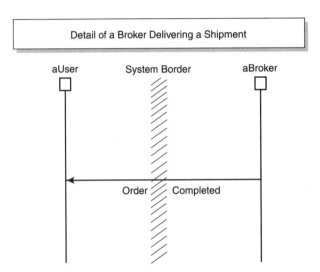

After the inspection step, the Broker receives a Shipment back that is now ready for delivery. The broker associates a Shipper for the delivery of the Shipment to its destination and provides the necessary output to the User of the System so that the completion of the Order is reported.

Chili Pepper Analysis State Model

The Analysis State Model presents the five major states of the Shipment class instantiated by a Broker, loaded by a Grower, inspected by an Inspector, insured by an Agent, and sent to a Shipper.

A state model describes the lifecycle of a class. It represents the states that a class may reach and the transitions that cause the changes of state. The state transitions represent the external events that cause the changes of state. A state model can be represented by a state diagram, as done here, or by a state transition table.

Notation. The class states are represented by circles, rectangles or rounded rectangles. The transitions are shown as directed arcs or links between the states. The transitions in the Analysis Object Model are labeled as a description of a Doer performing an Action that causes the target state to be reached from the previous (source) state. Specific symbols represent the initial state, when the instance is created and not yet initialized, and the terminal state, when the instance is not used anymore, that is not referred to by any other objects or deleted.

Traceability. This work product is impacted by the:

- Problem Statement
- Analysis Guidelines
- Analysis Object Model
- Analysis Object Interaction Diagrams

and impacts the:

- Analysis Object Interaction Diagrams
- Design State Model
- Glossary

Analysis State Model for the class Shipment of the Chili Pepper Application.

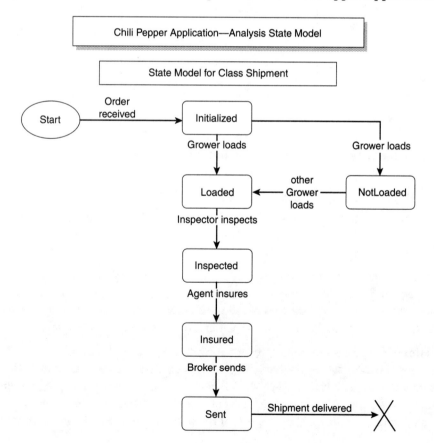

AOID

The AOIDs show the evolution of the Shipment in the business from the Broker to the Grower, to the Inspector and to the Agent before being sent by the Shipper. This sequence is recognized in this Analysis step as a series of logical states that are named with the corresponding business names: Loaded, Inspected, Insured and Sent.

Chili Pepper Design Work Products

The design work products presented here are the Design Object Model, associated Design Object Interaction Diagrams and the Design State Transition Diagram of the Shipment Object.

- Design Guidelines
- Design Object Model
- Design Object Interaction Diagrams
- Design State Model

Chili Pepper Design Guidelines

The Design Guidelines are the set of rules intended to define which design work products to produce and to report the rules as selected and agreed upon by the development team in order to facilitate the design process and, specifically, each design work product. In practice these guidelines refer to the analysis ones and have design specific extensions.

Notation. Free-format text paragraph per design work product.

Traceability. As with the Analysis Guidelines, this work product is not impacted here by other work products because the scope, scale and objectives of the project did not justify the production of formalized project-management work products.

This work product impacts the:

- Design Object Model
- Design Object Interaction Diagrams
- Design State Model

Design Guidelines Work Product of the Chili Pepper Application. The design work products presented next are: the Design Object Model (DOM), a sample Design Object Interaction Diagrams (DOID) , the Design State Model (DSM) of the Shipment class that had an Analysis State Model (ASM).

Because of the specific Bean Orientation of the Development, it has appeared during the implementation phase of the prototype scenario that views of the work product in terms of design components (beans) instead of classes could be an appropriate help for the application builders. Indeed, the designers involved in reusing software components need to view the model of the solution they are composing, both in terms of the bean-oriented static models and bean-oriented interactions. These decisions in the project could be developed into an iterative rework of the design guidelines that would specify the Bean Model (BM) and Bean Interaction Diagrams (BIDs). This has not been implemented for the coverage and scope of the first phase of Chili Pepper Application.

Chili Pepper Design Object Model

The Design Object Model (DOM) is a structural representation of the software objects (classes) that comprise the implementation of a system or application. It documents the static aspects of the envisaged solution in terms of attributes (properties), responsibilities, operations (methods), and interrelationships expressed as association, aggregation and inheritance links.

Notation. The DOM notation enhances the AOM notation with the emphasis on architecture and design class description. This enhancement, illustrated on the next two figures, includes:

- Three-pane (boxes) with the chosen attributes (properties) in the middle pane and the decided operations (methods) in the bottom pane.

- The attributes are explicitly typed in the diagram.

- The full signature (return type and parameter types) of the method are shown.

- Association shows the direction(s) of reference between the objects.

- Association with multiplicity are transformed into implementation choices like aggregation of a collection, for instance.

- Class abstraction is shown or explicitly labeled beside the name (UML convention).

- Interfaces are explicitly labeled. Interface implementations show as inheritance but with a full triangle instead of a hollow one as a distinct mark from class inheritance.

- Attribute accessibility should be specified. In practice, one will have nearly all the attributes private due to data hiding and accessed possibly through the public accessor methods imposed as a rule from the Coding Guidelines work product.

- The getters and setters (accessor methods) being systematically written for each property (attribute). One does not show them in the methods pane of the class to reduce detail in an overview diagram.

- Argument dependency and temporary variable dependency can be represented by a dotted line with an arrowhead. A class has an argument dependency on another class if one of its methods refers to the other class when defining its formal parameters. A class has a temporary variable dependency on another class, if it instantiates the class as a local, temporary variable.

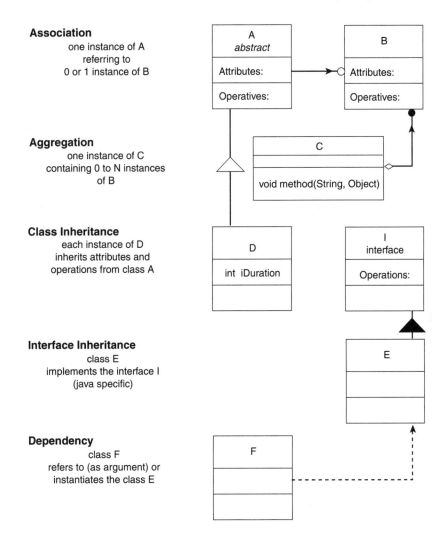

Our notation for interface implementation (interface inheritance) has been a triangle connecting a class to the interface it implements. For instance, in the DOM all the classes implement the `java.io.Serializable` interface, as presented in the next figure; but this is better kept as a note to the diagram or as a coding guideline to prevent overloading the DOM with too general or unspecific information. A better example of interface implementation notation used in the Chili Pepper DOM is presented next along with the Broker class that implements the interface `java.beans.PropertyChangeListener`.

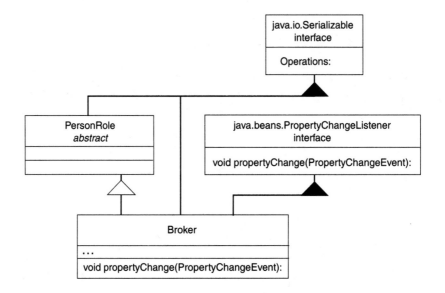

Traceability. This work product is impacted by:

- Analysis Object Model
- Design Guidelines
- Design OIDs

and impacts the:

- Design OIDs
- Design State Model
- Design Class Description
- Glossary

Design Object Model Work Product of the Chili Pepper Application.

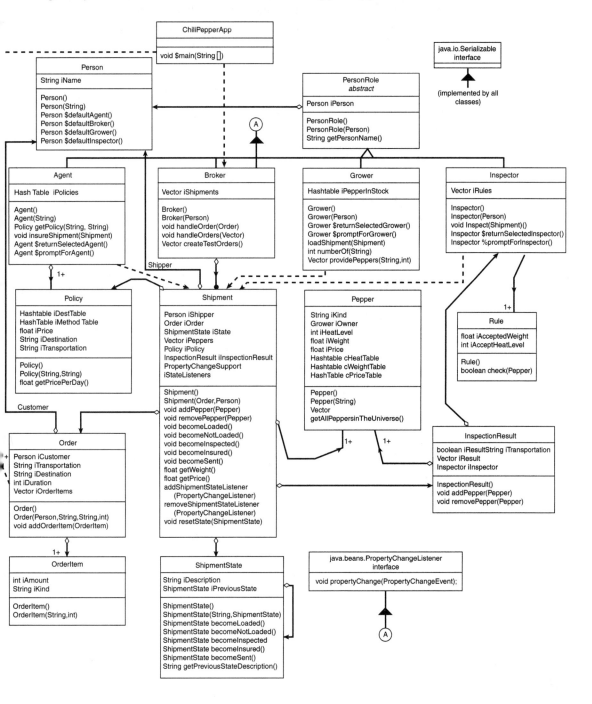

The Design Object Model of the Chili Pepper Application presents the design decisions and the specific Java Implementation decisions taken. The Event mechanism used between Shipment (Event Source) and Broker (Event Listener) has brought the implementation of Events into the picture.

See the section on Events for the mechanisms of this Event notification scheme.

Chili Pepper Design Object Interaction Diagrams

The DOIDs illustrate the collaboration of the pepper business objects for the sunny case of the main flow (scenario) of the application. The reader will recognize, in the Jacobson notation, the distribution of responsibilities and control among objects. The practicality and the limited scope of the prototype did not justify the extensive development of all the DOIDs. Thus, we decided to present below the first DOID that matches the first AOID for the sake of completeness of the basic work products coverage.

A Design Object Interaction Diagram (DOID) is a graphical representation of object collaborations in a design scenario in terms of design objects and their interactions (dynamic modeling). It is the result of transforming the corresponding AOID with the emphasis on the design classes intended for implementation and localization of control.

Notation. DOID notation is mostly the same as the AOID notation. The architectural additions are the representation of the focuses of control, the concurrency of tasks and the boundaries of subsystems.

Traceability. This work product is impacted by the:

- Analysis Object Interaction Diagrams
- Design Guidelines
- Screen Layout
- Design State Model

and impacts the:

- Design Object Model
- Design State Model
- Design Class Description

Design Object Interaction Diagram of the Chili Pepper Application–Example.

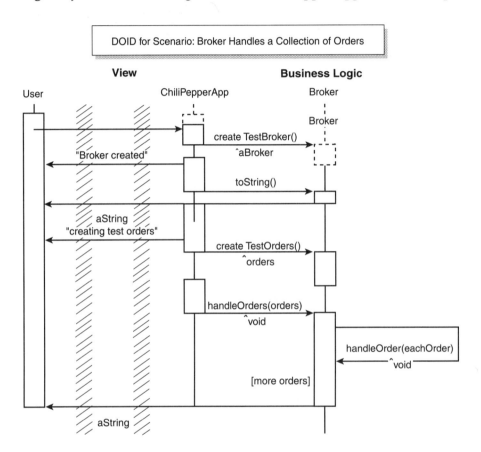

Chili Pepper Design State Model

The Design State Model presents the states of the class `Shipment`, the causes of the transitions and the methods called for the state transition to take place.

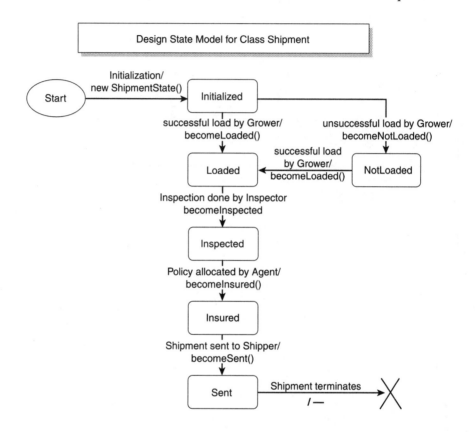

Each state of shipment is represented by a new instance of `ShipmentState`.

Chili Pepper Implementation Work Products

The implementation work product used before coding the Chili Pepper application has been the Coding Guidelines. After the first prototype, the `JavaDoc`-based documentation was generated. The specific bean implementation features are included in the Design work products.

- Coding Guidelines
- `JavaDoc` Documentation as Design Class Description
- Source Code

- Package JavaBean

- Application Glossary

- Executables

Chili Pepper Coding Guidelines Work Product

Coding Guidelines take the form of a set of documented rules and recommendations addressing the programming style to be used within a software development project.

Notation. Coding Guidelines are organized and distributed for easy reference. In the guidelines document, each guideline should be formatted with a Guideline, a Reason and an Example section.

Traceability. This work product is not impacted here by another work product, but it impacts the:

- Source Code

Coding Guidelines Work Product, Chili Pepper Application. This critically important Design work product has not been started before the implementation work products though it belongs normally to the Design-phase work products. This has been due to the specific prototyping, limited scope and Java-oriented nature of the Chili Pepper Application. Indeed, because the small development team did the analysis and design as a team, each programmer had a shared understanding of the wanted application and an easy communication path to any other member of the team. Also, since the major work products were dynamically updated on the walls of a commonly accessed room, the need of the duplication in a Design Class work product did not appear. A shared document was needed throughout the concurrent and iterative development of the different classes parted among the programmers and took form in a permanently updated Java-Doc documentation file on the shared server. As such, our Design Class work product happens to be a reverse-engineering document from the iterated Source Code work product.

Chili Pepper Design Class Descriptions Work Product and JavaDoc Documentation

Design Class Descriptions are containers of all the information known about a class at design level. Comments written at Analysis level are valid here, too, such as those from the Analysis Class Descriptions, CRC cards or Analysis Object Model.

Notation. Design Class Descriptions drive low-level design activity in the subsequent implementation phase and are necessarily sensitive to the target programming language.

Traceability. This work product is impacted here by the:

- Design Guidelines
- Design Object Model
- Design Object Interaction Diagrams
- Design State Models

and it impacts:

- Source Code. See the Java Documentation of the Chili Pepper Application

Chili Pepper Source Code Work Product

Source Code is the actual implementation of the application design in a programming language.

Notation. The coding notation is the usage of the Java language with compliance to the Coding Guidelines.

Traceability. This work product impacts no work product, but is impacted by the:

- Coding Guidelines
- Design Class Descriptions

Source Code Work Product of the Chili Pepper Application. The Source Code work product presents the Java source file of each Java class of the Chili Pepper Application. The classes listed next are all grouped in the application-specific Chili Pepper package.

- Agent
- Broker
- ChiliPepperApp
- Grower
- Inspector
- InspectionResult
- Order
- OrderItem
- Pepper

- Person
- PersonRule
- Policy
- Rule
- Shipment
- ShipmentState

Package Chili Pepper

This package contains all the business object model classes of the Chili Pepper Application.

Chili Pepper Application Glossary

A project Glossary defines all the terms used during the project. For each term it provides a short definition entry. The Glossary is used to record design and analysis definitions and normally contains only class and actor names.

Notation. Free-text format.

Traceability. This work product impacts no work product, but is impacted by the:

- Problem Statement
- Analysis Object Model
- Analysis State Model
- Design Object Model
- Design State Model

Glossary Work Product of the Chili Pepper Application.

Agent: the application class responsible for the allocation of an Insurance Policy to a Shipment. It is implemented as a `PersonRole` subclass.

Broker: the application class responsible for the creation and preparation of Shipments, such as dispatching them successively to Grower (for loading), to Inspector (for Food Regulations), to an Agent (for Insurance Policy) and to a Shipper (for delivery to the destination demanded by the Customer). It is implemented as a `PersonRole` subclass.

Customer: the application actor representing the origin of an Order for Peppers. Customer is implemented as an instance of Person.

Grower: the application class providing loads of Peppers for the Shipments. Grower is implemented as a `PersonRole` subclass.

Inspector: the application class providing the validation of a Shipment against Food Commerce Rules. Inspector is implemented as a `PersonRole` subclass.

Initialized: the state of the `Shipment` class

Inspected: the state of the `Shipment` class

Insured: the state of the `Shipment` class

Loaded: the state of the `Shipment` class

NotLoaded: the state of the `Shipment` class

Pepper: the application class representing the merchandise unit of Chili Pepper Broker and Insurance Co. Peppers exist in different specializations available from the Growers, such as Jalapeño, Habanero and Red Bell, for instance.

Policy: the application class representing the specifics of an Insurance Policy in terms of rate or price per day for a shipment of peppers.

Rule: the application class representing a Commerce or Food regulation to be met for the authorized shipment of a kind of peppers.

Sent: the state of the `Shipment` class

Shipment: the application class associated with an Order of Peppers. A Shipment is created and prepared by a Broker. It is loaded with Peppers from a Grower, controlled by an Inspector, associated with an Insurance Policy by an Agent, and sent to a Shipper for delivery at the destination demanded by the Customer. The `ShipmentState` class implements the six different states a `Shipment` instance can present in the application.

ShipmentState: the application class aggregated in the `Shipment` class and of which each instance represents one of the six possible following states of the Shipment: Initialized, Loaded, NotLoaded, Inspected, Insured and Sent.

Shipper: the application actor responsible for the delivery of a Shipment to the appropriate destination through the required transportation media (for example, air or truck) within a specified delivery time. Shipper is implemented as an instance of Person.

User: the application actor that operates the system for the handling of an Order of Peppers from the loading to the delivery of a Shipment (main Scenario).

Acronyms

AOID
    Analysis Object Interaction Diagrams
AOM
    Analysis Object Model
API
    Application Programming Interface
ASM
    Analysis State Model
BID
    Bean Interaction Diagrams
BM
    Bean Model

CAE
> Client Application Enabler

CORBA
> Common Object Request Broker Architecture

CD
> Compact Disk

CRC
> Class/Responsibilities/Collaborators

DBMS
> DataBase Management System

DOM
> Design Object Model

DSM
> Design State Model

GIF
> Graphics Interchange Format

GUI
> Graphical User Interface

HTML
> Hyper Text Markup Language

IDL
> Interface Definition Language

ITSO
> International Technical Support Organization

JAR
> Java ARchive

JDBC
> Java Database Connection

JSQL
> Java Structured Query Language

JVM
> Java Virtual Machine

NC
> Network Computer or Network Computing

OID
  Object Interaction Diagrams
OMG
  Object Group Management
OMT
  Object Modeling Technique
RDBMS
  Relational DataBase Management System
RMI
  Remote Method Invocation
ROM
  Read Only Memory
SQL
  Structured Query Language
TCP
  Transmission Control Protocol
TCPIP
  Transmission Control Protocol/Internet Protocol
UML
  Unified Model Language
URL
  Unified Resource Locator
XOR
  eXclusive OR

Bibliography

Flanagan, D., *Java in a Nutshell*, O'Reilly and Associates, 1996

Gamma, E., Helm, R., Johnson, R. and Vlissides, J., *Design Patterns, Elements of Reusable Object-Oriented Software*, Addison-Wesley, 1995.

Lindholm, T. and Yellin, F., *The Java Virtual Machine Specification*, Addison-Wesley, 1997.

McGraw, G. and Felten, E., *Java Security*, John Wiley and Sons, 1996.

Niemeyer, P. and Peck, J., *Exploring Java*, O'Reilly and Associates, 1996.

Object-Oriented Technology Center, *Developing Object-Oriented Software, An Experience Based Approach*, Prentice Hall, 1997.

Sun Microsystems (1996), *Java Beans 1.0 API*, Web document URL http://java.sun.com/beans/spec.html.

Sun Microsystems (1997), *Java Core Reflection Specification*, Web document URL http://java.sun.com/products/JDK/1.1/docs/guide/reflection/index.html.

Sun Microsystems (1997), *Java Object Serialization Specification*, Web document URL http://java.sun.com/products/JDK/1.1/docs/guide/serialization/index.html.

Sun Microsystems (1997), *Java Remote Method Invocation Specification*, Web document URL http://java.sun.com/products/JDK/1.1/docs/guide/rmi/index.html.

Sun Microsystems (1996), *JDK 1.1 Internationalization Specification*, Web document URL http://javasoft.com:80/products/jdk/1.1/intl/html/intlspecTOC.doc.html.

Sun Microsystems (1997), *Manifest File Specification*, Web document URL http://java.sun.com/products/JDK/1.1/docs/guide/jar/index.html.

van der Linden, P., *Just Java*, Sunsoft Press, 1996.

The Chile-Heads home page, Web document URL http://neptune.netimages.com/~chile/.

Index

LICENSE AGREEMENT AND LIMITED WARRANTY

READ THE FOLLOWING TERMS AND CONDITIONS CAREFULLY BEFORE OPENING THIS DISK PACKAGE. THIS LEGAL DOCUMENT IS AN AGREEMENT BETWEEN YOU AND PRENTICE-HALL, INC. (THE "COMPANY"). BY OPENING THIS SEALED DISK PACKAGE, YOU ARE AGREEING TO BE BOUND BY THESE TERMS AND CONDITIONS. IF YOU DO NOT AGREE WITH THESE TERMS AND CONDITIONS, DO NOT OPEN THE DISK PACKAGE. PROMPTLY RETURN THE UNOPENED DISK PACKAGE AND ALL ACCOMPANYING ITEMS TO THE PLACE YOU OBTAINED THEM FOR A FULL REFUND OF ANY SUMS YOU HAVE PAID.

1.   **GRANT OF LICENSE:** In consideration of your payment of the license fee, which is part of the price you paid for this product, and your agreement to abide by the terms and conditions of this Agreement, the Company grants to you a nonexclusive right to use and display the copy of the enclosed software program (hereinafter the "SOFTWARE") on a single computer (i.e., with a single CPU) at a single location so long as you comply with the terms of this Agreement. The Company reserves all rights not expressly granted to you under this Agreement.

2.   **OWNERSHIP OF SOFTWARE:** You own only the magnetic or physical media (the enclosed disks) on which the SOFTWARE is recorded or fixed, but the Company retains all the rights, title, and ownership to the SOFTWARE recorded on the original disk copy(ies) and all subsequent copies of the SOFTWARE, regardless of the form or media on which the original or other copies may exist. This license is not a sale of the original SOFTWARE or any copy to you.

3.   **COPY RESTRICTIONS:** This SOFTWARE and the accompanying printed materials and user manual (the "Documentation") are the subject of copyright. You may not copy the Documentation or the SOFTWARE, except that you may make a single copy of the SOFTWARE for backup or archival purposes only. You may be held legally responsible for any copying or copyright infringement which is caused or encouraged by your failure to abide by the terms of this restriction.

4.   **USE RESTRICTIONS:** You may not network the SOFTWARE or otherwise use it on more than one computer or computer terminal at the same time. You may physically transfer the SOFTWARE from one computer to another provided that the SOFTWARE is used on only one computer at a time. You may not distribute copies of the SOFTWARE or Documentation to others. You may not reverse engineer, disassemble, decompile, modify, adapt, translate, or create derivative works based on the SOFTWARE or the Documentation without the prior written consent of the Company.

5.   **TRANSFER RESTRICTIONS:** The enclosed SOFTWARE is licensed only to you and may not be transferred to any one else without the prior written consent of the Company. Any unauthorized transfer of the SOFTWARE shall result in the immediate termination of this Agreement.

6.   **TERMINATION:** This license is effective until terminated. This license will terminate automatically without notice from the Company and become null and void if you fail to comply with any provisions or limitations of this license. Upon termination, you shall destroy the Documentation and all copies of the SOFTWARE. All provisions of this Agreement as to warranties, limitation of liability, remedies or damages, and our ownership rights shall survive termination.

7.   **MISCELLANEOUS:** This Agreement shall be construed in accordance with the laws of the United States of America and the State of New York and shall benefit the Company, its affiliates, and assignees.

8.   **LIMITED WARRANTY AND DISCLAIMER OF WARRANTY:** The Company warrants that the SOFTWARE, when properly used in accordance with the Documentation, will operate in substantial conformity with the description of the SOFTWARE set forth in the Documentation. The Company does not warrant that the SOFTWARE will meet your requirements or that the operation of the SOFTWARE will be

uninterrupted or error-free. The Company warrants that the media on which the SOFTWARE is delivered shall be free from defects in materials and workmanship under normal use for a period of thirty (30) days from the date of your purchase. Your only remedy and the Company's only obligation under these limited warranties is, at the Company's option, return of the warranted item for a refund of any amounts paid by you or replacement of the item. Any replacement of SOFTWARE or media under the warranties shall not extend the original warranty period. The limited warranty set forth above shall not apply to any SOFTWARE which the Company determines in good faith has been subject to misuse, neglect, improper installation, repair, alteration, or damage by you. EXCEPT FOR THE EXPRESSED WARRANTIES SET FORTH ABOVE, THE COMPANY DISCLAIMS ALL WARRANTIES, EXPRESS OR IMPLIED, INCLUDING WITHOUT LIMITATION, THE IMPLIED WARRANTIES OF MERCHANTABILITY AND FITNESS FOR A PAR-TICULAR PURPOSE. EXCEPT FOR THE EXPRESS WARRANTY SET FORTH ABOVE, THE COM-PANY DOES NOT WARRANT, GUARANTEE, OR MAKE ANY REPRESENTATION REGARDING THE USE OR THE RESULTS OF THE USE OF THE SOFTWARE IN TERMS OF ITS CORRECTNESS, ACCURACY, RELIABILITY, CURRENTNESS, OR OTHERWISE.

IN NO EVENT, SHALL THE COMPANY OR ITS EMPLOYEES, AGENTS, SUPPLIERS, OR CONTRACTORS BE LIABLE FOR ANY INCIDENTAL, INDIRECT, SPECIAL, OR CONSEQUEN-TIAL DAMAGES ARISING OUT OF OR IN CONNECTION WITH THE LICENSE GRANTED UNDER THIS AGREEMENT, OR FOR LOSS OF USE, LOSS OF DATA, LOSS OF INCOME OR PROFIT, OR OTHER LOSSES, SUSTAINED AS A RESULT OF INJURY TO ANY PERSON, OR LOSS OF OR DAM-AGE TO PROPERTY, OR CLAIMS OF THIRD PARTIES, EVEN IF THE COMPANY OR AN AUTHO-RIZED REPRESENTATIVE OF THE COMPANY HAS BEEN ADVISED OF THE POSSIBILITY OF SUCH DAMAGES. IN NO EVENT SHALL LIABILITY OF THE COMPANY FOR DAMAGES WITH RESPECT TO THE SOFTWARE EXCEED THE AMOUNTS ACTUALLY PAID BY YOU, IF ANY, FOR THE SOFTWARE.

SOME JURISDICTIONS DO NOT ALLOW THE LIMITATION OF IMPLIED WARRAN-TIES OR LIABILITY FOR INCIDENTAL, INDIRECT, SPECIAL, OR CONSEQUENTIAL DAMAGES, SO THE ABOVE LIMITATIONS MAY NOT ALWAYS APPLY. THE WARRANTIES IN THIS AGREE-MENT GIVE YOU SPECIFIC LEGAL RIGHTS AND YOU MAY ALSO HAVE OTHER RIGHTS WHICH VARY IN ACCORDANCE WITH LOCAL LAW.

ACKNOWLEDGMENT

YOU ACKNOWLEDGE THAT YOU HAVE READ THIS AGREEMENT, UNDERSTAND IT, AND AGREE TO BE BOUND BY ITS TERMS AND CONDITIONS. YOU ALSO AGREE THAT THIS AGREEMENT IS THE COMPLETE AND EXCLUSIVE STATEMENT OF THE AGREEMENT BETWEEN YOU AND THE COMPANY AND SUPERSEDES ALL PROPOSALS OR PRIOR AGREE-MENTS, ORAL, OR WRITTEN, AND ANY OTHER COMMUNICATIONS BETWEEN YOU AND THE COMPANY OR ANY REPRESENTATIVE OF THE COMPANY RELATING TO THE SUBJECT MAT-TER OF THIS AGREEMENT.

Should you have any questions concerning this Agreement or if you wish to contact the Company for any reason, please contact in writing at the address below.

Robin Short
Prentice Hall PTR
One Lake Street
Upper Saddle River, New Jersey 07458

Java™ Development Kit
Version 1.1.1
and
BDK Version 1.0 Combined
Binary Code License

This binary code license ("License") contains rights and restrictions associated with use of the accompanying software and documentation ("Software"). Read the License carefully before installing the Software. By installing the Software you agree to the terms and conditions of this License.

1. Limited License Grant. Sun grants to you ("Licensee") a non-exclusive, non-transferable limited license to use the Software without fee for evaluation of the Software and for development of Java™ compatible applets and applications. Licensee may make one archival copy of the Software. Except for the foregoing, Licensee may not re-distribute the Software in whole or in part, either separately or included with a product. Refer to the Java Runtime Environment Version 1.1 binary code license (http://www.javasoft.com/products/JDK/1.1/index.html) for the availability of runtime code which may be distributed with Java compatible applets and applications.

2. Redistribution of Demonstration Files. Sun grants Licensee the right to use, modify and redistribute the Beans example and demonstration code, including the BeanBox ("Demos"), in both source and binary code form provided that (i) Licensee does not utilize the Demos ina manner which is disparaging to Sun; and (ii) Licensee indemnifies and holds Sun harmless from all claims relating to any such use or distribution of the Demos. Such distribution is limited to the source and binary code of the Demos and specifically excludes any rights to modify or distribute any graphical images contained in the Demos.

3. Java Platform Interface. Licensee may not modify the Java Platform Interface ("JPI", identified as classes contained within the "java" package or any subpackages of the "java" package), by creating additional classes within the JPI or otherwise causing the addition to or modification of the classes in the JPI. In the event that Licensee creates any Java-related API and distributes such API to others for applet or application development, Licensee must promptly publish an accurate specification for such API for free use by all developers of Java-based software.

4. Restrictions. Software is confidential copyrighted information of Sun and title to all copies is retained by Sun and/or its licensors. Licensee shall not modify, decompile, disassemble, decrypt, extract, or otherwise reverse engineer Software. Software may not be leased, assigned, or sublicensed in whole or in part. **Software is not designed or intended for use in on-line control of aircraft, air traffic, aircraft navigation or aircraft communications; or in the design, construction, operation or maintenance of any nuclear facility. Licensee warrants that it will not use or redistribute the Software for such purposes.**

5. Trademarks and Logos. This License does not authorize Licensee to use any Sun name, trademark or logo. Licensee acknowledges that Sun owns the Java trademark and all Java-related trademarks, logos and icons including the Coffee Cup and Duke ("Java Marks") and agrees to: (i) to comply with the Java Trademark Guidelines at http://java.com/trademarks.html; (ii) not do anything harmful to or inconsistent with Sun's rights in the Java Marks; and (iii) assist Sun in protecting those rights, including assigning to Sun any rights acquired by Licensee in any Java Mark.

6. Disclaimer of Warranty. Software is provided "AS IS," without a warranty of any kind. ALL EXPRESS OR IMPLIED REPRESENTATIONS AND WARRANTIES, INCLUDING ANY IMPLIED WARRANTY OF MERCHANTABILITY, FITNESS FOR A PARTICULAR PURPOSE OR NON-INFRINGEMENT, ARE HEREBY EXCLUDED.

7. Limitation of Liability. SUN AND ITS LICENSORS SHALL NOT BE LIABLE FOR ANY DAMAGES SUFFERED BY LICENSEE OR ANY THIRD PARTY AS A RESULT OF USING OR DISTRIBUTING SOFTWARE. IN NO EVENT WILL SUN OR ITS LICENSORS BE LIABLE FOR ANY LOST REVENUE, PROFIT OR DATA, OR FOR DIRECT, INDIRECT, SPECIAL, CONSEQUENTIAL, INCIDENTAL OR PUNITIVE DAMAGES, HOWEVER CAUSED AND REGARDLESS OF THE THEORY OF LIABILITY, ARISING OUT OF THE USE OF OR INABILITY TO USE SOFTWARE, EVEN IF SUN HAS BEEN ADVISED OF THE POSSIBILITY OF SUCH DAMAGES.

8. Termination. Licensee may terminate this License at any time by destroying all copies of Software. This License will terminate immediately without notice from Sun if Licensee fails to comply with any provision of this License. Upon such termination, Licensee must destroy all copies of the Software.

9. Export Regulations. Software, including technical data, is subject to U.S. export control laws, including the U.S. Export Administration Act and its associated regulations, and may be subject to export or import regulations in other countries. Licensee agrees to comply strictly with all such regulations and acknowledges that it has the responsibility to obtain licenses to export, re-export, or import Software. Software may not be downloaded, or otherwise exported or re-exported (i) into, or to a national or resident of, Cuba, Iraq, Iran, North Korea, Libya, Sudan, Syria or any country to which the U.S. has embargoed goods; or (ii) to anyone on the U.S. Treasury Department's list of Specially Designated Nations or the U.S. Commerce Department's Table of Denial Orders.

10. Restricted Rights. Use, duplication or disclosure by the United States government is subject to the restrictions as set forth in the Rights in Technical Data and Computer Software Clauses in DFARS 252.227-7013(c)(1)(ii) and FAR 52.227-19(c) (2) as applicable.

11. Governing Law. Any action related to this License will be governed by California law and controlling U.S. federal law. No choice of law rules of any jurisdiction will apply.

12. Severability. If any of the above provisions are held to be in violation of applicable law, void, or unenforceable in any jurisdiction, then such provisions are herewith waived to the extent necessary for the License to be otherwise enforceable in such jurisdiction. However, if in Sun's opinion deletion of any provisions of the License by operation of this paragraph unreasonably compromises the rights or increases the liabilities of Sun or its licensors, Sun reserves the right
to terminate the License and refund the fee paid by Licensee, if any, as Licensee's sole and exclusive remedy.

JDK1.1 BCL 2-9-97#

Use of this software is subject to the Binary Code License terms and conditions on this and the preceding pages. Read the license carefully. By opening this package, you are agreeing to be bound by the terms and conditions of this license from Sun Microsystems, Inc.

What Is in the CD-ROM

You will find the following directories:

\com\ibm\db2nt212	: IBM DATABASE SERVER FOR WINDOWS NT 2.1.2
\com\ibm \db2v5nt	: IBM DB2 UNIVERSAL DATABASE VERSION 5.0 FOR WINDOWS NT** (complimentary)
\com\ibm\ebeans	: IBM VisualAge WebRunner Bean Extender (complimentary)
\com\ibm\vajava	: IBM VisualAge for Java Entry (complimentary)
\com\javasoft\jdk1.1	: Java** Development Kit (JDK**) 1.1.4 for Windows 95 / NT 4.0
\com\javasoft\bdk	: Beans Development Kit (BDK) June, '97
\com\ptr\lastjdbcdrivers	: Java JBDC used in the book
\com\ptr\samples	: Java examples introduced in the book

Note: Please see the following Trademark section.

Installation

Each main product is located in its own directory in either a .zip format or an .exe autoextractable format.

When the file is in a .zip format, simply extract the file to a temporary directory and then proceed to the installation.

When the file is in an .exe format, simply double-click on it.

The samples introduced in the book just need to be copied to your hard drive in your favorite place. Then set your CLASSPATH env variable.

Trademarks

The following terms are trademarks of the IBM Corporation in the United States or other countries or both: AIX, DATABASE 2, DB2, IBM, MVS/ESA, OS/2, OS/390, OS/400, PS/2, VM/ESA, VSE/ESA. Microsoft, Windows, Windows NT, and the Windows 95 logo are trademarks or registered trademarks of Microsoft Corporation. Java, JavaBeans, JDK are trademarks or registered trademarks of Sun Microsystems, Inc. Other company, product, and service names, which may be denoted by a double asterisk (**), may be trademarks or service marks of others.

This no-charge Entry product is for internal use only and it is not transferable. The Entry product restricts the number of classes to 100.

Technical Support

Prentice Hall does not offer technical support for this software. However, if there is a problem with the media, you may obtain a replacement copy by e-mailing us with your problem at:

```
discexchange@phptr.com
```